Hoang Khanh Linh Nguyen

Detecting and Modeling the Changes of Land Use and Land Cover for Land Use Planning in Da Nang City, Vietnam

ERDSICHT - EINBLICKE IN GEOGRAPHISCHE UND GEOINFORMATIONSTECHNISCHE ARBEITSWEISEN

Schriftenreihe des Geographischen Instituts der Universität Göttingen, Abteilung Kartographie, GIS und Fernerkundung

Herausgegeben von Prof. Dr. Martin Kappas

ISSN 1614-4716

17 *Matthias Stähle*
   Trinkwasser in Delhi
   Versorgungsproblematik einer indischen Megastadt
   ISBN 978-3-89821-827-6

18 *Roland Bauböck*
   Bioenergie im Landkreis Göttingen
   GIS-gestützte Biomassepotentialabschätzung anhand ausgewählter Kulturen, Triticale und Mais
   ISBN 978-3-89821-959-4

19 *Wahib Sahwan*
   Geomorphologische Untersuchungen mittels GIS- und Fernerkundungsverfahren unter Berücksichtigung hydrogeologischer Fragestellungen
   Fallbeispiele aus Nordwest Syrien
   ISBN 978-3-8382-0094-1

20 *Julia Krimkowski*
   Das Vordringen der Malaria nach Mitteleuropa im Zuge der Klimaerwärmung
   Fallbeispiel Deutschland
   ISBN 978-3-8382-0312-6

21 *Julia Kubanek*
   Comparison of GIS-based and High Resolution Satellite Imagery Population Modeling
   A Case Study for Istanbul
   ISBN 978-3-8382-0306-5

22 *Christine von Buttlar, Marianne Karpenstein-Machan, Roland Bauböck*
   Anbaukonzepte für Energiepflanzen in Zeiten des Klimawandels
   Beitrag zum Klimafolgenmanagement in der Metropolregion Hannover-Braunschweig-Göttingen-Wolfsburg
   ISBN 978-3-8382-0525-0

23 *Daniel Karthe, Sergey Chalov, Nikolay Kasimov, Martin Kappas (eds.)*
   Water and Environment in the Selenga-Baikal Basin:
   International Research Cooperation for an Ecoregion of Global Relevance
   ISBN 978-3-8382-0853-4

Hoang Khanh Linh Nguyen

DETECTING AND MODELING THE CHANGES OF LAND USE AND LAND COVER FOR LAND USE PLANNING IN DA NANG CITY, VIETNAM

ibidem-Verlag
Stuttgart

Bibliografische Information der Deutschen Nationalbibliothek
Die Deutsche Nationalbibliothek verzeichnet diese Publikation in der Deutschen Nationalbibliografie; detaillierte bibliografische Daten sind im Internet über http://dnb.d-nb.de abrufbar.

Bibliographic information published by the Deutsche Nationalbibliothek
Die Deutsche Nationalbibliothek lists this publication in the Deutsche Nationalbibliografie; detailed bibliographic data are available in the Internet at http://dnb.d-nb.de.

∞

Gedruckt auf alterungsbeständigem, säurefreien Papier
Printed on acid-free paper

ISSN: 1614-4716

ISBN-13: 978-3-8382-1136-7

© *ibidem*-Verlag
Stuttgart 2018

Alle Rechte vorbehalten

Das Werk einschließlich aller seiner Teile ist urheberrechtlich geschützt. Jede Verwertung außerhalb der engen Grenzen des Urheberrechtsgesetzes ist ohne Zustimmung des Verlages unzulässig und strafbar. Dies gilt insbesondere für Vervielfältigungen, Übersetzungen, Mikroverfilmungen und elektronische Speicherformen sowie die Einspeicherung und Verarbeitung in elektronischen Systemen.

All rights reserved. No part of this publication may be reproduced, stored in or introduced into a retrieval system, or transmitted, in any form, or by any means (electronic, mechanical, photocopying, recording or otherwise) without the prior written permission of the publisher. Any person who does any unauthorized act in relation to this publication may be liable to criminal prosecution and civil claims for damages.

Printed in the EU

Dedication

To my beloved mother,
who has sacrificed all her life for my progress in study.

Acknowledgment

I would like to express my sincere gratitude to Prof. Martin Kappas for giving me opportunity and encouraging me to develop out this book.

Nguyen, Hoang Khanh Linh

April 2018

Preface

The new publication inside the book series „Erdsicht"focuses on the very hot topic of worldwide urban development (urban sprawl) and its relation to the surrounding countryside. Cities and climate change research are foci of the global research action agenda (e.g. from Future Earth).

On the "Cities and Climate Change Science Conference (CitiesIPCC)" held in Edmonton, Canada, from March 5-7th 2018 a new action agenda was submitted to bring this research forward and stimulate the generation of knowledge on cities and climate change, encourage science- and evidence-based climate action in cities, and create and strengthen partnerships in these areas.

The new "Erdsicht"-book No 24 about "Detecting and Modeling the Changes of Land Use and Land Cover for Land Use Planning in Da Nang City, Vietnam" reacts to this new research agenda and helps to find solutions for fast growing cities and for monitoring the changes in the environment. In short, the book is an example of science we need for the cities we want. Cities account for over 70% of global energy related CO2 emissions and are vulnerable hotspots of climate change impacts (e.g. weather extremes with severe flooding). The scale of ongoing urban expansion and associated infrastructure provides an opportunity for cities to avoid further dangerous climate change and environmental change. Cities and their surrounding regions may also be cornerstones of future mitigation and adaptation measures.

Using the model CLUE (The conversion of Land Use and its Effects) the Land use change in the Da Nang region was analyzed over a decade of years. The CLUE model is a flexible, generic land use modeling framework which allows scale and context specific specification for regional applications. Typical applications include the simulation of deforestation, land degradation, urbanization, land abandonment and integrated assessment of land use / land cover change (LULC).

To simulate the future changes of LULC at Da Nang City from 2009 to 2030, three scenarios with different missions were developed, namely, scenario A Development as usual, scenario B Aggressive development, and scenario C Optimal development. All scenarios give a continuous increase in urban area, and a gradual decrease in agriculture, barren, and shrub areas.

Major results are: The change of urban area in 2030 is the highest under scenario B with 17,152.7 ha (99.16%) and the lowest under scenario C with 9,794.23 ha (56.62%). Scenario B results in a major loss of agricultural area 6,098.96 ha (83.61%), while scenario C shows minor loss of agricultural area 1,996.98 ha (27.40%) during the simulated period. Particularly, forest areas decrease by 5,269.19 ha (9.1%) and 5,125.59 ha (8.85%) under scenarios A and B, respectively; meanwhile, scenario C, emphasizing the environmental issue, shows no change in forest area (57,936.2 ha) during the simulated period.

Finally Da Nang belongs to the fastest growing cities in South-East-Asia and the current study is a good example how knowledge about Land Use / Land Cover change and urban growth can be used to achieve a better and more sustainable oriented urban planning in line with its environmental surroundings.

Martin Kappas
April 2018

Abstract

Da Nang City is located in the South Central Coast region of Vietnam, between 15°55'19" to 16°13'20"N and 107°49'11" to 108°20'20"E, and covers an area of approximately 1,283.42 km², including Paracel Islands (Hoang Sa) of 305 km². Since the adoption of DOI MOI policy in economy by the national assembly in 1986, changing from a centrally planned economy to a market-oriented economy, Da Nang has developed in many aspects. Da Nang has been known as one of the five independent municipalities of Vietnam, after separating from Quang Nam Province on January 1, 1997. From then, it has asserted its position at the national level and today constitutes the Key Economic Zone in Central Vietnam. Consequently, rapid industrialization and urbanization have caused incessant change of land use/land cover (LULC) in Da Nang City. However, less attention has been paid to assess the long-term development and driving forces of LULC. In this context, the study aims to (1) detect, quantify, and characterize the changes of LULC in the Da Nang City region by using multitemporal images from 1979 to 2009; (2) explore the effects of LULC changes on landscape structure through spatial landscape metrics; (3) simulate the changes of LULC under different scenarios by the integration of the model of system dynamics and the model of dynamic conversion of land use and its effects.

The results of this thesis show that a total of 35,689.79 ha or 37% of the total land has undergone change. The analysis indicates a notable decrease of agriculture, forest, barren, and shrub due to the expansion of urban areas. The speed and transformation trends of LULC varied in different research periods. Before being separated from Quang Nam Province (1979–1996), the LULC in Da Nang City changed gradually. However, after becoming an independent municipality, the LULC changed with rapid speed, especially in the urban areas. Within 13 years (1996–2009), urban area grew up to 86.6% of net increase of urban area. This could be caused by a strong focus of economic development. Conversely, agriculture, and forest had a high rate of change, with a decreasing trend. In the meantime, key

Abstract

landscape indices were performed to further understand the spatial distribution of three main classes: urban, agriculture, and forest. The dynamic change of landscape indices revealed that agriculture areas were brokeninto smaller patches. However, except agriculture, patches of forestry and urban spaces tended to have a uniform landscape configuration.

To simulate the future changes of LULC at Da Nang City from 2009 to 2030, three scenarios with different missions were developed, namely, scenario A *Development as usual*, scenario B *Aggressive development*, and scenario C *Optimal development*. All scenarios give a continuous increase in urban area, and a gradual decrease in agriculture, barren, and shrub areas. The change of urban area in 2030 is the highest under scenario B with 17,152.7 ha (99.16%) and the lowest under scenario C with 9,794.23 ha (56.62%). Scenario B results in a major loss of agricultural area 6,098.96 ha (83.61%), while scenario C shows minor loss of agricultural area 1,996.98 ha (27.40%) during the simulated period. Particularly, forest areas decrease by 5,269.19 ha (9.1%) and 5,125.59 ha (8.85%) under scenarios A and B, respectively; meanwhile, scenario C, emphasizing the environmental issue, shows no change in forest area (57,936.2 ha) during the simulated period.

Keywords: land-use/cover change, land-use planning, landscape, simulate, Da Nang

Zusammenfassung

Da Nang City liegt in der südlich zentralen Küstenregion von Viet Nam, zwischen 15°55'19" bis 16°13'20" N und 107°49'11" bis 108°20'20" E, und umfasst eine Fläche von ca. 1,283.42 km^2, einschließlich des Bezirks Paracel Islands mit 305 km^2. Seit der wirtschaftlichen Kontrolle durch die DOI MOI Politik in der Nationalversammlung im Jahre 1986, wurde die zentrale Planwirtschaft in eine marktorientierte Wirtschaft verändert, wodurch sich Da Nang in vielen Aspekten entwickelt hat. Am 1. Januar 1997 ist Da Nang offiziell eine von fünf selbstständigen Gemeinden in Viet Nam geworden. Seit dem hat sie ihre Position auf nationaler Ebene ausgebaut und ist heute Key Economic Zone in Zentral-Viet Nam. Folglich haben die rasche Industrialisierung und Urbanisierung einen unaufhörlichen Wandel der Landnutzung/Bodenbedeckung (LULC-Land use/land cover) in Da Nang Stadt verursacht. Allerdings ist wenig Aufmerksamkeit auf die langfristige Entwicklung und die treibenden Kräfte der LULC Veränderungen gelegt worden. In diesem Zusammenhang soll diese Studie (1) zum Erfassen, zum Quantifizierten und zum Charakterisieren der Veränderungen durch LULC in Da Nang City mit multi-temporalen Bildern von 1979 bis 2009, (2) zum Untersuchung der Auswirkungen der LULC Änderung auf die Landschaftsstruktur durch Raumlandschaftsmetriken und (3) zum Simulieren der Veränderungen der Landnutzung/Bodenbedeckung unter verschiedenen Szenarien durch die Kombination von SD-Modell und Dyna-CLUE Modell dienen.

Die Ergebnisse dieser Arbeit zeigen, dass insgesamt 35.689,79 ha oder 37% der gesamten Landfläche von Veränderungen betroffen sind. Die Analyse ergab, dass ein deutlicher Rückgang der landwirtschaftlicher Fläche, des Waldes sowie unfruchtbarer Gebiete und Strauchvegetation auf den Ausbau der Städte zurückzuführen ist. Die Geschwindigkeits und Transformations Trends der LULC variiern in verschiedenen Forschungsperioden. Bevor Da Nang von der Provinz Quang Nam (1979–1996) abgetrennt wurde, änderte sich die LULC nur allmählich. Doch nachdem die Stadt zur eigenständigen Gemeinde wurde, änderte sich die LULC besonders im Stadtgebiet

Zusammenfassung

mit rasanter Geschwindigkeit. Innerhalb von 13 Jahren (1996–2009) wuchs das Stadtgebiet mit einen Netto-Zunahme der städtischen Bereiche von 86.6%. Dies kann durch die starke Konzentration auf wirtschaftliche Entwicklung verursacht worden sein. Durch die urbanisierte Fläche ergab sich eine hohe Veränderungsrate für landwirtschaftlicher Fläche und Waldgebiete, mit abnehmender Tendenz. In der Zwischenzeit wurden Indizes für die Landbedeckung festgelegt, um die räumliche Verteilung der drei Hauptklassen, Stadt, Landwirtschaft und Wald ab zu leiten. Die dynamische Veränderung der Landschaft Indizes von Landwirtschaft Klasse zeigte die Aufspaltung der Flächen in kleinere Segmente. Dennoch lässt sich mit Ausnahme der Landwirtschaft, eine einheitliche Tendenz in der Landschaftskonfiguration für Wald und Stadtgebiete erkennen.

Um die zukünftigen Veränderungen der LULC bei Da Nang von 2009 bis 2030, vorherzusagen wurden drei Szenarien mit unterschiedlichen Annahmen entwickelt, nämlich: Szenario A "Normale Entwicklung," Szenario B "Aggressive Entwicklung" und Szenario C "Optimale Entwicklung." Alle Szenarien ergeben einen kontinuierlichen Anstieg im städtischen Bereich, und eine allmähliche Abnahme der landwirtschaftlicher Fläche, sowie der unfruchtbaren Gebiete und in Bereichen mit Strauchvegetation. Die Veränderung im städtischen Gebiete bis zum Jahr 2030 ist am höchsten im Szenario B mit 17,152.7 ha (99.16%) und am niedrigsten im Szenario C mit 9.794.23 ha (56.62%). Im Szenario B ergibt sich der größte Verlust an landwirtschaftlicher Fläche mit 6098.96 ha (83.61%), während im Szenario C der geringste Verlust landwirtschaftlicher Fläche, mit 1996.98 ha (27.40%) zu verzeichnen ist. Ein Verlust von Waldgebieten zeigt sich besonders in den Szenarien A und B mit 5,269.19 ha (9.1%) bzw. 5,125.59 ha (8.85%), während im Szenario C, welches den ökologischen Aspekt betont, keine Veränderung der Waldgebiete (57,936.2 ha) bis 2030 zu verzeichnen ist.

Schlagwort: Bodennutzung/Bodenbedeckung, Wandel, Raumplanung, Landschaft, simulieren, Da Nang

Table of contents

Acknowledgment vii

Preface... ix

Abstract xi

Zusammenfassung xiii

Abbreviations xix

List of Tables... xxi

List of Figures xxiii

Chapter 1 Introduction.. 1

1.1 Study background 1

1.2 Statement of the problem 3

1.3 Research objectives 5

    1.3.1 General objectives 5

    1.3.2 Specific objectives... 5

1.4 Outline of thesis.. 6

Chapter 2 Theoretical Background 7

Abstract 7

2.1 Land use and land cover 7

    2.1.1 Definition and clarifications 7

    2.1.2 LULC change 8

    2.1.3 LULC change causes and consequences ... 9

    2.1.4 Driving factors of LULC change 9

2.2 Combination of remote sensing
and geographic information systems 10

2.3 Definition of landscape metric 11

2.4 Model and modeling 13

    2.4.1 Definition 13

Table of contents

      2.4.2 Kinds of models 13
      2.4.3 LULC modeling 14

Chapter 3 Study Area 19

  3.1 Natural conditions 19
      3.1.1 Location and area 19
      3.1.2 Topography 21
      3.1.3 Meteorological conditions 22
      3.1.4 Hydrologic conditions 23
      3.1.5 Natural resources 24
  3.2 Social and economic conditions 28
      3.2.1 Economic development 28
      3.2.2 Economic structure 30
      3.2.3 The situation of economic sectors 31
      3.2.4 Population, labor, employment, and income 32
      3.2.5 The situation of infrastructure 35
  3.3 General assessment of natural, socioeconomic condition .. 40

Chapter 4 Data and Methodology 43

  Abstract 43
  4.1 Sensor systems 43
  4.2 Data collection 46
  4.3 Image preprocessing 53
      4.3.1 Geometric correction 53
      4.3.2 Radiometric normalization 53
  4.4 Image classification and accuracy assessment 55
      4.4.1 Image classification 55
      4.4.2 Accuracy assessment 57
  4.5 Change detection 61
  4.6 Landscape metrics 61
  4.7 Modeling LULC change 65
      4.7.1 Nonspatial model 67

	4.7.2 Spatial model 78
	4.7.3 Accuracy assessment of model 84
4.8	ANOVA analysis for landscape metrics under scenarios..... 90

Chapter 5 Land-Use/Cover Changes 93

Abstract 93

5.1	Spatial-temporal dynamics and evolution of LULC changes .. 93
	5.1.1 Urban.. 99
	5.1.2 Agriculture 103
	5.1.3 Forest 105
	5.1.4 Shrub.. 106
	5.1.5 Barren.. 106
	5.1.6 Water.. 107
5.2	Landscape pattern analysis at class level........................ 108
5.3	Discussions and conclusions 110

Chapter 6 Modeling Land Use/Cover Changes 113

Abstract 113

6.1	Demands of land-use/cover types....................................... 113
	6.1.1 Demands of land-use/cover types from 1996 to 2009 . 113
	6.1.2 Demands of land-use/cover types from 2009 to 2030 . 116
6.2	Driving factors for allocation 119
6.3	Logistic regression analysis 124
6.4	Elasticity coefficients 127
6.5	Conversion matrix 128
6.6	Validation output from the Dyna-CLUE model 128
	6.6.1 Visual comparison.. 128
	6.6.2 Agreement components 130
6.7	Analysis of the changes of scenarios................................. 131
	6.7.1 LULC changes under different scenarios................ 131
	6.7.2 LULC changes according to administration boundary.. 138
6.8	Landscape structure of scenarios 141

      6.8.1 At landscape level 141

      6.8.2 At class level 144

      6.8.3 Effects of land-use scenarios to landscape structure ... 154

  6.9 Discussions and conclusions 156

      6.9.1 Discussions 156

      6.9.2 Conclusions... 157

Chapter 7 Conclusions 159

Abstract 159

  7.1 General conclusions 159

  7.2 Future works 163

References 165

Appendices 185

Appendix 1 Accuracy assessment error matrices 185

      LULC 1979 185

      LULC 1996 189

      LULC 2003 193

      LULC 2009 197

Appendix 2 Scenarios of land-use/cover types from 1996 to 2030 . 201

Appendix 3 Logistic regression of land-use/cover types 205

Appendix 4 Area under the curve of land-use/cover types 208

Appendix 5 Main parameters of Dyna-CLUE model 211

Appendix 6 Main results obtained with ANOVA 213

Abbreviations

ANOVA	Analysis of variance
ASTER	Advanced Space-borne Thermal Emission and Reflection Radiometer
AUC	Area under the curve
CLUE	Conversion of land use and its effects
DEM	Digital elevation model
Dyna-CLUE	Dynamic conversion of land use and its effects
ETM⁺	Enhanced Thematic Mapper Plus
FAI	Fixed-assets investment of construction
FAO	Food and Agriculture Organization of the United Nations
FPR	False-positive rate
GDP	Gross domestic product
GIS	Geographic information system
GloVis	Global visualization
GOI	Gross output industry
IDS	Institute of Development Studies
IFOV	Instantaneous field of view
IR-MAD	Iteratively reweighted multivariate alteration detection
LULC	Land use/land cover
MAD	Multivariate alteration detection
MCK	Map Comparison Kit
MSS	Multispectral scanner
PIFs	Pseudoinvariant features
RMSE	Root mean square error
ROC	Relative operating characteristic
SD	System dynamics
SPOT	System Probatoire d'Observation de la Terre
SWIR	Short-wave infrared

Abbrevations

TM	Thematic mapper
TPR	True-positive rate
USGS	United States Geological Survey
VND	Vietnamese Dong
VNIR	Visible and near infrared

List of Tables

Table 2.1 Overview of land-use/cover model 17
Table 3.1 GDP and development of economics during
the period 2000–2010 29
Table 3.2 Economic structures during the period 2000–2010 30
Table 3.3 Population structure during the period 2000–2010 33
Table 3.4 Quantity of transported passengers and goods by airlines .. 35
Table 3.5 Quantity of transported passengers and goods by train .. 37
Table 3.6 Quantity of transported goods by waterway 38
Table 4.1 Characteristics of Landsat sensors 45
Table 4.2 Characteristics of ASTER 46
Table 4.3 Characteristics in satellite datasets used 52
Table 4.4 Illustration of error matrix with j classes
and N reference samples 57
Table 4.5 Formulas of quantity disagreement
and allocation disagreement indices 60
Table 4.6 Descriptions of landscape pattern metrics 65
Table 4.7 Example of conversion matrix with three land-use types . 84
Table 4.8 Two-by-two contingency table 85
Table 5.1 Kappa scores obtained from the assessment
of four different land-use maps 94
Table 5.2 Land use/cover in Da Nang City from 1979 to 2009 95
Table 5.3 Land-use/cover transformation matrices 101
Table 5.5 Metrics of landscape structure at the class level 108
Table 6.1 SD model results and validations 116
Table 6.2 Parameter settings for scenarios 116
Table 6.3 Temporal simulation of land-use/cover system
in Da Nang City 119
Table 6.4 Logistic regression of land-use/cover type 124
Table 6.5 Elasticity coefficient of land-use/cover type 127
Table 6.6 Conversion matrix of land-use/cover type 128
Table 6.7 Accuracy assessment indices
of land-use change modeling 130

List of Tables

Table 6.8 Comparison of land-use/cover changes in 2030 under three scenarios 137

Table 6.9 Comparison of land-use/cover types in 2030 under three scenarios according to administration boundary 140

Table 6.10 Descriptive values of landscape metrics obtained with one-way ANOVA 154

Table 6.11 Obtained landscape metrics of scenarios 155

Table A2.1 Demand of land-use/cover types in scenario 1 202

Table A2.2 Demand of land-use/cover types in scenario 2 203

Table A2.3 Demand of land-use/cover types in scenario 3 204

Table A3.1 Available land-use/cover types in logistic regression mode 205

Table A3.2 Available driving factors in logistic regression mode ... 205

Table A3.3 Logistic regression for agriculture 205

Table A3.4 Logistic regression for barren 206

Table A3.5 Logistic regression for urban 206

Table A3.6 Logistic regression for forest 206

Table A3.7 Logistic regression for shrub 207

Table A3.8 Logistic regression for water 207

List of Figures

Figure 3.1 Location of Da Nang City, Vietnam 20
Figure 4.1 Subset of Landsat MSS image (July 24, 1979), RGB 754 ... 48
Figure 4.2 Subset of mosaic Landsat TM images
(July 07 & 14, 1996), RGB 432 images 49
Figure 4.3 Subset of mosaic Landsat ETM+ images
(March 04 & April 14, 2003), RGB 432 50
Figure 4.4 Subset of ASTER image (April 02, 2003), RGB 321 51
Figure 4.5 Moving window computation 62
Figure 4.6 Flowchart of modeling land-use/cover changes
used in the study 66
Figure 4.7 Example of SD model used in the study 68
Figure 4.8 The SD model for simulating the demands
of land use/cover in Da Nang City 71
Figure 4.9 Framework of the Dyna-CLUE model 80
Figure 4.10 Flowchart of the Dyna-CLUE model 80
Figure 4.11 Example of ROC curve = 0.970,
area under the curve (forest) 86
Figure 4.12 Flowchart of calibration and validation process 90
Figure 5.1 Percentage of land use/land cover extracted
from remote sensing data 95
Figure 5.2 Trends of land use/cover from multitemporal images and
statistic data: (a) Agriculture; (b) Barren; (c) Urban; (d) Forest;
(e) Forest and shrub; and (f) Water 96
Figure 5.3 Classified land use/cover maps
from multi-temporal images 98
Figure 5.4 Gross domestic product (GDP) and its growth
in Da Nang City from 1990 to 2009 102
Table 5.4 Measuring the changes
of urban area in different districts 102
Figure 5.5 Development of the economic structure
in Da Nang City from 1997 to 2009 105
Figure 6.1 Comparison between actual and predicted values of (a)
population, (b) gross output industry, and (c) fixed-assets
investment construction 115

List of Figures

Figure 6.2 Comparison between actual and predicted values of land-use/cover area 115

Figure 6.3 Driving factors: (a) urban rate, (b) mean density of population, (c) slope, (d) elevation; (e) distance to urban, (f) distance to water, and (g) distance to road. 123

Figure 6.4 Visual comparison between the pairs of maps 129

Figure 6.5 Simulated LULC maps in scenario A 132

Figure 6.6 Simulated LULC maps in scenario B 133

Figure 6.7 Simulated LULC maps in scenario C 134

Figure 6.8 Land-use/cover types under different scenarios: (a) Scenario A; (b) Scenario B; and (c) Scenario C 135

Figure 6.9 Comparisons of land use/cover in three scenarios: (a) Agriculture, (b) Barren, (c) Urban, (d) Forest, (e) Shrub, and (f) Water 136

Figure 6.10 Landscape metrics at landscape level under scenarios (a) Number of patches, (b) Patch density, (c) Mean proximity, (d) Mean patch area, (e) Interspersion and juxtaposition index, (f) Largest patch index, and (g) Largest shape index .. 142

Figure 6.11 Landscape metrics at agriculture class under scenarios (a) Number of patches, (b) Patch density, (c) Mean proximity, (d) Mean patch area, (e) Interspersion and juxtaposition index, (f) Largest patch index, and (g) Largest shape index .. 146

Figure 6.12 Landscape metrics at barren class under scenarios (a) Number of patches, (b) Patch density, (c) Mean proximity, (d) Mean patch area, (e) Interspersion and juxtaposition index, (f) Largest patch index, and (g) Largest shape index .. 147

Figure 6.13 Landscape metrics at urban class under scenarios (a) Number of patches, (b) Patch density, (c) Mean proximity, (d) Mean patch area, (e) Interspersion and juxtaposition index, (f) Largest patch index, and (g) Largest shape index .. 149

Figure 6.14 Landscape metrics at forest class under scenarios (a) Number of patches, (b) Patch density, (c) Mean proximity, (d) Mean patch area, (e) Interspersion and juxtaposition index, (f) Largest patch index, and (g) Largest shape index .. 150

Figure 6.15 Landscape metrics at shrub class under scenarios (a) Number of patches, (b) Patch density, (c) Mean proximity, (d) Mean patch area, (e) Interspersion and juxtaposition index, (f) Largest patch index, and (g) Largest shape index .. 151

Figure 6.16 Landscape metrics at water class under scenarios (a) Number of patches, (b) Patch density, (c) Mean proximity, (d) Mean patch area, (e) Interspersion and juxtaposition index, (f) Largest patch index, and (g) Largest shape index .. 153

Chapter 1
Introduction

1.1 Study background

As stated in *Competitive Cities in the Global Economy* (OECD, 2006) and *State of the World's Cities 2008/2009: Harmonious Cities* (UN, 2008), urbanization is a global phenomenon that is expected to continue for the next few decades. According to the United Nations, roughly half of the world's population lives in urban areas, and, in 2030, it will have increased to 60%. This increase in urbanization will mainly happen in developing countries (OECD 2010). As pointed out by Elvidge et al. (2004), human beings tend to live in spatially limited habitats, called the urban environment, where most people live and work. Hence, urban areas concentrate not only on people but also on economic density and productivity (OECD, 2009), which is the reason for changes in lifestyles, high consumption of energy, transportation, infrastructure, and production of waste (Angel et al., 1998; Collier, 1997; Collier and Löfstedt, 1997; DeAngelo and Harvey, 1998; Harvey, 1993; Lambright et al., 1996; McEvoy et al., 1999; Wilbanks and Kates, 1999).

Urbanization is believed to be one of the most prevalent anthropogenic causes of arable land loss, habitat devastation, and natural vegetation-cover loss (Dewan and Yamaguchi, 2009). As a matter of course, rural areas have been converted into urban areas through development at an unprecedented rate, which has had a noted effect on the natural functioning of ecosystems (Turner, 1994). In other words, "the phenomenon of urban development is one of the major forces driving land use change" (Wu et al., 2006). What is more, urban growth is a very complex process that is jointly influenced by social, economic, historical, and biophysical factors. Hence, a profound understanding of land-use/cover (LULC) change is very important to be able to have proper land-use planning and sustainable development policies (Braimoh and Onishi, 2007).

To fulfill a sustainable development plan, Myint and Wang (2006) asserted that such a plan must be consolidated from numerous factors extracted from various data sources. These factors could represent the physical, biological, and social settings of areas in the continued spectrum of spatial and temporal domains. Therefore, it is important to have an effective spatial dynamic tool, which is used to understand the changes of LULC.

Since the launch of the first Earth Resources Technology Satellite in 1972 (ERTS-1, later renamed Landsat 1), remote sensing has become an important research branch in mapping and monitoring environmental changes due to anthropogenic pressures and natural processes (Treitz and Rogan, 2004). In the last three decades, the technologies of remote sensing have incessantly evolved, including a suite of sensors operating at a wide range of imaging scales, lower data price, and high resolution (Rogan and Chen, 2004). Hence, remote sensing data offer spatially consistent datasets of large areas with high spatial detail and high temporal frequency. Undoubtedly, remote sensing is an ideal means for providing consistent historical time series data which can be seen as a "unique view" of spatial and temporal patterns in the process of LULC change (Xiao et al., 2006). Accordingly, remote sensing is well known as a technique used in detecting and monitoring the change at various scales with useful results (Stefanov et al., 2001; Wilson et al., 2003). In addition, with strong development, geographic information systems (GIS), a powerful spatial analysis function, can be used to convert the discrete statistical data and survey data into spatially continuous distribution data. GIS effectively reflects the spatial difference by using certain spatial calculation methods (Peng and Lu, 2007). Of the many technological and conceptual approaches to spatial data analysis, GIS, the most promising tool, can give reliable information for both planning and decision-making tasks (Michalak, 1993).

Landscape ecological studies have been focused upon as a new dimension of land management in recent years. The recognition of the importance of the "landscape perspective" is growing (Apan et al., 2000). Studying landscape change is absolutely necessary for sustainable management; it helps decision makers obtain a complete view of the LULC change system and its components (Keleş et al., 2008). Regarding this term, ecological perspectives have been addressed by the questions "How does urbanization influence land-ecosystem services" and "How does urbanization impact landscape structures/land architecture?" (Fragkias et al., 2012). To answer these questions and to increase effectiveness in managing environmental sustainability, it is necessary to understand the links between LULC and landscape pattern (Antrop and Van Eetvelde, 2000). What is more interesting is that spatial metrics could be a useful tool to characterize the differences between plan and design alternatives. As a result, spatial metrics are required for land-use planning and design (Lin et al., 2007).

According to Jat et al. (2008), for balanced development after monitoring to know how the land is currently used, the municipal authorities or decision makers must assess future demand and take steps to assure adequacy of future supply. Hence, to answer the question as to how LULC is likely to move in the next several years to come, a modeling approach is believed to be a useful tool. Simulating LULC dynamics by models can help municipal authorities or decision makers perceive the characteristics and interdependencies of the components that constitute spatial systems. This could give valuable insights into possible LULC configurations in the future (Koomen et al., 2007). Consequently, policy makers could evaluate different scenarios of LULC change and their effects, which could then be used to support land-use planning and policy (Rafiee et al., 2009).

1.2 Statement of the problem

Da Nang, the fourth largest city of Vietnam and the largest urban area in the Central region, is in a favorable geographical location, including the national transport axis with road, rail, sea, and air transportation links as well as serving as the gateway to the Central Highlands (Nguyen, 2003).

In the late 1980s and early 1990s, the Vietnamese government adopted the economic reform policy (namely, DOI MOI), changing from a centrally planned economy to a market-oriented one (Que and Phuc, 2003). However, Da Nang had not been able to grow its economy compared to Ho Chi Minh city and Ha Noi capital. On January 1, 1997, Da Nang was separated from Quang Nam Province and officially became one of five independent municipalities of Vietnam that directly belongs to the government (The Statistics department, 2005). This marked an important turning point in the socioeconomic development of Da Nang because the government would like to push the city into an economic hub to boost the development of the Central region (Nguyen, 2003). During this development period, Da Nang has experienced its highest economic growth rates, with an annual increase of the gross domestic product (GDP) of 11.43%. Together with the growth of the economy, rapid industrialization and urbanization have caused the incessant change of LULC in Da Nang City.

With this change, Da Nang has asserted its position of importance at the national level and today constitutes the key economic zone in Central Vietnam. Nevertheless, as the Institute of Development Studies reports (IDS, 2007), Da Nang City has been confronted with many environmental problems and natural disasters that impact not only socioeconomic development but also the environment. Different conflicts have been arising, such as the conflict between land resources and demand for development versus the vulnerability of the coastal zone (Ding et al., 2007; Huang et al., 2010; Käyhkö et al., 2011; Lyons et al., 2012; Quan et al., 2006; Shalaby and Tateishi, 2007; Weng, 2002). Like other provinces in Vietnam, the land-use planning in Da Nang City was generated basically on the increase of population, the development of economics, characteristics of topography, and experiments of local planners without scientific support. Thus, sustainable development is put at risk due to inadequate planning, increasing human activity, interagency conflicts, and lack of a coordinated management approach. Consequently, it is necessary to obtain complete measures to arrest and reverse the declining environmental conditions (IDS, 2007). In this case, a complete research study in assessing and simulating LULC dynamics in Da Nang City is needed to help the local decision-making processes and influence land managers to carefully consider land-use planning and design.

1.3 Research objectives

1.3.1 General objectives

Guided by the matters stated earlier, the objectives of this dissertation are to address and simulate the changes of LULC in Da Nang City. A deep understanding of the complex changes over time could support land-use planners or decision makers in the formulation of locally adapted policy interventions. It is expected to have an efficient LULC management manner that benefits both local and national economies.

The proposed research will be guided by the following questions:

- What is the current system of LULC in Da Nang City and how has the spatial and temporal distributions altered over time?

- What are the driving factors of LULC changes within Da Nang City? What are the critical developments, and can the effects of change over time be quantified? How to identify the local effects of vulnerable and sustainable components to interacting perturbations?

- How does the trend of spatial land use help political decision-making variables and land-use planning?

1.3.2 Specific objectives

In order to achieve the aforementioned general objectives, the operational steps are formulated as follows:

- Assessing the change of LULC, in particular urban land use under the impacts of urbanization by using time series remotely sensed images from 1979 to 2009

- Analyzing patterns of changes in landscape within the study area during the last three decades

- Determining the underlying and proximate causes of LULC changes

- Simulating and locating the changes of LULC within the study area during the period 2009–2030

The outcome of this study is to support the sustainable development of urbanization. Understanding of the complex interactions of these changes over time could assist local decision makers in the formulation of regionally adapted policy interventions.

1.4 Outline of thesis

In the framework of dissertation, this research consists of seven chapters that discuss the major components. This chapter defines the problem statements and the main objectives of the study. Chapter 2 reviews shortly the conceptual background often used in assessing the change of LULC and landscape structure. In addition, this chapter also includes a brief literature review on land-use modeling approaches. Chapter 3 introduces an overview of study area based on its biophysical and socioeconomic characteristics. In Chapter 4, data used for this research are presented. Importantly, this chapter fully discusses the applied methods for processing the remote sensing dataset, the approaches for detecting the changes of LULC and landscape structure, and the modeling techniques. The dynamics of LULC and landscape structure within the study area over the last three decades are presented in Chapter 5. The resulting output of modeling, the validation results, as well as landscape structure analysis under different LULC scenarios are detailed in Chapter 6. Finally, general conclusions and recommendations are outlined in Chapter 7.

Chapter 2
Theoretical Background

Abstract

This chapter introduces and provides some of the fundamental terms related to land-use/land cover (LULC) concepts, remote sensing, geographic information system (GIS), combination of remote sensing and GIS in LULC change analysis, landscape metrics analysis, and LULC modeling.

2.1 Land use and land cover

2.1.1 Definition and clarifications

The Food and Agriculture Organization of the United Nations (FAO, 1995) defined land as follows:

> "Land is a delineable area of the earth's terrestrial surface, encompassing all attributes of the biosphere immediately above or below this surface including those of the near-surface climate the soil and terrain forms, the surface hydrology (including shallow lakes, rivers, marshes, and swamps), the near-surface sedimentary layers and associated groundwater reserve, the plant and animal populations, the human settlement pattern and physical results of past and present human activity (terracing, water storage or drainage structures, roads, buildings, etc.)."

Land use/cover (LULC) is one of the important pieces of information for land-use planning and management. The concepts "land use" and "land cover" have a close relationship to each other; therefore, in many cases, they are often confused and have been used interchangeably (Anderson et al., 1976b; Zhan, 2003). As a matter of fact, "land cover and land use are two linked components" (Müller, 2003).

As mentioned by Campbell (1996, 2002), land use is defined as the use of land by humans and refers to how the land is being used, which often refers to the use of land for economic activities. On the other hand, land cover designates the visible evidence of land use or refers to the biophysical materials found on the land that can be directly observed, such as roads, buildings, parking lots, forests, and rivers. Hence, land use is an abstract term while land cover is a concrete one without economic function. For example, a state park may be used for recreation but have a deciduous forest cover. One method of organizing LULC information is to use a classification system.

Many different classification systems, based mainly on various requirements of planners or other businesses, have been created in different countries. These classification systems are actually quite detailed and not suitable for applying remote sensing or visual aerial interpretation (Zhan, 2003). To have useful information from remote sensing data for different applications, therefore, a proper standardized land-use or land-cover classification scheme must be organized (Jensen, 2000). For this reason, the first "Land use/Land cover classification system for use with remotely sensed data" was developed by Anderson et al. (1976b). After that, it was modified by the United States Geological Survey (USGS) in 1992 with four system levels (I–IV). The main source of this classification system at that time was Landsat MSS with 79 m spatial resolution (Zhan, 2003). Up to now, despite the adapted classification system for high-resolution images (0.5–4 m), the classification of USGS is still useful for coarse and medium spatial resolution of remotely sensed images.

2.1.2 LULC change

In order to detect the dynamics of LULC, it is necessary to differentiate the types of change. Regarding land cover, the change can be distinguished as two types: conversion and modification (Lambin et al., 2003; Turner et al., 1995).

Land-cover conversion is known as the complete transformation of one cover type to another, whereas land-cover modification replaces the structure or function from one type to another without a total change, which could cause the changes in productivity, biomass, or phenology (Sloke, 1994) (i.e., forest succession under slash-and-burn cultivation) (Lambin et al., 2001).

Likewise, land-use conversion may be understood as the transformation of one type of land use to another one. The changes in land-use modification involve the intensity of the use and the alterations of their qualities or attributes (e.g., the use of suburban forest is changed from natural conservation to recreation purpose by remaining unchanged in area) (Orekan, 2007).

2.1.3 LULC change causes and consequences

To improve the models or projections of LULC, it is important to understand the causes of changes (Committee on Global Change Research, 1999). LULC change is the consequence of human activities in direct or indirect manner. It is known as a complex process by the mutual interactions between environmental and social factors on different spatial and temporal scales (Jokar Arsanjani, 2012). Lambin et al. (2001) summarized the changes of LULC for the following reasons: "tropical deforestation, rangeland modifications, agricultural intensification and urbanization."

Changes in LULC are so pervasive; therefore, when aggregated globally, they significantly affect the functioning of the Earth's systems (Lambin et al., 2001), such as directly impacting biotic diversity worldwide (Sala et al., 2000), contributing to local and regional climate change (Chase et al., 2000) or global climate warming (Houghton et al., 1999), being the primary source of soil degradation (Tolba and El-Kholy, 1992), and affecting the ability of biological systems to support human needs by altering ecosystem services (Vitousek et al., 1997).

2.1.4 Driving factors of LULC change

As pointed out by Priyanto (2010), the perspective of regional planning is used to manage human activities development to reduce the impacts of environmental degradation and achieve sustainable development. In order to have a practical planning, the driving forces behind the changes of LULC in the past patterns should be clarified.

There are a variety of driving forces on LULC changes relating to environmental, social, and economic variables. Turner et al. (1995) categorized the forces into following groups: "(a) Factors that affect the demands that will be placed on the land: population and affluence; (b) Factors that control the intensity of exploitation of the land: through technology; (c) Factors that are related to access to or control over land resources: the political economy; (d) Factors create the incentives that motivate individual decision makers: the political structure attitudes and values."

To investigate the interrelation between the drivers of land change, a thorough knowledge of methods and effective variables from the natural and social sciences is required, such as climatology, soil science, ecology, environmental science, hydrology, geography, information systems, computer science, anthropology, sociology, and policy science (Ellis, 2010).

2.2 Combination of remote sensing and geographic information systems

Wilkinson (1996) ascertained that there are three different approaches for integrating remote sensing and geographic information system (GIS) technologies to enhance each other.

(1) Remote sensing data can be seen as input datasets for use in GIS

From remote sensing data, thematic information can be extracted to create GIS layers via three different methods as Campbell (2007) summarizes. First, after interpreting remote sensing images, a set of maps depicting boundaries between categories of land use are digitized to make appropriate input digital files for GIS. Second, by using automated methods, paper maps and images generated from analyzing and classifying digital remote sensing data are digitized for data entry in GIS. Finally, after analysis and classification, digital remote sensing data are converted directly into GIS.

The automated extraction of cartographic information is also an important application of remote sensing for GIS. By using pattern recognition, edge extraction, and segmentation algorithms, lines, polygons, and other geographical features are generated. Therefore, satellite images have been recognized as a great information provider in creating and revising base maps. In addition, satellite images have been demonstrated as cost-effective sources to update GIS databases and maps by their temporal resolution. This could be used to detect changes within a particular area. Moreover, the fourth application of remote sensing imagery as an input of GIS is cartographic representation (Weng, 2010).

(2) GIS datasets are one piece of ancillary information used in remote sensing

GIS datasets can be applied to remote sensing image processing at various stages. First, GIS datasets (vector polygons) are used to select the area of interest to restrict the area of an image to be processed. This will make the image processing much more efficient due to the faster processing time (Weng, 2010). The second use of GIS datasets such as vector points, polygons, and digital elevation model is in applying geometric and radiometric correction at the stage of image preprocessing (Hinton, 1996). At the stage of image classification, independent ancillary datasets are useful in assisting the selection of training samples (Mesev, 1998). Moreover, GIS technology also offers a flexible environment for entering, analyzing, managing, and displaying digital data from various sources to enhance the functions of remote sensing image processing at various stages (Weng, 2010).

(3) Remote sensing and GIS are applied as input of modeling

According to the studies of many authors (Ehlers et al., 1990; Harris and Ventura, 1995; Treitz et al., 1992; Weng, 2002), the integration of remote sensing and GIS has been widely used as an effective tool for analysis and modeling of the changes of LULC in general, urban in particular. Multitemporal images are processed in order to understand and monitor the change of LULC and then the data area can be abstracted into suitable form of GIS. Based on this information, different models of geographical space can be conceptualized more easily (Weng, 2010).

2.3 Definition of landscape metric

In general, the study of spatial structure and pattern is central to many types of geographical research. Many approaches have been implemented to analyze the spatial structure as well as pattern, including spatial metric method. This perspective is used to measure the spatial configuration of vegetation in natural landscapes. Hence, spatial metrics are also known under the name of landscape metrics (Herold et al., 2005). A definition of landscape metrics is portrayed in the work of McGarigal and Marks (1995b), where the landscape metrics (indices) are numeric measurements that are used to quantify the spatial pattern of land-cover patches, land-cover classes, or entire landscape mosaics of a geographical area. The metrics have been applied in landscape ecology (Forman and Gordon, 1986) to specify the important relationships in ecology (Bhatta, 2010).

Recently, the combination of remote satellite imagery and spatial metrics has been widely examined. Analyzing the changes in spatial metrics can help broaden the knowledge of spatial configuration and change processes and, therefore, can support the modeling processes for guiding planning and management efforts (Bhatta, 2010).

Landscape metrics are supposed to numerically interpret the spatial structure of landscape, by which we can be well aware of the effects of structure system to heterogeneous landscape (O'Neill et al., 1999; Turner, 1989; Turner et al., 2001). Also, studying landscape structure can help the scientific transition from an inductive to deductive logic model, in which the hypotheses can be formed and tested (Curran, 1987; Dietzel et al., 2005). Commonly, landscape structure has two basic components: (a) composition and (b) configuration. According to Leitao and Ahern (2002), composition metrics are nonspatially explicit characteristics. They measure landscape characteristics (e.g., richness, evenness, dispersion, contagion, etc.) instead of reflecting patch geometry or geographical location. In contrast, configuration metrics refer to spatially explicit characteristics of land-cover types in a given landscape, which display the geometry or the spatial distribution of patches. They measure spatial characteristics (e.g., size, shape, perimeter, perimeter-area ratio, fractal dimension, etc.).

Many studies showed that landscape metrics can be utilized for examining the change of spatial heterogeneity in the degree when they were applied to multiscale or multitemporal datasets (Dunn et al., 1991; Herold et al., 2005; Wu et al., 2000). The work of O'Neill et al. (1988) showed many different metrics that were tested, modified, and developed (Hargis et al., 1998; McGarigal et al., 2002; Riitters et al., 1995). These metrics can be found in the statistical package FRAGSTATS (McGarigal et al., 2002).

2.4 Model and modeling

2.4.1 Definition

When searching for the definition of model, many concepts of this term can be found. According to *Webster's Dictionary*, a model is defined as "a description, a collection of statistic data, or an analogy used to help visualize often in a simplified way something that cannot directly observed (as an atom), or a theoretical projection in detail of a possible system of human relationships."

A similar definition of model can be also read in the *Collins English Dictionary*, in which a model is understood as a simplified representation or description of a system or complex entity, especially the one designed to facilitate calculations and predictions. From these definitions, Liu (2009) ascertained that a model is generally a simplified representation of reality, and modeling, therefore, is the process or behavior of producing models.

In geographical terms, model and modeling were mentioned in the 1960s. As pointed out in *Integrated Models in Geography* (Chorley and Haggett, 1967, 2013), a model could be a theory, a law, a hypothesis of data, a word, a map, a graph, or some type of computer or laboratory hardware arranged for experimental purposes. However, this definition was later narrowed to "any device or mechanism which generates a prediction" (Haines-Young and Petch, 1986). Consequently, modeling is "an activity that enables the theories to be examined critically" (Haines-Young, 1989).

2.4.2 Kinds of models

In general, there are two kinds of models: hardware and mathematics. Hardware models represent the real work situations as scaled-down versions. This model is applied when it is impossible to use the mathematical one due to the complexity, uncertainty, or lack of knowledge. Conversely, mathematical models are much more common, which are used to express the states and rates of change based on mathematical rules. Hence, mathematical models can encompass from simple equations through to complex software codes with various equations and rules over discrete areas of time and space. This kind of model can be distinguished asempirical, conceptual, or physical based.

In empirical models, only observed behaviors between variables are described by the simplest mathematical function, wherein physical laws or assumptions about the relationships between variables on the basis of observations are not considered. Therefore, empirical models are much better at predicting than explaining and have the capability to generalize data. The conceptual models describe the same behavior, but under different values of parameter, which reveal the observed relationship between the variables. This means that conceptual models have slightly greater explanatory depth but are not as general as empirical models. Physically based models are based on the deduction of physical principles and produce results. These models tend to have good explanatory power but low prediction power and often need to be calibrated against observations. In the case that they are not highly calibrated to observed data and have an appropriate and flexible structure, physically based models can generalize better than empirical models (Mulligan and Wainwright, 2004).

2.4.3 LULC modeling

Models on LULC change are believed to be powerful tools that can be used to reveal and analyze the links between socioeconomic processes associated with land development, agricultural activities, and natural resource management strategies (Roy and Tomar, 2001). In other words, the modeling of LULC change tries to solve at least one of the following questions: "(1) Which socio-economic and biophysical variables cause the change of land use/cover—why? (2) Which locations are affected by land use changes—where? (3) At what rate does land use/cover change progress—when?" (Lambin, 2004).

In addition, techniques using computers have erupted dramatically over the past few decades. As a result, research on modeling has increased exponentially. There are hundreds of LULC models that have been described in the literature on "landscape ecology, geography, urban planning, economics, regional science, computer science, statistics, geographic information science and other fields" (Brown et al., 2004). To bridge the information gap that many users must face when selecting a dynamic model, many authors tried to arrange or systematize the available LULC models (Agarwal et al., 2002; Lambin et al., 2000; Mondal et al., 2012; Verburg et al., 2004). In this situation, a new classification scheme of models was developed by Silva and Wu (2012). Accordingly, a comprehensive review of the models showed that models of LULC change could be arranged based on six important benchmarks: modeling approaches, level of analysis, spatial scales, temporal scales, spatial contexts, and planning tasks.

In the first benchmark, different modeling approaches were distinguished based on the methods of the models: mathematical/statistical models, GIS-based models, cellular automata-based models, agent-based models, rule-based models, and integrated models. Besides the traditional mathematical/statistical modeling approaches, there are an increasing number of dynamic models that use cellular automata or are agent based (Batty et al., 1999). Similar to GIS-based models, the new modeling approaches, rule-based models, also rely on the knowledge of experts and are based on explicit decision rules in which the model users can specify how the model will behave (Silva and Wu, 2012).

The second benchmark categorizes all models into three different levels: macro-level, micro-level, or cross-level (or multilevel). The macro-level models were developed based on macroeconomic theory or system approach. These models focus mainly on the macro-process of urban land-use change and hardly consider the micro-level interactions (Silva and Wu, 2012). According to Verburg et al. (2004), micro-level models are used to simulate the behavior of individuals and the upscaling of this behavior, through which changes of LULC can be revealed.

Similar to the second benchmark, models in benchmarks 3, 4, and 5 were categorized based on the scales of the simulated phenomena in terms of size of the application area and the prediction time. The group models of spatial scale were divided into four levels: regional (or national) scale, metropolitan scale, local scale, and multiscale. Depending on the time of the simulation, the temporal scale groups were divided into long-term models (more than 50 years), medium-term models (from 10 to 50 years), and short-term models (from zero to 10 years). In considering the spatial characteristics, models can be categorized into three groups:

(a) Spatial-oriented models: focusing on geographical patterns of LULC processes

(b) Nonspatial-oriented models: focusing on the interaction of commodity demand, production, and trade

(c) Integrated models: concerning both geographical and socioeconomic aspects

According to popular designed planning tasks, models were classified into five groups: LULC change, urban growth, transportation land use, impact assessment, and comprehensive projection (Silva and Wu, 2012). An overview of land-use change models are summarized in Table 2.1.

Model name	Benchmark						Total
	1	2	3	4	5	6	
Agent-LUC	x			x		x	3
BabyLOV	x	x			x	x	4
CARLOS			x			x	2
CUF	x		x			x	3
CUFM	x	x	x			x	4
CURBA	x	x	x		x	x	5
CLUE	x	x	x	x	x	x	6
Community Viz	x		x			x	3
CVCA	x	x	x	x	x	x	6
DG-ABC	x	x	x	x	x	x	6
DRAM	x		x			x	3
DELTA	x	x	x	x	x	x	6
DUEM	x		x			x	3
EMPIRIC	x				x	x	3
Environmental Explorer	x	x	x		x	x	5
GEOMODE2	x	x	x			x	4
GSM	x	x	x	x		x	5
INDEX	x					x	2
ILUTE	x	x			x	x	4
ITLUP	x					x	2

Chapter 2 Theoretical Background

Model name	Benchmark						Total
IMAGE-GTAP/LEI	x				x	x	3
IRPUD	x	x				x	3
IIASA		x				x	2
ILUMASS	x	x	x		x	x	5
IFDM			x			x	2
LOV	x	x				x	3
LEAM	x	x	x		x	x	5
LUSD	x		x			x	3
LINE	x				x	x	3
LUCAS	x				x	x	3
LUCIM	x			x		x	3
LTM	x	x			x	x	4
LUCITA	x					x	2
METROPILUS	x		x			x	3
METRSCOPE	x		x		x	x	4
METROSIM	x	x			x	x	4
MEPLAN	x			x	x	x	4
NELUP					x	x	2
Place3S	x		x			x	3
POL IS	x	x				x	3
PLUM	x				x	x	3
PUMA	x	x	x	x	x	x	6
FEARLUS	x		x	x	x	x	5
PECAS	x		x		x	x	4
SAM-IN	x		x	x	x	x	5
SLEUTH	x	x	x		x	x	5
SPARTACUS	x		x			x	3
SOLUTIONS	x		x			x	3
SelfCormas	x			x	x	x	4
SYPRIA	x					x	2
STIT	x					x	2
SIMLAND	x					x	2
SLUCE	x					x	2
SLUDGE	x					x	2
SIMPOP	x	x				x	3
TRANUS	x		x		x	x	4
TLUMIP	x	x				x	3
UrbanSim	x	x	x			x	4
UPLAN	x		x		x	x	4
UGM	x		x	x	x	x	5
UED	x	x			x	x	4
What if?	x					x	2
WiVsim		x		x		x	3

Table 2.1 Overview of land-use/cover model
Source: Silva and Wu (2012)

In terms of the main characteristics, only 12 of the total of 64 models seem to cover up to 6 of the main benchmarks defined for the analysis of the models, whereas the majority of the models cover only three benchmarks (and in many cases, only two). After reviewing the relevant literature, the conversion of land use and its effects (CLUE) model was chosen to estimate the changes of LULC area in the near future of Da Nang City. Orekan (2007) and Khoury (2012) showed some reasons that motivated the choice of using CLUE model:

- CLUE is a hybrid model using the parameters from the estimation models (scenarios) to simulate simultaneously the changes in spatial terms of multiple LULC types

- CLUE uses empirically quantified relation between variable factors of LULC change and statistical methods

- CLUE can be used at continental, national, and regional scales to define the change of LULC based on biophysical and socioeconomic factors

- CLUE can simulate cartographically the future LULC map as the continuation of the former one

- CLUE modeling was performed in different regions of the world and across various ranges of LULC change scenarios, such as "agricultural intensification, deforestation, land abandonment, and urbanization" (Verburg and Overmars, 2007)

- The output of CLUE may be used as a reference for land-use planners to decide the way developing for a desired LULC in the future

More details of the CLUE modeling approach will be presented in Chapter 4.

Chapter 3
Study Area

3.1 Natural conditions

3.1.1 Location and area

Da Nang is located in the Central Coast region of Vietnam, between 15°55'19" to 16°13'20" north latitude and 107°49'11" to 108°20'20" east longitude. It covers an area by approximately 1,283.42 km^2, including Paracel Islands (Hoang Sa) of 305 km^2. It is next to Thua Thien Hue Province to the north and Quang Nam Province to the south and west, and is washed by the Eastern Sea, along its 92 km seashore. Da Nang is located in the middle of the country and it is 764 km far from Ha Noi, the northern capital, and 964 km far from Ho Chi Minh city on the south (**Figure 3.1**). Sitting on the north-south road (National Road 1A), rail, sea, and air routes, Da Nang is an important gateway to the Central Highlands of Vietnam, and to the Northeast Asian countries (Laos, Cambodia, Thailand, and Myanmar) through economic corridor running east-west and the Tien Sa seaport. In addition, Da Nang is in the center of the well-known world cultural heritage sites, including the ancient capital of Hue, the ancient town of Hoi An and My Son Holy Land, and Phong Nha-Ke Bang National Forest. As one of the sea-lanes and international air routes, Da Nang's geographical location is particularly convenient for rapid development and sustainability (Danang Info, 2012).

Chapter 3 Study Area

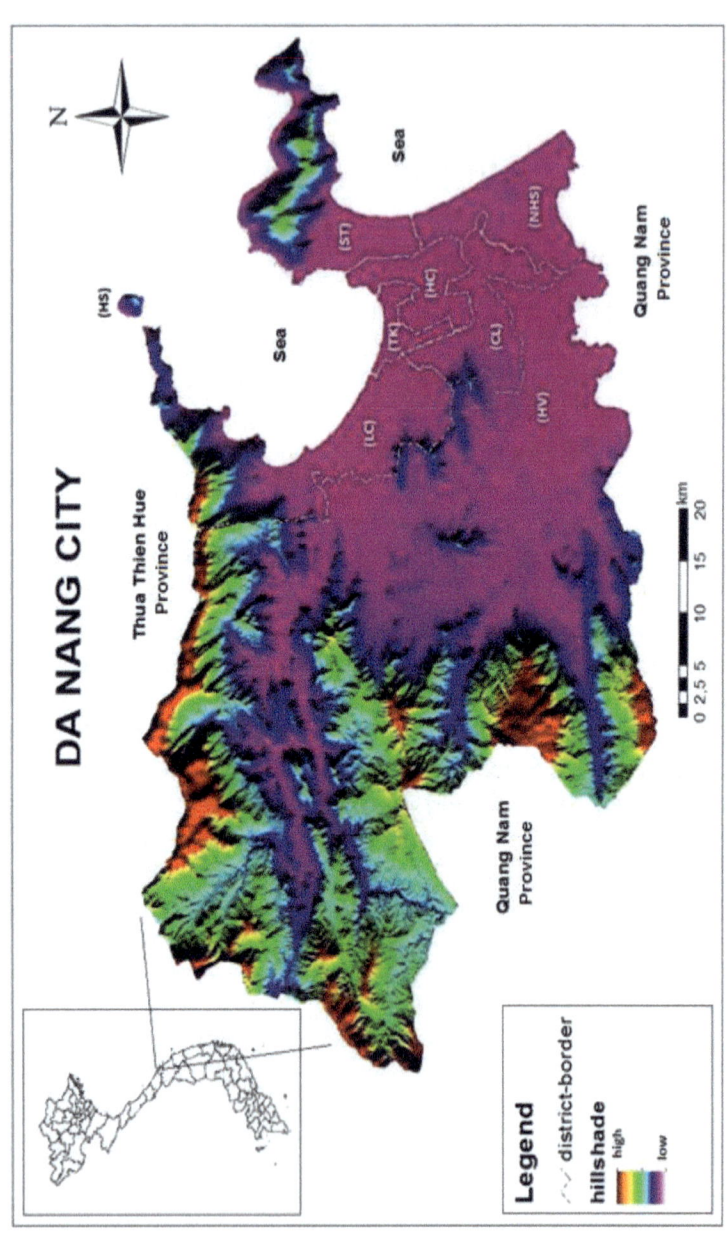

Figure 3.1 Location of Da Nang City, Vietnam
Source: Author's calculation

The city is divided into seven mainland districts and one island district, namely, Cam Le (CL), Hai Chau (HC), Hoa Vang (HV), Lien Chieu (LC), Ngu Hanh Son (NHS), Son Tra (ST), Thanh Khe (TK), Hoang Sa (HS). According to the *Statistical Yearbook* of Da Nang City in 2009, the total population of Da Nang City was about 890,490 and the population density was approximately 693.84 people per km^2, with 86.9% population in the urban area. The average annual population growth rate was 2.39%. It was the highest rate in the North and South Central Coast regions and the sixth highest in the country (Danang' Statistical Office, 2009).

3.1.2 Topography

The topographic structure of Da Nang City is multiform and strongly separated. Its direction of dip is from the northwest to southeast. It can be divided into three main types of topography: high and steep mountains, hills and mountains, and low-lying coastal plains. High and steep mountains range in the west and northwest of the city (in Hoa Bac, Hoa Lien, Hoa Ninh, and Hoa Phu communes) with average altitude from 500 to 1,500 m, including continuous ranges running into the sea. Some valleys are broken by high mountains, such as Ba Na (1,487 m), Hoi Mit (1,292 m), and Nui Mam (1,712 m). This area is primarily covered by forests with high value of biodiversity, natural resources, ecosystems, and environmental protection. Hills and mountains are located in the west and northwest of the city, including communes: Hoa Lien, Hoa Son, Hoa Nhon, Hoa Phong, and a part of Hoa Khuong, Hoa Ninh of Hoa Vang district. Hills and mountains are the area with a transition from high mountains to plains. Mountains in this area are specified by an inverse bowl shape with soil exhaustion and stones, average altitude changing from 50 to 100 m, slope from 3° to 8°. It is appropriate for developing fruit gardens and orchards.

Mainly in the eastern side of the city and along the coastal area and big rivers, such as Song Yen, Tuy Loan, Cam Le, Cu De, and Han, low-lying plains are separated by rivers as small and narrow areas, including many directions of dip. There are many large sand dunes along coastal regions, such as Xuan Thieu, Hoa Khanh, and Bac My An. The topography of this area is fairly low. Hence, residential quarters, agriculture services, industrial factories, and the functional area of government are mostly concentrated in this area.

3.1.3 Meteorological conditions

Da Nang is in a typical tropical monsoon region with high temperature and equable climate. The weather of city is a combination between climatic features of northern and southern Vietnam. There are two seasons: the wet season is from August to December and the dry from January to July. Occasional cold spells occur in winter but they are not severe and short. According to the statistics of Da Nang weather station at coordinates of 108°12' east longitude and 16°3' north latitude after 50 years, climatic weather of Da Nang City has been characterized as follows:

The annual average temperature is 25.6°C. The highest average temperature is about 29.8°C in June and July, and the lowest average temperature is 22.7°C in December and January. The absolute high temperature is 40.9°C, and the absolute low temperature is 10.2°C. The 1,500-m-high mountain Ba Na has an average temperature of 20°C.

The average moisture is 82% and the average humidity is 83.4%. The highest humidity appears in October and November, the average humidity of these months is about 85.67–87.67%, and the lowest humidity appears in June and July, average humidity of these months is about 76.67–77.33%.

The average rainfall in many years in the Ba Na Mountain is 2,642 mm, in Da Nang is 2,185 mm, and in Tien Sa is 2,456 mm. The highest rainfall is 550–1,000 mm per month in October and November and the lowest is 23–40 mm per month in January, February, March, and April.

The annual average sunshine hours are 2.158, with the maximum in May and June of 234–277 hours per month and the minimum in November and December of 69–165 hours per month. Gross annual radiation is 147.8 kcal/cm^2. Total sunshine hours in a year are 2.272 hours in average, and the average evaporation is 1,048 mm.

Based on measured data on wind speed, with the frequency corresponding to 0.5%, the strongest wind speed is 52 m/s; with a frequency of 1%, the wind speed is 47 m/s, and with the frequency of 5%, the wind speed was 39 m/s.

3.1.4 Hydrologic conditions

Within the city's territory, there are four large rivers, three of which are in the southeast of city, namely Vu Gia—Thu Bon river basin, including Vinh Dien River, Yen River, and Tuy Loan River. All of these rivers run to Han River before reaching the Da Nang gulf at the Han River mouth; basin area of Cu De River is 472 km^2 and this river flows from west to east.

+ Han River: Han River mouth is contiguous to the sea; therefore, it is strongly influenced by the tide. The Han River is the confluence of the Cau Do River and the Vinh Dien River. The highest water level is +3.45 m (1964), the lowest water level is +0.25 m.

+ Cu De River: Cu De River rises from the south of the Hai Van mountain pass, 38 km in length and 426 km^2 in area. Cu De River has the highest water level at +4.0 m and the lowest water level at +0.3 m. It includes two branches running in a west-east direction. The hydrographic varies swiftly according to the rains.

+ Vinh Dien River: Vinh Dien River is the confluence of Thu Bon River and Han River. The hydrograph varies according to the seasons. This is one of the rivers that caused formidable floods in Da Nang City during the last several years.

Topographical separation of the city was created to distinguish two river basins, the Cu De River basin in the North and Vu Gia-Thu Bon River basin in the South. Among eight districts, there are six districts in Vu Gia-Thu Bon River basin, accounting for 59.5% natural area. Therefore, Vu Gia-Thu Bon River basin plays an important role in the city's development. The flood season usually starts from September and continues to December.

In general, rivers flowing across Da Nang City have the common characteristics of rivers in the coastal region of Central Vietnam: short in length, large in depth, strongly fluctuating in water level and output, and poor alluviums. Da Nang Bay Sea has semidiurnal irregular tidal regime; on average, there are three diurnal tidal days in a month; the maximum month has eight diurnal tidal days, and the minimum month has one diurnal tidal day. Tidal amplitude at Da

Nang Port is 90 cm on average, the largest is 170 cm. Da Nang has many scattered small lakes, notably Xuan Ha, Thac Gian-Vinh Trung, Khue Trung, Bau Mac, Bau Vang, Bau Tram, Bau Gia Thuong, Bau Gia Ha, and so on. These lakes are generally small, with a surface area from 1 to 10 ha; the water level depends on the city's water level and season.

3.1.5 Natural resources

3.1.5.1 Soil resources

+ Sandy-bank and sandy-dunes group: This group is in the coastal region or in the river mouth, created by the influence of wind. The sandbank and sand dunes can be stable or mobile, located mainly in Lien Chieu, Son Tra, and Ngu Hanh Son districts. The sand-bank and sand dunes occupy about 10% of total area of Da Nang City. They are mainly in low-lying plains and used particularly in nonagriculture, exploiting for infrastructure construction, tourism, and habitat.

+ Salt soil group: This group is created from the penetration of the sea in the surface or artesian area. This kind of soil appears in sunken areas and concentrates in coastal regions or river mouths. The soil has brown-gray color, a salt layer in the surface, reaction from low aluminous to neuter, the mechanical composition from mix-sand to soil, the layer is deep from 50 to 100 cm.

+ Alkaline and salt soil group: Due to the disintegration of dead ocean animals in low-lying area, this kind of soil has brown, brown-gray color. This group is distributed in Hoa Xuan, Hoa Quy commune of Hoa Vang district. This group occupied about 2% of total area, mainly in low-lying plains, and most can be used for agriculture.

+ Alluvial soil group: This soil group is present mainly in lower sections of river streams. This kind of soil is appropriate for producing agriculture and occupied about 9% of total area of Da Nang City.

+ Slope gathering soil group: This kind of soil is normally distributed in the valleys. It is a thick layer with many organic substances. The fertility of the soil is good. This kind of soil has gray-brown, gray-black color; the mechanical composition includes softly soil to medium soil. It occupies about 1.8% of total area of Da Nang City and is good for agriculture. However, it has a scattered distribution across many complicated topographical areas and so can be difficult to access.

+ **Yellow and red humus soil group**: This kind of soil is distributed mainly in high mountains of Hoa Lien commune.

+ **Yellow and red soil group**: This group is the product of feralit process. The soil is created from weathered magma rock products; therefore, it has a red-yellow or yellow-red color. These soils are distributed in high mountains (including Hoa Vang and Son Tra districts) and occupied about 56.1% of total area of Da Nang City. They are mostly used in forestry and a little bit for agriculture.

3.1.5.2 Water resources

+ **Water surface**: Water for Da Nang City is supplied mainly from Cu De and Han Rivers.

- Cu De River is 38 km in length with total average of water volume of 0.7 billion m^3/year. The quality of water is quite good and now supplying for habitat activities and manufacturing in the north and northwest of city.

- Han River is the confluence of Cau Do and Vinh Dien rivers. Total average of the water volume is about 7.6 billion m^3/year. It is mainly used for supplying water in habitat activities and agricultural production.

In addition, the water supply in Son Tra Peninsula might be used for life activities; however, the reserves are quite low and depend on the seasons.

+ **Underground water**: According to the survey results of Planning Water Resource Association 709, the underground water in Da Nang City is quite shallow, various, and complicated. The underground areas exploited for water supply are in the Hoa Hai and Hoa Quy communes, with a depth of about 20–35 m and total average water volume of 5,000–10,000 m^3/day, and in Hoa Khanh with a depth about 30–90 m and total average water volume of 20,000,000 m^3/day for industrial places.

In general, the water source of Da Nang City is quite plentiful. However, in the dry season (May and June), the water source is salted because of tidal influence. The quality of water was quite good and might be used for life activities and developing economics.

3.1.5.3 Forestry and floristic cover resources

+ **Forestry resource**: Forest area occupied 59,127.27 ha, about 46.02% of total area. Natural forest in Da Nang City is at the confluence of north and south floras of Vietnam. All the trees are tropical evergreens and could be seen as the "Green Lung" of city. Ecological characteristic of forest is abundant and diversified, including:

- Protected forest, for the preservation of water resources, the prevention of erosion, natural disasters, climatic risks, and the overall protection of environment (8,624.55 ha)

- Special use of forest to conserve nature, plant, and animal species; to research; and to protect historic, cultural, and tourist sites (35,288.68 ha)

- Production of forest, for supplying timber and other forest products, and associated with other types of forest to protect environment (15,239.04 ha)

+ **Floristic cover resources:**

- **Mountains**: Due to the natural conditions, the ecology in the mountains is highly diverse and covered with many kinds of flora. However, the floristic cover resource has been strongly devastated because of the war and the exploitation by humans. At this time, the floristic cover has not been recovered to cover all the bare mountains yet. It can be divided into four levels:

- **Floristic cover of evergreen**: This is created from big standing timber and is green all year around. Therefore, the moisture in this area is high. In addition, floristic cover of evergreen supplies large amount of organic substance for soil.

- ***Floristic cover of sapling forestry***: Because of the war and the strong exploitation by humans, the forestry area was heavily devastated. For covering the mountains, many forest plantation programs were implemented in the late 1990s. Hence, the forest trees are still small, which is why the floristic cover of this forestry is thinner and the moisture is lower than that of the floristic cover of evergreen.

- ***Floristic cover of bamboos***: Besides sapling forestry, bare mountains are covered also by species of bamboo. However, the floristic cover is thinner and the moisture is lower than the floristic cover of sapling forestry.

- ***Floristic cover of shrub***: This area is contiguous to plains. Instead of trees, the surface in this area is covered by many kinds of shrub: *Rhodomyrtus tomentosa* (L.), *Melastoma dodecandrum Lour* (L.), *Melastoma candidum D. Don.* (L.), and *Imperata cylindrica* (L.). However, the layer of this cover is too thin which was caused by soil erosion when the rain falls down. Hence, it is difficult to plant in this area.

- ***Low-lying plains***: This is an agricultural area. The floristic cover includes mainly short-day crops and fruit trees. Because of the change in agricultural activities, the cover of this area is abundant and diversified. This area is closely connected with human life.

- ***River mouth area***: The area is covered by *Pinophyta*, *Poplar*, *Willow*, or *Halophyte* trees. There are also many kinds of alga or seaweed in the riverbed or the seabed, which are affected directly by human activities in the environment, in particular the water environment.

3.1.5.4 Sea and coastal region resources

Da Nang City has a coastal line of over 92 km in length, with a deepwater bay of 200 m and continental shelf outstretched over 125 km, which provides suitable conditions for developing maritime economics and doing business with foreign countries. According to the survey, the territorial seas of Da Nang City have high reserves of seafood, about 60,000-70,000 tons/year can be exploited (distributing in water at 50 m depth 31%, 50-200 m depth 48%, and over

200 m depth 21%). In addition, coastal region of Da Nang City is the right place for rearing aquatic products, such as fish and lobster in Tho Quang commune, shrimp in Nai Hien Dong, Hoa Hiep commune, Son Tra district.

Besides, various nice beaches with wonderful natural landscape along coastal line, such as Non Nuoc, My Khe, Pham Van Dong, Thanh Khe, Xuan Thieu, and Nam O, are good conditions for developing tourism.

3.1.5.5 Mineral resources

According to the survey documents, there is little mineral resource in Da Nang City, including stone for construction in Hoa Nhon, Hoa Phat, Hoa Son commune, granite in Non Nuoc commune, gold in Hoa Bac commune, white sand and peat in Hoa Khanh commune; however, the mineral reserve is negligible. The continental shelf promises petroleum and gas complex.

3.2 Social and economic conditions

3.2.1 Economic development

The economics of Da Nang City had many positive changes and obtained a remarkable growth rate, which met the basic demands in the short term and created impetus for development in the next years. In the period from 2001 to 2010, the city made many achievements in developing economics:

+ From 2001 to 2005 stage: The city gradually promoted the advantages of the new economic policy, mobilized all human and financial resources to give an impulse to trade and producing, and then could overcome all the difficulties of financial crisis. All economic indices of Da Nang City in this period achieved or exceeded the indices of the proposal. The annual development rate of GDP was about 12.89%, in which agriculture, forestry, and fishery increased to 6.3%, construction and industry increased to 18.95%, and services increased to 8.34%. The average GDP of each person in 2005 was 940 USD.

+ From 2006 to 2010 stage: In this period, there were many opportunities and challenges, such as Chanchu and Xangsane storms, and disease epidemics. Consequently, the price of raw materials increased, which heavily influenced to production and human life. Being an official member of World Trade Organization, it has given many chances for investment, developing production, economic development, and changing the economic structure of Vietnam in general, and of Da

Index	Unit	2000	2005	2010	Rate (%)		
					2001–2005	2006–2010	2001–2010
1. Population	10³ people	716.3	781.0	926.09	1.69	3.44	2.47
2. GDP (1994 price)	billion VND	3,390.2	6,214.3	10,275.45	12.89	10.31	11.74
– Agriculture, forestry, and fishery	–		276.3	373.5	308.12	6.30	-5.11	1.19
– Construction and industry	–		1,347.9	3,207.4	4,043.13	18.95	4.93	12.72
– Services	–		1,766.0	2,633.4	5,924.20	8.34	17.53	12.42
3. GDP/people							
– 1994 prices	10⁶ VND/person	4.73	7.97	11.56	11.00	6.73	9.10
– Current prices	–	6.91	15.01	35.87	16.83	16.82	16.82
– In USD	USD/person	488.0	940.0	1,795.0			

Table 3.1 GDP and development of economics during the period 2000–2010

Note: GDP, gross domestic product; VND, Vietnamese Dong; USD, US dollar.

Source: People's Committee Da Nang City (2010)

Nang city in particular: The annual development rate of GDP in this period was about 10.31%, in which agriculture, forestry, and fishery decreased to 5.11%, Construction and industry increased to 4.93%, and services increased to 17.53%. The average GDP of each person in 2010 was 1,795 USD. In general, from 2000 to 2010, the economics of Da Nang City achieved the annual rate at 11.74%, in which construction and industry increased to 12.72%, services increased to

12.42%, and agriculture, forestry, and fishery increased to 1.19%. The average income of each person was increased clearly, higher after each year. The average GDP was 488 USD/person in 2000, 940 USD/person in 2005, and 1,795 USD/person in 2010 (increased five times than in year 2010 and 1.91 times in year 2005).

3.2.2 Economic structure

During the period 2000–2010, the economic structure of Da Nang City has changed. The value of GDP in constructive and industry, and services increased strongly. The economic structure moved in both quality and quantity from "agriculture, forestry, and fishery-construction and industry-services" to "construction and industry-services-agriculture, forestry, and fishery" which satisfied the inherent demands of Da Nang City. As given in **Table 3.2**, the value of GDP in agriculture section decreased regularly from 7.9% (in 2000) to 3.91% (in 2010). Services section had the largest value of GDP, decreased from 50.19% (in 2000) to 44.68% (in 2005), and then increased to 51.51% (in 2010). The annual tempo-development of GDP in construction and industry section was quite good at 12.72% per year. The value of GDP in this section increased from 41.3% (in 2000) to 44.58% (in 2010).

Unit: %

Index	2000	2005	2010
Total	100	100	100
- Construction and industry	41.3	50.19	44.58
- Services	50.9	44.68	51.51
- Agriculture, forestry, and fishery	7.9	5.13	3.91

Table 3.2 Economic structures during the period 2000–2010
Source: People's Committee Da Nang City (2010)

The structure of economics by ownership also changed in a positive way. In the first period, the state-owned enterprise section still played an important role with the value of GDP increased from 54.86% (in 2000) to 58.5% (in 2003). However, since 2004, due to the promotion of arranging, renovating, and privatizing state enterprises, the value of GDP of this section decreased to 41.09% (in 2010), whereas the value of GDP in nonstate enterprises section increased gradually from 31.89% (in 2000) to 51.89% (in 2010). Although occupied just 8% of total GDP of Da Nang City, the foreign investment enterprises section was always kept in high level, which contributed to the development of economics of Da Nang City.

3.2.3 The situation of economic sectors

3.2.3.1 Agriculture, forestry, and fishery sector

In the 10-year period 2000–2010, the growth in gross output of agriculture, forestry, and fishery achieved the rate at 1.19% per year. The density of this section in total GDP of Da Nang City decreased from 7.9% (in 2000) to 3.91% (in 2010). The inherent structure of this section was changed by focusing on developing maritime economics, protecting the environment, increasing the density of fisheries, and decreasing the density of forestry and agriculture.

With a coastal line of over 92 km, fisheries were determined as a key in developing agriculture, forestry, and fishery section by exploiting seafood in the deep-sea instead of inshore fishing, investing and contributing the infrastructures and services for fish farming. Regarding agriculture and forestry, the decrease of agricultural area brought about the decrease in production of annual crops. Hence, the inherent structure of agriculture was changed by reducing the density in planting, raising the density in breeding. Forestry was strongly shifted from exploiting wood and forest products to protecting, afforesting, and covering the bare mountains.

3.2.3.2 Construction and industry sector

The gross output of construction and industry in the period of 10 years (2000–2010) increased at an annual rate of 12.72%. The density of this section in total GDP of Da Nang City increased from 41.3% (in 2000) to 44.58% (in 2010). The gross output of construction and industry section in 2010 was approximately 4,043.13 billion VND (Vietnamese Dong), over threefold than in 2000, which helped to shift the economic structure in the trend of increasing the density of construction and industry. Industry was the main force of Da Nang City and its gross output increased high every year. Many industrial parks and large projects have been invested. Nevertheless, the industry also faced many difficulties and challenges because of natural calamities, diseases, and the financial crisis in 2007.

3.2.3.3 Services sector

Because of its convenient geographical location and availability of all kinds of transportation, such as an airport, a seaport, and railways, Da Nang City had more advantages in transporting, importing, exporting, and tourism than any provinces in key economic zone of Central Vietnam. Therefore, almost all important service providers had their headquarters in Da Nang City to supply the services not only for Da Nang but also for the Central Zone. Including wholesale and retail trade, financial credit, real estate, tourism, transport, post, and others, the density of services section in total GDP of Da Nang City was always over 45%. During the 10-year period (2000–2010), the annual GDP rate of this section was 12.42%. The GDP of this section increased from 50.9% (in 2000) to 51.51% (in 2010).

3.2.4 Population, labor, employment, and income

3.2.4.1 Population

According to the *Statistical Yearbook of Da Nang 2010*, the population of Da Nang City on December 31, 2010, was 942,132, in which there were 458,605 men and 483,527 women, 819,332 people in urban (86.97% of total population), 122,800 people in rural (13.03% of total population). The natural growth rate of population in Da Nang City was 10.09%. The dweller distributed not equally between the area and districts. The highest density of people was 19,041 people/km^2 in Thanh Khe district; the lowest one was 166 people/km^2 in Hoa Vang district; the density of people in mainland was 960 people/km^2; the density of people in urban area was 3,364 people/km^2, over 20-fold the density of people in rural area. With the high urbanization rate, the population of Da Nang City will be further increased, which will bring about an increase in the density of people in the near future.

Number	District	Population (people)	Density (people/km²)
1	Hai Chau	197,922	8,500
2	Thanh Khe	179,810	19,041
3	Lien Chieu	140,500	1,775
4	Son Tra	135,300	2,280
5	Ngu Hanh Son	69,500	1,801
6	Cam Le	96,300	2,852
7	Hoa Vang	122,800	166
	Da Nang City*	942,132	960

* Calculated just in mainland.

Table 3.3 Population structure during the period 2000–2010
Source: People's Committee Da Nang City (2010)

3.2.4.2 Labor and employment

In 2010, the labor force of the whole city was 462,979 people (49.14% of total population), in which 440,500 people (95.14% of labor force) had stable employment, 148,050 people (33.61% of stable employment) worked in construction and industry section, 249,650 people (56.67% of stable employment) in services section, and 42,800 people (9.72% of stable employment) in agriculture, forestry, and fishery section.

Compared with the average standard for the whole country, the academic and technical standard of the labor force in Da Nang City was quite good. Most of the laborers were young. According to the statistics in 2010, over 83,498 laborers graduated from university and college education (18.03% of labor force), 26,039 laborers graduated from secondary vocational qualification (5.62% of labor force), and there were 37,914 technical workers (9.48% of labor force). In recent years, laborers in state-owned enterprises lessened strongly, whereas more and more laborers concentrated in nonstate and foreign investment enterprises.

In the 10-year period (2000–2010), Da Nang City provided jobs for 2.2 thousand laborers a year. Particularly, the number of laborers who obtained jobs significantly increased due to the adoption of the "Having Job" project. Accordingly, the rate of unemployment decreased from 5.42% (in 1997) to 4.95% (in 2005) and 4.86% (in 2010). It was assessed as a stable and reasonable condition for a developing city.

The unemployed individuals of Da Nang City in 2010 were numbered about 22,479 and most of them were in the urban area. In rural areas, the unemployment rate was lower. According to the statistical data, the coefficient of working day was about 85%. Da Nang City always concentrated in providing jobs for labors, combined with vocational and technical training. Therefore, the rate of educated labors increased from 21.6% (in 1997) to 24.4% (in 2000) and 50.16% (in 2010), over two times than in the first period of separating province in 1997.

Generally, the labor force of Da Nang City was quite plentiful, which provided good conditions for developing socioeconomics and constructing infrastructure. Nevertheless, the educated laborers were not enough. Hence, Da Nang City must concentrate more in vocational and technical training for the demands of development.

3.2.4.3 Income and life

Based on the reformation of economic policy and its own conditions, the economic growth rate of Da Nang City in the period 2000–2010 was 11.74% and reached the sixth position of the whole country after Ho Chi Minh, Ha Noi, Dong Nai, Binh Duong, and Ba Ria-Vung Tau. The average income increased from 6.91 million VND/person (in 2000) to 15.01 million VND/person (in 2005) and 35.87 million VND/person (in 2010).

The living conditions of all social classes were clearly improved and the comforts of life were ameliorated significantly. About 97% of households had solid or half-solid houses, and only 3% of households had rudimentary houses. About 95% of households could use electricity and 93% of households had running water. The habitat area also increased noticeably; the average habitat area of low-income groups was 13 m^2/person; the average habitat area of the whole city was 20.3 m^2/person, which was quite high, compared with other provinces and the whole country (Ho Chi Minh city: 12.27 m^2/person; cities in Central Zone: 9.02 m^2/person; the whole country: 9.67 m^2/person). Therefore, Da Nang City has continued to implement the aims of the "Having House" project in order to increase the living conditions of its inhabitants.

3.2.5 The situation of infrastructure

After Da Nang was recognized as a centrally governed city in 1997, the city concentrated more in constructing infrastructure, improving most streets within the city. However, these measures were not enough for a big city. The infrastructure satisfied just a part of urgent demand of city.

3.2.5.1 Transport

+ Airline: Far away from the center of the city, about a distance of 5 km, Da Nang airport has an important position, compared with other airport systems in the Central Zone. It is used for civil and military transport, with an area of 1,100 ha, 850 ha for the airport and 37 ha for civilian use. Da Nang airport is the aid point that supplies air-traffic services for international flights and has the capability of receiving up to 400,000 tons of goods per year and 2.5 million passengers per year. Because of the location of airport in the city, there are many advantages for passengers. However, this also causes many obstacles for people living near the airport as well as the development of the city. In the long term, the noise of airplanes will significantly affect the environment.

Year	Passenger (person)		Goods (ton)	
	Departure	Arrival	Departure	Arrival
2000	240,024	233,145	1,092	1,128
2001	338,843	328,651	2,186	2,089
2002	336,170	321,063	1,601	2,303
2003	314,585	295,385	2,047	2,484
2004	445,994	404,800	2,727	3,406
2005	524,708	485,561	2,385	3,932
2006	626,577	580,726	2,779	4,891
2007	613,336	571,818	2,597	5,902
2008	904,426	797,332	3,410	6,689
2009	791,000	778,000	3,097	8,976
2010	974,189	937,381	3,057	7,458

Table 3.4 Quantity of transported passengers and goods by airlines
Source: Da Nang's Statistical Office, Statistic Year Books

+ *Road network*: Highway 1A is the communication axis running from North to South Vietnam. Part of the highway across Da Nang City begins from the Hai Van Pass to Hoa Phuoc commune at 35.5 km in length and carries interprovincial traffic. It has been improved by mineral pitch concrete composition and widened to 28 m. Highway 14B (32 km in length) runs along Son Tra and Ngu Hanh Son districts, crosses Tuyen Son Bridge, and reaches to the crossroads of Hoa Cam, Tuy Loan, and Hoa Khuong. This route connects Da Nang City with the Central Highlands as well as with the overland network to Cambodia, Thailand, and so on. The province road network includes roads 601, 602, 604, and 605 which are 83.8 km in length, 7 m wide (601 and 602), or 15 m wide (604 and 605). Most roads have been improved by mineral pitch concrete composition. The road network within the city has a total length of 268 km. Most of the roads were improved and fixed for traffic in the city itself. The rural road network includes district roads that are 69 km in length, commune roads that are 84 km in length, and rural roads 272 km that are in length. Most of the rural road network was covered by mineral pitch composition; in particular, about 90% of rural roads were concreted. In addition, there are 35 kinds of bridges that have just been improved and/or constructed. As a whole, the road network of about 850 km in length in Da Nang City was synchronously connected, improved, fixed, and renewed. Fifty percent of the road networks are main roads, which help to develop socioeconomics not only for the urban area but also for the rural and mountainous region.

+ *Railway*: Railway runs across Da Nang City, 36 km in length, and has the capability of 22 couple of trains for over a 24-hour period. It includes three main railway stations: Kim Lien station in the south of Hai Van Pass, Le Trach in Hoa Tien commune (the south of city), and Da Nang station in the central of city with an area of 240,000 m^2 is responsible for transporting passengers and goods.

Year	Passenger departure (1,000 person)	Package departure (ton)	Goods (1,000 ton)	
			Departure	Arrival
2000	363.0	5,320	10,046	58,225
2001	403.1	6,101	10,506	107,190
2002	415.6	5,172	23,989	195,543

2003	414.9	4,573	50,622	220,055
2004	444.5	5,718	40,576	170,720
2005	445.8	3,939	30,604	174,089
2006	364.4	2,863	65,277	207,119
2007	342.3	2,294	113,659	208,454
2008	313.5	1,945	123,557	197,403
2009	290.3	2,083	135,741	220,885
2010	315.3	2,139	131,091	216,994

Table 3.5 Quantity of transported passengers and goods by train
Source: Da Nang's Statistical Office, Statistic Year Books

+ Waterway: The inland waterway is 60 km in length and can be used to transport goods when it is not convenient to transport by land, including Han, Cu De, Cam Le, Yen, Tuy Loan Rivers, and the transported goods are mainly consumer products, fuel, and sand. Due to the advantages of the road network, transporting by inland waterway decreases with every passing day. Da Nang City seems to have many advantages for developing the seaport and river port. They play important roles in the Central Zone for domestic transport and international exporting, including Tien Sa seaport and Han River port. Han River port has an area of 3 ha, in which 8,000 m^2 is used for storage area and 8,225 m^2 for storehouses. The river port can accept ships with an aggregate tonnage of 5,000 tons. Tien Sa seaport is in Da Nang bay with two wharfs (183 m in length and 27.5 m in width), three large storehouses (15,875 m^2), and one storage area (17 ha). The seaport can accept ships with an aggregate tonnage of 20,000–30,000, which is used for container goods, over-length or overweight goods.

Unit: 1,000 tons

Year	Total	Dividing				Turn-around
		International export	International import	Domestic export	Domestic import	
2000	1,410.6	421.6	333.5	65.9	589.6	1,847.1
2001	1,709.8	428.6	646.2	76.1	558.9	2,232.3
2002	2,074.0	511.2	802.7	159.9	600.2	2,644.9
2003	2,178.6	554.1	824.3	231.1	569.0	2,768.8
2004	2,308.9	739.9	724.7	146.0	698.4	3,086.9

2005	2,256.1	778.4	595.2	95.4	787.3	3,021.3
2006	2,371.0	891.6	414.8	72.2	992.4	3,145.3
2007	2,736.9	1,241.2	489.3	106.3	900.1	4,056.2
2008	2,742.3	1,230.8	525.9	85.6	899.9	4,188.1
2009	3,150.4	1,370.6	630.3	102.0	1,074.5	4,179.2
2010	3,304.0	1,388.0	645.0	136.0	1,232.0	4,591.0

Table 3.6 Quantity of transported goods by waterway
Source: Da Nang's Statistical Office, Statistic Year Books

Generally, the traffic in Da Nang City has many advantages and ability in exploiting effectively by the connection between mountainous regions, midland, coastal region, tourism area, and center city. It can be developed and integrated easily with national and international traffic. However, there are many problems that need to be solved, such as the placement of the airport and railway station in the center of the city. Although it is convenient for passengers, there are many obstacles in developing the city and protecting environment.

3.2.5.2 Irrigation

The irrigation systems in Da Nang City include 2 big water reservoirs (HoaTrung and Dong Nghe), 21 medium and small water reservoirs, 27 spillways and 27 feed-pump stations, 13 km of seawalls, and 630 km of canals (452 km interior field canals). Total capable design of irrigation systems is 12,500 ha; real capability of irrigation is 8,500 ha (68% of total design capacity) that satisfies 72% of the cultivated area. There are 139 km permanent canals (71% of total canals).

3.2.5.3 Education and training

The education and training systems of Da Nang City have all kinds of school, such as public, semiofficial, private, day-boarder. These schools are distributed widely across Da Nang city. Therefore, 100% of children from six years old come to school. Illiteracy disappeared in 100% of the communes. There are 124 kindergartens, 99 primary education schools, 55 junior high schools, 21 senior high schools, 8 technical secondary schools, 10 colleges, and 5 universities. In general, the education and training network in Da Nang City developed quite well, which satisfied the demand of study for the inhabitants and supplied thousands of educated laborers for not only Da Nang City but also neighboring provinces. In addition, the education systems supported the farmer who lost cultivated land, the rural laborer, the poor, or the handicapped people who now have new jobs.

3.2.5.4 Health and medicaments

The public health of Da Nang City has 22 hospitals (including 4 private hospitals), 3 health centrals, and 56 communal health stations. The total number of beds is 3,819, that is, 43 beds/10,000 people. About 56/56 (100%) communes attained the national standard of health and medicaments. The health network in Da Nang City was carefully planned, and the number of beds and physician doctors increase every year. In addition, the preventive health services were also concerned. Consequently, the disease prevention projects have been implemented and all kinds of vaccine have been widely used.

3.2.5.5 Electricity

+ **Power source**: The main power source of Da Nang City belongs is the National Grid 500 kV through transformer stations, including a 500-kV station with two transformer machines (+500/200 kV -450 MVA and +220/110 -125 MVA), Xuan Ha station with two transformer machines (2 × 25 MVA -110/35/6 kV). In addition, there are spare diesel source in Cau Do (12 MW) and airport (3.5 MW) for supplying in peak hours.

   + **Electric network**: Currently, Da Nang City has 448.9 km in length of electric network (110 kV – 385 km, 35 kV – 63.9 km), 362.37 km in length of supply network (15 KV – 206.9 km, 6 KV – 125.3 km, 22 KV – 30.17 km), 29 km in length of step-low network (0.4 and 0.2 kV), and 1,310 transformer machines (220/0.4 kV station: 19, 15/0.4 kV station: 428, 0.6/0.4 kV station: 863).

3.2.5.6 Telecommunication

The telecommunications of Da Nang City has been modernized in recent years and became the third large telecommunication center of the whole country. The network distributes widely across the whole city with one central post office, four district post offices, 57 posts, and 14 communal cultural stations. Currently, the communication system includes 146 telecommunication centrals, 449 telecommunication stations, 45 switchboards with 275,218 telephones and fax machines, and 48 public telephone stations, which satisfy the communicating demand of inhabitants in Da Nang City.

3.3 General assessment of natural, socioeconomic condition

Based on the conditions of nature and socioeconomics, we can summarize the advantages and disadvantages of developing economics of Da Nang City in the following statements:

+ **Advantages**:

- By the favorable geographical location with all kinds of traffic conditions, such as national transport axis with major road, railroad, sea and air transport links, and the gateway to Central Highlands as well as trans-network to East-West Economic Corridor, Da Nang City has conditions that allow easy exchange with other countries (Lao, Thailand, Myanmar, and so on). It has the capability of being in the first position in developing economics in the Central Region and Highlands.

- With a coastline of 92 km, Da Nang City has advantages in developing maritime economics as well as tourism.

- The temperate weather, together with the big potentiality of seafood and large fishing ground, is a good condition to develop fisheries.

- Being the center of famous cultural and natural heritage sites such as the ancient capital of Hue, Hoi An ancient town, My Son sanctuary, and Phong Nha-Ke Bang National Forest, and having many beautiful beaches, Da Nang City attracts numerous tourists coming to visit and relax.

- Da Nang has made a good start by building hard infrastructure with multiform transport network, synchronously electricity and water systems, and modern telecommunications.

These conditions attracted both domestic and foreign investments.

- There are many kinds of education and training, including university, college, technical training, as well as research centers, which help to have educated laborers to high level and attract more and more research staff working in Da Nang City.

+ *Disadvantages*:

- In the wet season, downpours cause floods in low-lying plains, whereas exhausted sources of water in dry season cause salty in lower river section that give troubles for farming.

- Complicated topography with high and steep mountains, in company with heavy rains, is the reasons of destroying floristic cover, through landslide and erosion in the areas of Da Nang City.

- The degradation of water, soil, and air has been more and more serious due to the human activities in development and construction. Like other cities in Vietnam, Da Nang City also faces these problems. If there is not any timely solution for preventing natural degradations, it will diminish the ability in developing the economics of the city.

Chapter 4
Data and Methodology

Abstract

This chapter presents the remote sensing collection used in this study. Computational methods applied for processing data, detecting changes in land use/cover, and landscape structure, together with modeling land-use change are explained in detail.

4.1 Sensor systems

Initially, three satellite sensor systems were chosen for land-cover mapping: Landsat, SPOT (System Probatoire d'Observation de la Terre), and ASTER (Advanced Space-borne Thermal Emission and Reflection Radiometer). However, SPOT data could not be used due to incomplete availability. Landsat satellite data were the best alternative choice owing to their long existence. The chosen Landsat scenes for this study include data of all three Landsat systems, namely Landsat multispectral scanner (MSS), Landsat thematic mapper (TM), and Landsat enhanced thematic mapper plus (ETM$^+$).

According to Jensen (2000), the Landsat MSS sensor was set for Landsat satellites 1–5. Landsat MSS used an optical-mechanical system in which a mirror scans the terrain perpendicular to the flight direction. Energy reflected or emitted from the terrain is obtained onto discrete detector elements in scanning. Then, the radiant flux measured within each instantaneous field of view (IFOV) in the scene has been converted into an electronic signal by the detectors. The IFOV of each detector element is squared and measured in a ground resolution by approximately 79 × 79 m. The MSS scanning mirror oscillates through an angular displacement of ±5.78° off nadir. The 11.56° field of view resulted in a swath width of 185 km during each orbit. Six parallel detectors sensitive to four spectrums viewed the ground simultaneously: 0.5–0.6 µm (green), 0.6–0.7 µm (red), 0.7–

0.8 µm (reflective near-infrared), and 0.8–1.1 µm (reflective near-infrared), namely, 4, 5, 6, and 7 bands, respectively.

The Landsat TM sensor was placed on the Landsat 4 and 5 platforms. This records energy in the visible, reflective infrared, mid-infrared, and thermal-infrared (TIR) regions of the electromagnetic spectrum as an optical mechanical whisk-broom sensor. The Landsat TM sensor can obtain multispectral images with higher spatial, spectral, temporal, and radiometric resolution compared to Landsat MSS. Landsat TM has seven bands: band 1: 0.45–0.52 µm (blue), band 2: 0.52–0.60 µm (green), band 3: 0.63–0.69 µm (red), band 4: 0.76–0.90 µm (near-infrared), band 5: 1.55–1.75 µm (mid-infrared), band 6: 10.4–12.5 µm (TIR), and band 7: 2.08–2.35 µm (mid-infrared). The TIR band 6 has been excluded as it has a spatial resolution of 120 × 120 m, whereas band 1 through band 5 and band 7 have a ground projected IFOV of 30 × 30 m.

The ETM$^+$ sensor was launched on the Landsat-7 platform. The ETM$^+$ sensor has the same mirror and detector design, and is based on the same push-broom technology which is derived from Landsat TM. The ETM$^+$ has the same 7 bands than its predecessor TM, in which bands 1 through 5 and 7 have the same 30 × 30 m spatial resolution and TIR band 6 has 60 × 60 m spatial resolution instead of 120 × 120 m. Moreover, there is a notable band with 15 × 15 m resolution, namely panchromatic band: 0.52–0.9 µm. However, the ETM$^+$ Scan Line Corrector was defected in 2003, resulting in imagery with significant missing data. Consequently, an ASTER image was used to discover the changes of land use/cover (LULC) for the period after 2003 instead of Landsat ETM$^+$.

	Landsat MSS		Landsat TM		Landsat ETM⁺	
	Band	Spectral resolution (μm)	Band	Spectral resolution (μm)	Band	Spectral resolution (μm)
	4	0.5–0.6	1	0.45–0.52	1	0.45–0.52
	5	0.6–0.7	2	0.52–0.6	2	0.52–0.6
	6	0.7–0.8	3	0.63–0.69	3	0.63–0.69
	7	0.8–1.1	4	0.76–0.9	4	0.76–0.9
			5	1.55–1.75	5	1.55–1.75
			6	10.4–12.5	6	10.4–12.5
			7	2.08–2.35	7	2.08–2.35
					8 (panchromatic)	0.50–0.9
IFOV at nadir	79×79 band 1–7 240×240 band 8		30×30 band 1–5, 7 120×120 band 6		30×30 band 1–5, 7 60×60 band 6 15×15 band 8	
Data rate	15 Mb/s		85 Mb/s			
Quantization	6-bits (values 0–63)		8-bits (values 0–255)		8–9-bits (values 0–255)	
Earth coverage	18 days (Landsat 1, 2, 3) 16 days (Landsat 4, 5)		16 days (Landsat 4, 5)		16 days	
Altitude	919 km		705 km		705 km	
Swath width	185 km		185 km		185 km	
Inclination	99°		98.2°		98.2°	

Table 4.1 Characteristics of Landsat sensors

Note: MSS, multispectral scanner; TM, thematic mapper; ETM⁺, enhanced thematic mapper plus; IFOV, instantaneous field of view.
Source: Jensen (2000)

ASTER is the product of cooperation between National Aeronautics and Space Administration and Japan's Ministry of International Trade and Industry. ASTER records information on land surface temperature, emissivity, reflectance, and elevation. ASTER consists of 14 bands from visible through TIR regions of the electromagnetic spectrum, dividing as three separate instrument subsystems: VNIR (visible and near infrared), SWIR (short-wave infrared), and TIR. The technical details of the ASTER system are summarized in **Table 4.2**.

ASTER					
Band	VNIR (µm)	Band	SWIR (µm)	Band	TIR (µm)
1 (nadir)	0.52–0.60	4	1.600–1.700	10	8.125–8.475
2 (nadir)	0.63–0.69	5	2.145–2.185	11	8.475–8.825
3 (nadir)	0.76–0.86	6	2.815–2.225	12	8.925–9.275
3 (backward)	0.76–0.86	7	2.235–2.285	13	10.25–10.95
		8	2.295–2.365	14	10.95–11.65
		9	2.360–2.430		
Detector	Push-broom		Push-broom		Whisk-broom
Spatial resolution	15 × 15		30 × 30		90 × 90
Swath width	60 km		60 km		60 km
Quantization	8-bits		8-bits		12-bits

Table 4.2 Characteristics of ASTER

Note: ASTER, advanced space-borne thermal emission and reflection radiometer; VNIR, visible and near-infrared; SWIR, short-wave infrared; TIR, thermal infrared.
Source: Jensen (2000)

4.2 Data collection

In this study, four base years were defined to analyze LULC changes in Da Nang City. The determination of these base years is a result and compromise of project needs and satellite data availability. Among all available satellite data, the following scenes were chosen: Landsat-3 MSS July 24, 1979; Landsat-5 TM July 7, 1996; Landsat-5 TM July 14, 1996; Landsat-7 ETM+ March 4 and April 14, 2003; and ASTER April 2, 2009. Details of these satellite images can be found in **Table 4.3**. Landsat images were downloaded for free from Earth Explorer (http://earthexplorer.usgs.gov/) and the United States Geological Survey (USGS) Global Visualization (http://glovis.usgs.gov/). ASTER images were purchased from the Japan Space Systems/Earth Remote Sensing Division. Nevertheless, the SWIR data (bands 4–9) of ASTER are unusable (USGS, 2009) due to the increase of the SWIR detector's temperature after April 2007.

Because of the geographic location and the tropical climate, the area of Da Nang City is frequently covered by cirrus and cumulus clouds. As a consequence, only a limited number of cloud-free optical satellite images were available for the study area. The data acquisitions used in this study cover different seasons (dry season to wet season), which has to be accounted for in the change detection analysis due to seasonal effects. Detailed training and reference data together with local knowledge were used in order to deal with this problem (Kashaigili and Majaliwa, 2010).

The mosaic of Landsat TM images of 1996 was chosen to map the state of LULC in the study area before separating from the Quang Nam Province. In 2003, the new Land Law was approved by the national assembly and a new land-use system was created. Land use in Da Nang City was inventoried for these special times by the National Department of Geodesy and Cartography. Hence, LULC maps resulting from these inventories could be used later as reference data (Figures 4.1–4.4).

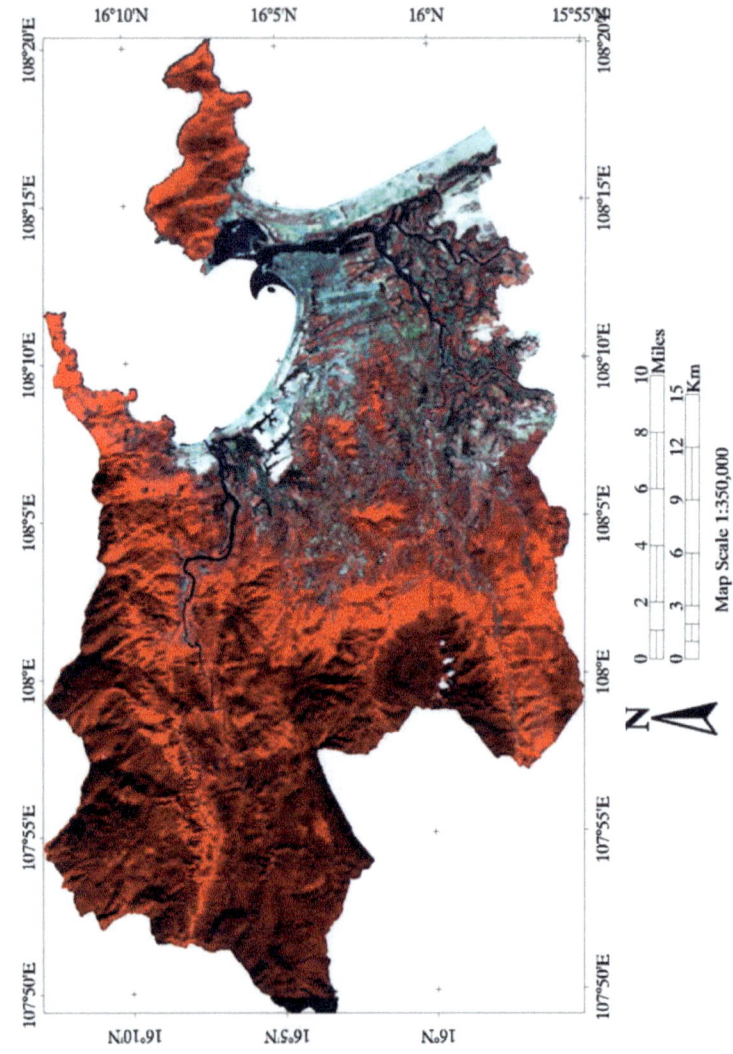

Figure 4.1 Subset of Landsat MSS image (July 24, 1979), RGB 754
Source: Author's calculation

Chapter 4 Data and Methodology

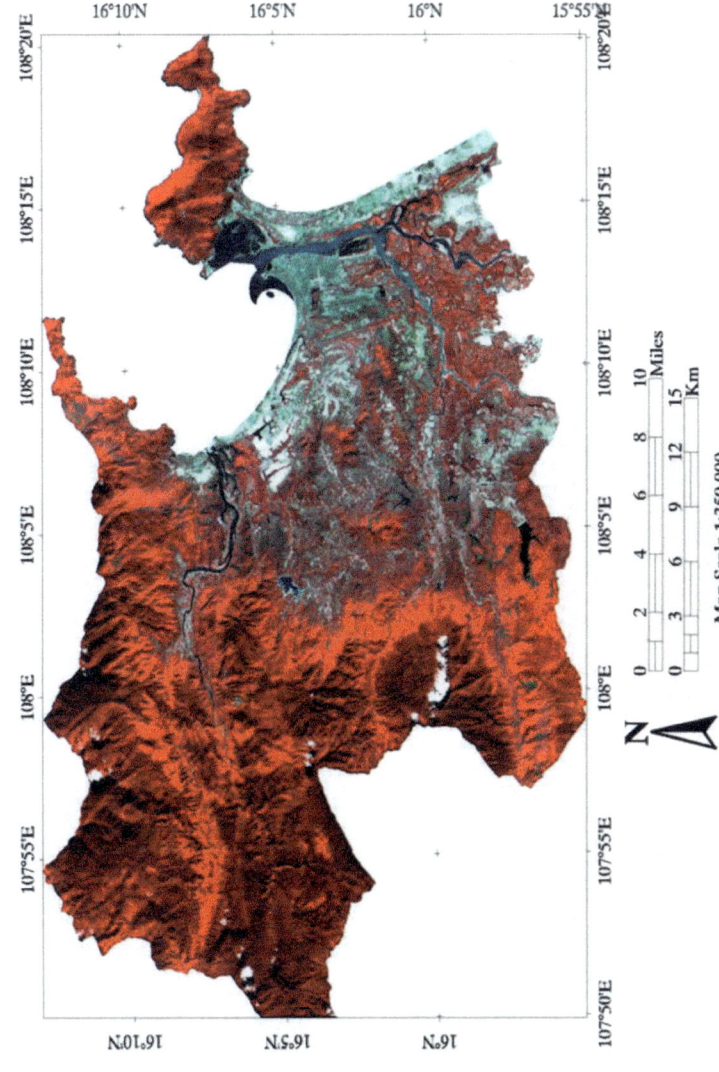

Figure 4.2 Subset of mosaic Landsat TM images (July 07 & 14, 1996), RGB 432 images
Source: Author's calculation

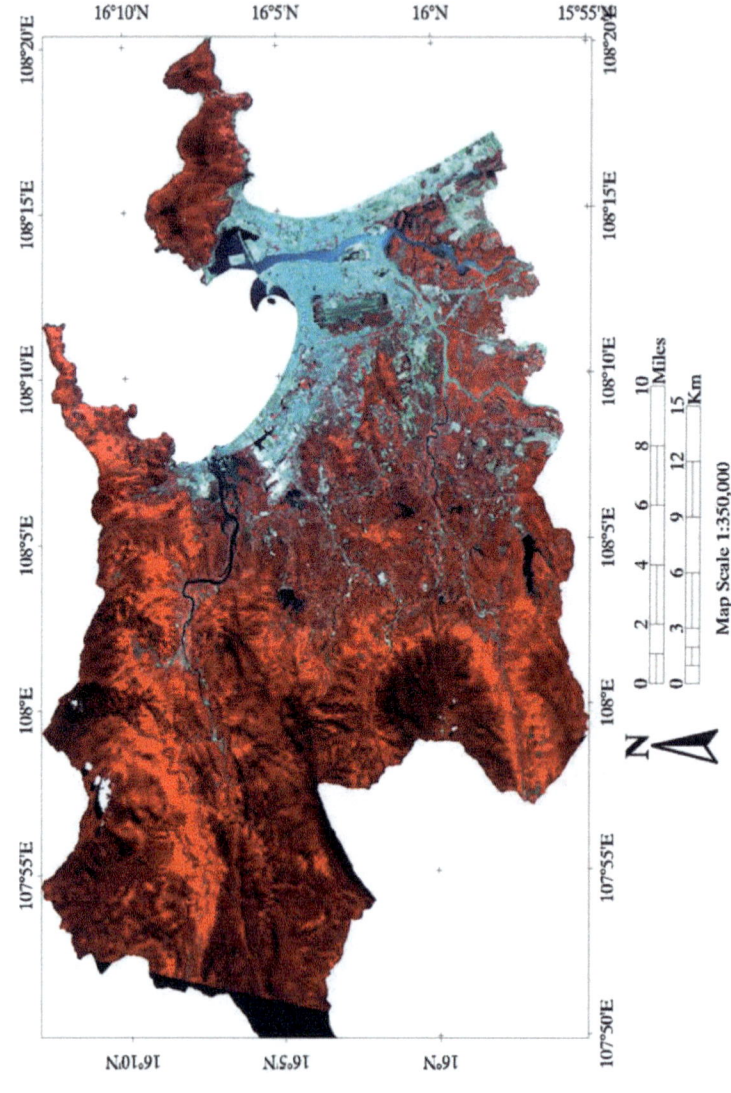

Figure 4.3 Subset of mosaic Landsat ETM+ images (March 04 & April 14, 2003), RGB 432
Source: Author's calculation

Chapter 4 Data and Methodology

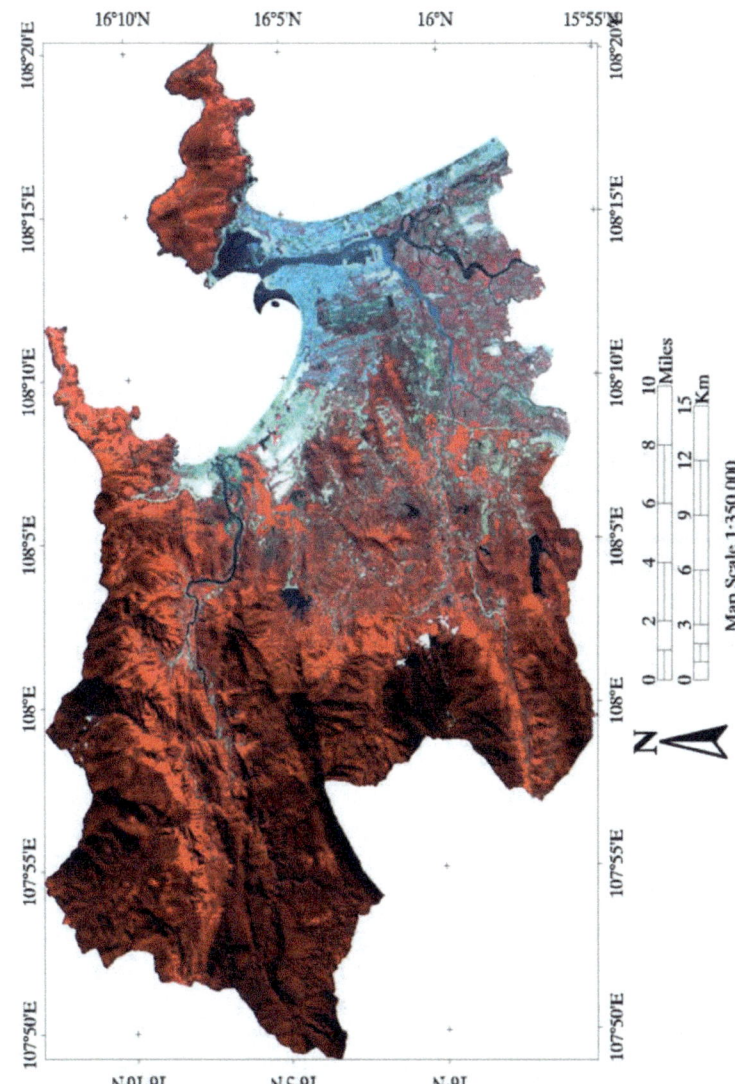

Figure 4.4 Subset of ASTER image (April 02, 2003), RGB 321
Source: Author's calculation

In this study, ancillary data included topographical map 2001 (scale 1:50.000), land-use map 1997, 2003, 2010 (scale 1:25.000), and an administrative map. These maps were used to correct the geometry of the satellite images and assess the accuracy of land-use maps. In addition, a panchromatic SPOT 5 image acquired on February 12, 2009 (2.5 m), was also used as reference images for satellite images interpretation. SPOT image was purchased from Vietnam National Remote Sensing Centre. In addition to remote satellite data, social statistics and economic data for Da Nang City were collected from Da Nang Statistics Yearbooks in different years. Due to the rapid growth of the city, the administrative boundaries of districts in this study area have been changed. In 2005, a part of Hoa Vang district was separated as one new, namely, Cam Le. Consequently, social statistics and economic data were inconsistent in parts. Population data and the GDP of agriculture, industry, and service sectors were gathered. Also, land-use planning guidelines of Da Nang City were collected to analyze the driving factors of LULC changes in Da Nang City.

Type of sensor	Spatial resolution (m)	Band	Date	Path	Row	Average cloud coverage (%)
Landsat-3 MSS	79	4–8	July 24, 1979	134	49	20
Landsat-5 TM	30	1–5, 7	July 14, 1996	125	49	11
	30	1–5, 7	July 07, 1996	124	49	0
Landsat-7 ETM+	28.5	1–5, 7	March 04, 2003	125	49	34.65*
	28.5	1–5, 7	April 14, 2003	124	49	0.34
ASTER (VNIR)	15	1–3	April 02, 2009	–	–	4

Table 4.3 Characteristics in satellite datasets used

Note: MSS, multispectral scanner; TM, thematic mapper; ETM+, enhanced thematic mapper plus;
*Although the average cloud coverage of Landsat-7 ETM+ is very high, there is almost no cloud in the study area at that time.

4.3 Image preprocessing

4.3.1 Geometric correction

For producing spatially corrected LULC maps through time, it is important to register multiple data imageries to a single map coordinate system (Yang and Lo, 2002). In this study, the digital topographical map 1/50,000 of 2001 was used as reference data. The ASTER image was georeferenced to Universal Transverse Mercator coordinate system, Datum World Geodetic System 1984, Zone 48 North by image-to-map rectification. Then, the ASTER-registered image was used as the base image to co-register all Landsat images. An average of 25 well-distributed ground control points were used. A first-degree polynomial transform was applied to transform the image coordinates. The achieved root mean square error (RMSE) value of all transformations was below 0.5 pixels. According to Lunetta et al. (1998), an ideal RMSE of any two date images used for change detection should be less than 0.5 pixel.

Due to the different spatial resolution and seasonal acquisitions of the remote satellite imagery, a radiometric normalization was required in order to study change detection. For this reason, the nearest-neighbor resampling was used to avoid changing the radiometric characteristic of original remote satellite images (Crocetto and Tarantino, 2009). All satellite images were resampled to 30 m pixel size.

4.3.2 Radiometric normalization

As pointed out by Chen et al. (2005), radiometric correction should be performed on multitemporal images to increase the sensitivity of LULC changes and simultaneously reduce the impact of environmental and sensor factors like sensor characteristics, atmospheric condition, solar angle, and sensor view angle.

Conghe Song et al. (2001) evaluated different absolute and relative radiometric normalization techniques. This preprocessing method is significant for land-cover change and other studies, such as mosaicking imageries and tracking indices of vegetation over times (Caprioli et al., 2008).

Conghe Song et al. (2001) asserted that in the absolute radiometric correction approach, the digital brightness value of a pixel has been recorded by the remote sensing system. In which, established transformation equations and atmospheric models are used to convert digital brightness value as a percent reflectance value. Thus, it needs information of both the sensor spectral characteristic and the properties of atmosphere at the time of the acquired image. According to Caprioli et al. (2008), data for characterization of the relevant atmosphere include "aerosols, ozone, or water vapor in different atmospheric layers." However, it is impossible to determine these data for the historic satellite images, because atmospheric properties are not available (Du et al., 2002).

To overcome this problem, relative radiometric correction can be considered as an alternative approach, which is discovered by the radiometric information intrinsic of images (Caprioli et al., 2008). Relative radiometric correction is applied for (a) normalizing the intensities of different bands in a single-date image or (b) normalizing the intensities of different bands in multiple-date images to a standard selected image (Jensen, 2005). Yuan and Elvidge (1996) ascertained that this procedure maintains the original radiometric value of the reference image. Thus, it obviates the computation in converting image to the unit of radiance or reflectance. The relative correction approach for multiple-date images has been suggested by authors such as Jensen (2005) with multiple-date empirical radiometric normalization or Schott et al. (1988), Caselles and García (1989), Conel (1990), and Hall et al. (1991) with pseudoinvariant features (PIFs). These methods involve in selecting a base image, and then the spectral characteristics of all other images recorded on different dates are transformed to have approximately the same radiometric as the standard scale. Within radiometric normalization approach, the selection of ground targets is generated from the knowledge and abilities of the analyst about local area (Janzen et al., 2006). Nevertheless, those approaches are limited with satellite imagery under climatic conditions, such as clouds or snow covers in the acquisition phase (Caprioli et al., 2006; Moran et al., 1992).

For ameliorating such matters, different techniques to select PIFs were developed by Heo and FitzHugh (2000). Later, Du et al. (2002) used the principal component analysis to select PIFs. In

2004, Canty et al. raised a new automatic radiometric normalization for multitemporal satellite imagery, based on MAD (multivariate alteration detection) transformation and later IR-MAD (iteratively reweighted multivariate alteration detection) transformation; see also Canty and Nielsen (2008). IR-MAD transformation is known as a fully automatic approach and overcomes the aforementioned limited problems, in which "no change pixels" are identified. Based on the earlier discussions, IR-MAD transformation was chosen as the radiometric normalization approach for this study.

The remote satellite images used in this thesis were attained from various sensors at different dates spanning a period of 30 years. In order to have a meaningful detection of LULC change, the second step in the preprocessing images involved in compensating the inhomogeneous of the time series of satellite images. The ASTER 02/04/2009 image was selected as a reference image or "target" image, which was used to correct the rest of the images based on IR-MAD method by means of ENVI extensions (Canty and Nielsen, 2008). As requirement of radiometric normalization approach, all images must have the same dimensions and spectral resolution. Hence, a subset of 1,800 × 1,100 pixels with resampled 30 m spatial resolution including 968.17 km^2 was chosen for investigation. In addition, a composite of standard false color was applied for individual images: Landsat MSS (754), Landsat TM/ETM+ (432), and ASTER (321). After radiometric normalization, the multi-images in the same period of years 1996 and 2003 were mosaicked as a new single seamless composite image and then the study area was extracted in the image for further analysis

4.4 Image classification and accuracy assessment

4.4.1 Image classification

According to Anderson's classification scheme level I (Anderson et al., 1976a), six LULC classes were defined in this study: (1) agriculture, (2) barren, (3) urban area, (4) forest, (5) shrub, and (6) water. The fact that there were some clouds and cloud shadows in remote satellite imagery, all potential clouds and cloud shadows were detected. However, all of these clouds and cloud shadows persisted in the northern and western parts of study area covered by forest. Consequently, all clouds and shadow cloud categories were combined to forestry classes.

For classification, different training areas of each LULC class were delineated and verified by reference maps and the visual interpretation of each image (Bakr et al., 2010). The number of pixels for Landsat 1979, Landsat 1996, Landsat 2003, and ASTER 2009 were 11,701, 16,389, 11,927, and 10,693, respectively. Based on supervised classification using maximum likelihood algorithm, six LULC types were derived from the classification maps of 1979, 1996, 2003, and 2009.

Due to the capability in minimizing the problems that are encountered in radiometric calibration of imagery of two days, post-classification comparison was employed for LULC maps extracted from satellite imageries to detect the changes of LULC in four intervals of time: 1979–1996, 1996–2003, 2003–2009, and 1979–2009. Based on pixel-by-pixel approach, a change detection matrix of the classification results in two days was inspected, from which from-to-change of LULC types were identified. It means that the accuracy of each individually classified map decides the accuracy of change detection (Jensen, 2005). Therefore, it requires accurate geometric correction, proper radiometric correction, a good quality training sample, and suitable classification methods in order to increase the image classification accuracy and improve/achieve acceptable change detection results (Chen and Wang, 2010).

The second part of this study is related to investigating the change of landscape pattern; it is worthy to perceive the "salt-and-pepper" effect observed in per-pixel classification approach. In some cases, a single pixel could be ranged as one patch of land-cover type. Such occurrence can result in scattered patches of very small sizes, which have potential in reducing the effectiveness of patch metrics to analyze landscape patterns. Thus, it is needed to generate classified LULC maps as less impact of the "salt-and-pepper" effect as possible by carefully evaluating and manipulating the spectral signatures of each LULC type. To do this, a 3 × 3 majority filtering of post-classification was applied on the binary images to reduce the occurrences of patches with a single pixel or a small number of pixels (Ji et al., 2006).

4.4.2 Accuracy assessment

		Reference classes				
	Class	1	2	3	j	Row total
Remote sensing classification	1	$p_{1,1}$	$p_{1,2}$	$p_{1,3}$	$p_{1,j}$	p_{1+}
	2	$p_{2,1}$	$p_{2,2}$	$p_{2,3}$	$p_{2,j}$	p_{2+}
	3	$p_{3,1}$	$p_{3,2}$	$p_{3,3}$	$p_{3,j}$	p_{3+}
	j	$p_{j,1}$	$p_{j,2}$	$p_{j,3}$	$p_{j,j}$	p_{j+}
	Column total	p_{+1}	p_{+2}	p_{+3}	p_{+j}	N

Table 4.4 Illustration of error matrix with j classes and N reference samples
Source: Jensen (2005)

As pointed out by Johannsen et al. (2003), remotely sensed/remote sensing image data have become more and more important for environmental models at local, regional, and global scales. Many significant decisions are made throughout the world using derived information from remotely sensed data (Kyriakidis et al., 2004; Muchoney and Strahler, 2002). Hence, it is needed to assess the accuracy of thematic maps and give evidence for implementing the next steps.

A total of 300 stratified random samples of pixels were assigned to each LULC map extracted from satellite image and checked their labels based on reference data, from which overall accuracy of each LULC map was calculated. The 1996 classified Landsat images were compared to land-use map of 1997; the 2003 classified Landsat images were compared to land-use map 2003 and topographic map 2000; the 2009 classified ASTER image was compared to land-use map 2010 and SPOT-5 images 2009. It is more difficult to assess the accuracy for the 1979 LULC map due to the lack of reference data. To overcome this circumstance, the overall accuracy of LULC map 1979 would be determined as the work of Yang and Lo (2002). Accordingly, it is believed that the comparison of LULC map 1979 to LULC map 1996 is the sufficient way to shed light on accuracy.

Comparison of samples from classification or modeling system results with the reference data prevailing at the same location on ground is accepted as the most widely used approach to calculate the accuracy classification (Leinenkugel, 2010). Comparisons of both samples labeled correctly and erroneously of each class are presented in the error matrix. Through this, a tabular range of descriptive and analytical statistical accuracies of each class are computed based on commission errors and omission errors (Colgalton and Green, 1999; Leinenkugel, 2010).

The overall accuracy represents the percentage of correctly classified samples. It can be calculated by dividing the total number of sample points correctly classified using the total number of pixels in the entire error matrix (Colgalton and Green, 1999):

$$\text{Overall accuracy} = \frac{\sum_{i=1}^{j} p_{ii}}{N} \quad [4.1]$$

Together with overall accuracy, the Kappa coefficient (K) has been believed to be a powerful tool for such a long time, which is used to indicate the level of classification accuracy compared to a classification obtained by chance. However, Pontius and Millones (2011) ascertained some of conceptual flaws with the standard kappa and its variations. According to these authors, instead of revealing the difference from correct proportion in a manner which helps practical decisions about image classification, kappa coefficient just gives redundant or misleading information for practical decision making. They found that the standard kappa and its variations are complicated in computing, difficult in understanding, and unhelpful in interpreting. Thus, a more useful and simpler tool focusing on two components of disagreement between maps in terms of the quantity and spatial allocation of the categories marks the end of the use of kappa. Quantity disagreement is defined as the amount of difference between the reference map and classified map based on the less than perfect match in the proportions of the categories. On the other hand, allocation disagreement is defined as the amount of difference between the reference map and classified map based on the less than optimal match in the spatial allocation of the categories. Pontius and Millones (2011) defined five types of indices ($K_{standard}$, K_{no}, $K_{allocation}$, K_{histo}, and $K_{quantity}$), which are used to explore the observed agreement between the comparison map and the reference map, where 1 indicates that the agreement is perfect and 0 indicates that the observed agreement is equivalent to the statistically expected random agreement. $K_{standard}$ is an index that accounts for the expected agreement because of random spatial reallocation of categories in the comparison map, through which the proportion of categories in the comparison and reference maps can be given without regarding the size of the quantity disagreement. K_{no} is the statistical index that measures the expected overall agreement based on the randomly selection of both the quantity and allocation of categories in the comparison map. $K_{allocation}$ is computed to have an index of pure allocation, where 1 shows optimal spatial allocation as constrained by the observed proportions of the categories and 0 shows the observed overall agreement that is equal to the agreement expected under random spatial reallocation within the comparison map given the proportion of categories in the comparison and reference maps. K_{histo} index defines the separation of quantity and allocation. Contrary to $K_{allocation}$, $K_{quantity}$ is computed to have an index of pure quantity which defines the accuracy of the allocation. Thus, Pontius and Millones (2011) stated that these statistics could be used to answer two critical questions: (1) How well does a pair of maps agree in terms of the quantity of cells in each category? and (2) How well do a pair of maps agree in terms of the allocation of cells in each category? In short, how well the comparison map agrees with the reference map could be explored by these kappa statistics (Ahmed et al., 2013).

The formulas in calculating the observed agreement indicators are briefly presented in **Table 4.5**. For more details about this method please see Pontius (2000, 2002), Pontius and Millones (2011) and Pontius et al. (2004).

Index	Formula	
$K_{standard}$	$\dfrac{C-E}{1-E} = \dfrac{(1-Q-A)-(1-R)}{1-(1-R)} = \dfrac{R-(Q+A)}{R} = \dfrac{R-D}{R}$	[4.2]
K_{no}	$\dfrac{C-1/J}{1-1/J} = \dfrac{(1-Q-A)-(1/J)}{1-1/J} = \dfrac{(1-1/J)-(Q+A)}{1-1/J} = \dfrac{(1-1/J)-D}{1-1/J}$	[4.3]
$K_{allocation}$	$\dfrac{C-E}{(1-Q)-E} = \dfrac{(1-Q-A)-(1-R)}{(1-Q)-(1-R)} = \dfrac{R-(Q+A)}{R-Q} = \dfrac{R-D}{R-Q}$	[4.4]
K_{histo}	$\dfrac{(1-Q)-E}{1-E} = \dfrac{(1-Q)-(1-R)}{1-(1-R)} = \dfrac{R-Q}{R}$	[4.5]

Index	Formula
K_{quantity}	$\dfrac{C-Z}{Y-Z}$ [4.6]
where	(1) $p_{ij} = \left(\dfrac{n_{ij}}{\sum_{j=1}^{J} n_{ij}}\right)\left(\dfrac{N_i}{\sum_{i=1}^{J} N_i}\right)$ [4.7] p_{ij} is the estimated proportion of study area that is category *i* in the comparison map and category *j* in the reference map *J* is the number of categories *i* is the category in the comparison map (ranges from 1 to *J*) *j* is the category in the reference map (ranges from 1 to *J*) *Ni* is the number of pixels in each stratum *nij* is the number of observations in row *i* and column *j* of sample matrix (2) $C = \sum_{j=1}^{J} p_{jj}$ [4.8] *C* is the proportion correct (3) $E = \sum_{g=1}^{J} e_g$ [4.9] *E* is the overall expected agreement of all *J* categories (4) $e_g = \left(\sum_{i=1}^{J} p_{ig}\right)\left(\sum_{j=1}^{J} p_{gj}\right)$ [4.10] e_g is the expected agreement for category *g* (5) $Q = \dfrac{\sum_{g=1}^{J} q_g}{2}$ [4.11] *Q* is the overall quantity disagreement of all *J* categories (6) $q_g = \left|\left(\sum_{i=1}^{J} p_{ig}\right) - \left(\sum_{j=1}^{J} p_{gj}\right)\right|$ [4.12] q_g is the quantity disagreement q_g for an arbitrary category *g* (7) $A = \dfrac{\sum_{g=1}^{J} a_g}{2}$ [4.13] *A* is the overall allocation disagreement of all *J* categories (8) $a_g = 2\min\left[\left(\sum_{i=1}^{J} p_{ig}\right) - p_{gg}, \left(\sum_{j=1}^{J} p_{gj}\right) - p_{gg}\right]$ [4.14] a_g is the allocation disagreement for an arbitrary category *g* (9) $R = 1 - E$ [4.15] *R* is the overall expected disagreement of all *J* categories (10) $D = 1 - C = Q + A$ [4.16] *D* is the total disagreement of quantity and allocation (11) $Y = \left\{\sum_{j=1}^{J}\left[\left(\sum_{i=1}^{J} p_{ij}\right)^2\right]\right\} + K_{\text{allocation}}\left\{1 - \sum_{j=1}^{J}\left[\left(\sum_{i=1}^{J} p_{ij}\right)^2\right]\right\}$ [4.17] *Y* is the proportion correct with perfect ability to specify quantity and medium ability to specify location (12) $Z = (1/J) + K_{\text{allocation}}\left\{\sum_{j=1}^{J}\min\left[(1/J), \sum_{i=1}^{J} p_{ij}\right] - (1/J)\right\}$ [4.18] *Z* is the proportion correct with no ability to specify quantity and medium ability to specify location

Table 4.5 Formulas of quantity disagreement and allocation disagreement indices

Source: Adapted from Pontius and Millones (2011)

4.5 Change detection

The next step is post-classification comparison which was carried out for LULC maps extracted from remote satellite imageries to detect the changes of LULC in four interval times: 1979–1996, 1996–2003, 2003–2009, and 1979–2009. Based on a pixel-by-pixel approach, a change detection matrix of the classification results was generated, from which the tendency and amount of LULC change were identified (Jensen, 2005).

4.6 Landscape metrics

Landscape metrics are usually used to objectively quantify landscape composition and configuration, which are main descriptions of landscape pattern (Deng et al., 2009; Lin et al., 2007; Turner et al., 2001). According to McGarigal et al. (2002), landscape composition describes the abundance and variety of patches in the landscape, whereas landscape spatial configuration characterizes the spatial character and arrangement, position, or orientation of patches in the landscape.

Herold et al. (2005) evinced that the combination of remote satellite imagery and spatial metrics could give more detailed information about landscape structure and their changes than either of the methods that are used independently. In this regard, FRAGSTATS 4.1® (McGarigal et al., 2002), a spatial pattern analysis program, was used to evaluate the changes of landscape pattern in the study area based on the output of the remote sensing mappings. The FRAGSTATS software was developed by McGarigal and Marks (1995a) of the Forest Science Department of Oregon State University. As output, a continuous landscape metric surface for statistical analysis is created by using square moving window computing technique (**Figure 4.5**). The selected index is calculated within each window, and then the value returned to the focal (central) cell. Continuously, the moving window goes through the grid until all valued cells containing a full window are mostly calculated. A new grid for each selected metric is the output of studying (Xinping Ye, 2008).

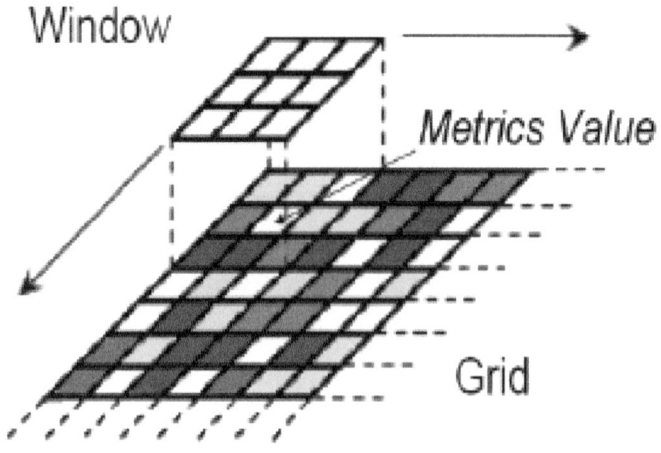

Figure 4.5 Moving window computation
Source: Xinping Ye (2008)

According to Antrop and Van Eetvelde (2000), all elements in the spatial structure of the landscape pattern are related to each other. One single metric alone cannot clarify the spatial characteristics of a landscape. So far, the few published studies have compared and suggested some different sets of metrics in analyzing landscape structure. Especially, these studies were focused more on economic landscape functions and LULC pattern (Herold et al., 2005). Most importantly, Parker et al. (2001) stated that there is no standard set of metrics that is best suited for a particular region because the significance of specific metrics is varied upon the objectives of research as well as the characteristics of study area. Thus, the eight major landscape metrics were selected for studying based on own characteristics of study area and objectives of the thesis, including (1) percentage of landscape, (2) number of patches, (3) largest patch index, (4) average size of patches, (5) patch density, (6) proximity index, (7) interspersion and juxtaposition index, and (8) landscape shape index (**Table 4.6**). These metrics were of particular interest for this study because they offer additional attributes for landscape types or region (Antrop and Van Eetvelde, 2000). In addition, their values deliver statistically meaningful information about the change of LULC over long period of times (Olsen et al., 2007).

According to McGarigal et al. (2012), some landscape metrics are partially or completely redundant. It means that these metrics quantify a similar or identical feature of landscape pattern. In some particular applications, metrics are used for a particular landscape under investigation instead of using to measure the same aspect of landscape pattern. In this case, the different aspects of landscape pattern are statistically correlated. However, it is also important to understand the redundancy, because little can be learned by interpreting metrics that are inherently redundant, but much can be learned about landscapes by interpreting metrics that are empirically redundant. In this study, we focus on the change of landscape structure between 1979 and 2009. Consequently, LULC maps of 1979 and 2009 were converted into Grid format by using ArcGIS 10.1 software for computing landscape metrics in FRAGSTATS®. Further explanations and formulas of the metrics are presented by McGarigal et al. (2012), as follows:

Index	Unit	Description	Range
PLAND	Percent	Percentage of landscape equals the sum of the areas (m²) of all patches of the corresponding patch type, divided by the total landscape area (m²), multiplied by 100 to convert to a percentage	0 < PLAND ≤ 100
Formula	\multicolumn{3}{c}{ $$PLAND = P_i = \frac{\sum_{j=1}^{n} a_{ij}}{A}(100) \qquad [4.19]$$ P_i = proportion of the landscape occupied by patch type (class) i a_{ij} = area (m²) of patch ij A = total landscape area (m²) }
NP	None	Number of patches equals the number of patches of the corresponding patch type (class)	NP ≥ 1, no limit
Formula	\multicolumn{3}{c}{ $$NP = n_i \qquad [4.20]$$ n_i = number of patches in the landscape of patch type (class) i }
LPI	Percent	Largest patch index equals the area (m²) of the largest patch of the corresponding patch type divided by the total landscape area (m²), multiplied by 100 to convert to a percentage	0 < LPI ≤ 100

Index	Unit	Description	Range
Formula	$$LPI = \frac{max_{j=1}^{n}(a_{ij})}{A}(100)$$ a_{ij} = area (m²) of patch ij A = total landscape area (m²)		[4.21]
AREA_MN	Hectares	Mean patch area – average size of patches	AREA_MN≥ 0, no limit
Formula	$$AREA = a_{ij}\left(\frac{1}{10,000}\right)$$ a_{ij} = area (m²) of patch ij		[4.22]
PD	Number per 100 ha	Patch density equals the number of patches of the corresponding patch type divided by the total landscape area (m), multiplied by 10,000 and 100 (to convert to 100 ha)	PD ≥ 0, no limit
Formula	$$PD = \frac{n_i}{A}(10,000)(100)$$ n_i = number of patches in the landscape of patch type (class) i A = total landscape area (m²)		[4.23]
PROX_MN	Meters	Mean proximity equals the sum of patch area (m²) divided by the nearest edge-to-edge distance squared (m²) between the patch and the focal patch of all patches of the corresponding patch type whose edges are within a specified distance(m) of the focal patch; average proximity index for all patches in a class	PROX_MN ≥ 0, no limit
Formula	$$PROX = \sum_{s=1}^{n}\frac{a_{ijs}}{h_{ijs}^{2}}$$ a_{ijs} = area (m²) of patch ijs within specified neighborhood (m) of patch ij h_{ijs} = distance (m) between patch ijs and patch ijs, based on patch edge-to-edge distance, computed from cell center to cell center		[4.24]
IJI	Percent	Interspersion and juxtaposition index measures the juxtaposition of a focal patch class with all other classes	0 < IJI ≤ 100
Formula	$$IJI = \frac{-\sum_{k=1}^{m}\left[\left(\frac{e_{ik}}{\sum_{k=1}^{m}e_{ik}}\right)ln\left(\frac{e_{ik}}{\sum_{k=1}^{m}e_{ik}}\right)\right]}{ln(m-1)}(100)$$ e_{ik} = total length (m) of edge in landscape between patch types (classes) i and k m = number of patch types (classes) present in the landscape, including the landscape border, if present		[4.25]
LSI	None	LSI equals 0.25 (adjustment for raster format) times the sum of the entire landscape	LSI ≥ 1, no limit

Index	Unit	Description	Range
		boundary (regardless of whether it represents "true" edge or not, or how the user specifies how to handle boundary/background) and all edge segments (m) within the landscape boundary involving the corresponding patch type, including some or all of those bordering background (based on user specifications), divided by the square root of the total landscape areas (m²)	
Formula		$$LSI = \frac{.25 \sum_{k=1}^{m} e_{ik}^{*}}{\sqrt{A}}$$ [4.26] e^{*}_{ik} = total length (m) of edge in landscape between patch types (classes) *i* and *k*; includes the entire landscape boundary and some or all background edge segments involving class *i* A = total landscape area (m²)	

Table 4.6 Descriptions of landscape pattern metrics
Source: Adapted from Keleş et al. (2008) and McGarigal et al. (2012)

4.7 Modeling LULC change

The flowchart of the methodology used to simulate the changes of LULC in this study is presented in **Figure 4.6**. It includes two main parts: simulating temporal demand of LULC under various scenarios (nonspatial analysis) and simulating the allocation of LULC depending on scenarios (spatial analysis).

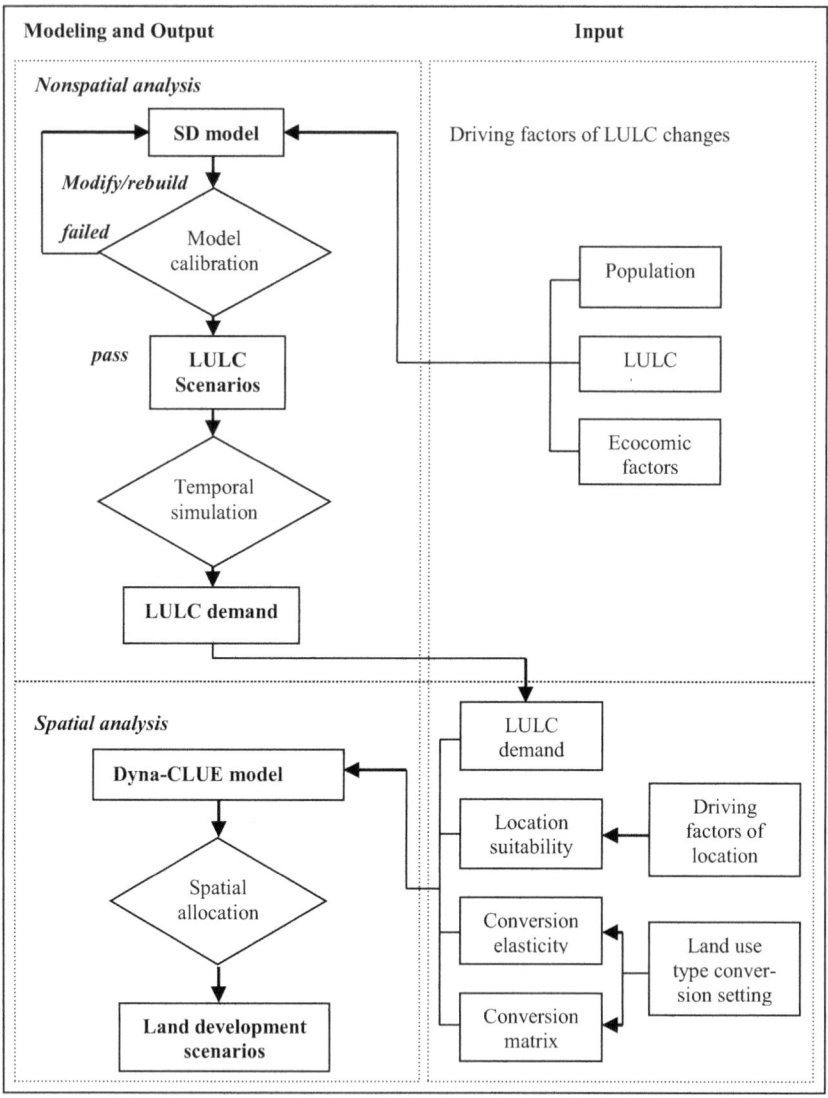

Figure 4.6 Flowchart of modeling land-use/cover changes used in the study
Source: Adapted from Zheng et al. (2012)

According to Verburg and Overmars (2007), the demands for LULC types are calculated by the user in advance with different techniques, ranging from simple trend extrapolation (e.g., linear trend) to advanced models (e.g., macroeconomic modeling changes). In this study, the system dynamics (SD) model is chosen for setting various control factors, which allows observing and predicting the changes of LULC. Zheng et al. (2012) asserted that the SD model can help answer the questions, "When and how much does the land development take place according to different scenarios?" In contrast to this, the Dyna-CLUE (dynamic conversion of land use and its effects) model is applied to solve the question "Where does the land development possibly take place?" due to its capacity in describing the microcosmic and spatial factors. Consequently, the Dyna-CLUE model is created as a way of bridge building between temporal land demand and spatial supply.

4.7.1 Nonspatial model

4.7.1.1 Conceptual model

As pointed out by Radzicki and Taylor (2008), SD is a methodology and mathematical model technique to frame, understand, discuss, and simplify complex problems over time. This method was originally developed by Jay Forrester (1961) of the Massachusetts Institute of Technology, in which the interactions among various components of the system are studied by internal feedback loops and time delays. They are the two important components that reflect the behavior of the entire system. In the SD model, the real world is represented in terms of causal loop diagrams, flow and stock diagrams, and different equations. A causal loop diagram is a simple map of a system which is used to visualize all its constituent components and their interactions. Hence, it is possible to discover the system's behavior over a certain time period (Meadows, 2008). The correlational relationship between variables can be symbolized by arrows in positive or negative directions. It is indicated that in positive arrow two nodes change in the same direction; meanwhile, the two nodes change in opposite directions in negative arrow. For more detailed quantitative analysis, a stock and flow diagram is performed. A stock is considered as any entity that accumulates or depletes over time; meanwhile, a flow is considered as the rate of change in a stock (Steven N. Durlauf and Blume, 2008). Once the model is structurally established, it needs a set of equations to describe each relationship. The equation is a simple algebraic expression to calculate the values of a specific variable, defining one variable in terms of others that are causally connected (http://vensim.com/docs/). An example of SD model is presented in **Figure 4.7**.

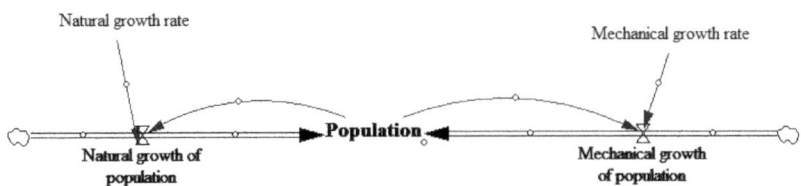

In which:

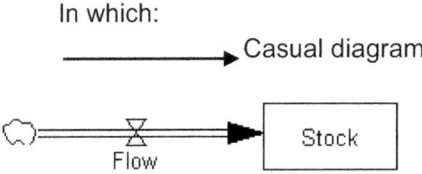

Figure 4.7 Example of SD model used in the study
Source: Author's calculation

To look at the sketch view, *mechanical growth rate* has no cause; hence, it is a constant in the model and has a numerical value. *Mechanical growth of population* is calculated as follows:

Mechanical growth of population = Population × mechanical growth rate   [4.27]

User-friendly SD software was developed in the 1990s and has been applied in a wide range of areas such as population, environmental management, ecosystem assessment, and economic systems. Some researchers have recently applied SD to predict the demands of LULC for land-use planning and management by using social-economic conditions (Luo et al., 2010), for example, He et al. (2006) modeled urban expansion by using SD model and cellular automata model in Beijing, China; Lee et al. (2009) coupled system modeling and spatial system modeling for simulating land-use change of Taipei metropolitan area; and Wang et al. (2011) applied SD model for changes in land-use patterns under drought scenarios. It proves that the SD model is a useful tool to analyze the demands of LULC.

Generally, the SD model simulates the demand of LULC types based on natural and social-economic parameters. The natural driving forces may cause climate, landform conditions, distance conditions, and water availability (Wang et al., 2011); social-economic driving forces include population density, population growth rate, economic factors, marketing conditions or technology advances, and macro-policy constraints (Luo et al., 2010). The natural factors are more stable and have a cumulative trend; socioeconomic factors are more active in contrast (Wang et al., 2011). According to Lambin et al. (2001), the changes of LULC types in short term are mostly dominated under human activities. In this sense, only socioeconomic factors are supposed to affect LULC changes.

4.7.1.2 SD model setting

The Ventana Vensim PLE v6.1 program (http://vensim.com) is used to construct system variables in different scenarios for the study. The SD model includes three subsystems, namely, population, economic factors, and LULC types. As shown in **Figure 4.8**, population is the main social factor that affects the land-use system from many aspects because of human life demands. The increase in population causes the growth of built-up areas for residential demand or constructing factories. The larger population requires the higher demand of primary products, for example, meat, food, and water; hence, demanding areas for breeding and cultivation are increased (Zheng et al., 2012). In this study, the economy subsystem relates to the growth rate of gross output industry (GOI) and fixed-assets investment (FAI) of construction. The increase in the rate of GOI and FAI could lead mostly to the growth of demand in land use for construction. Generally, urban areas are expanded more and more at the expense of other LULC types such as agriculture or forestry. Consequently, changes in population and economic subsystem result in the increment or decrement in area of each dependent LULC type. More details about the relation among three kinds of subsystem are presented in **Figure 4.8**.

(1) Predicted population

The future population of Da Nang City is simulated as extrapolative approach according to the natural and mechanical growth (Da Nang's Committee, 2012):

$$P_{(t)} = P_{(0)} \cdot e^{rt} \quad [4.28]$$

where $P_{(t)}$ is the simulated population at given time (2030); $P_{(0)}$ is the population at the start of the simulation (1996); e = 2.718 (Euler's number); r is the growth rate of population; t represents 35 years of simulation (from 1996 to 2030).

Figure 4.8 shows that the increase of population in Da Nang City is calculated based on the natural growth rate and mechanical growth rate of population. Here, natural growth rate is the rate of birth and death; mechanical growth rate is the rate of immigration and transmigration.

(2) Cultivated area demand

The demand of cultivated area can be obtained based on food security. The required number of land resources is achieved under the circumstances of ensuring the healthy life of the total population and the food demand in their basic development (Yang Long-fei et al., 2010). The calculation formula is given as follows:

$$A_d = \frac{P_t \cdot F_c \cdot D_s}{Y_a \cdot R_s} \quad [4.29]$$

where A_d is the regional land demand (ha); P_t is the total population (person); F_c is the per capita food demand (kg/per capita); D_s is the food self-sufficiency ratio (%); Y_a is the yearly food yield per unit area (kg/ha); and R_s is the rate of grain sowing (%).

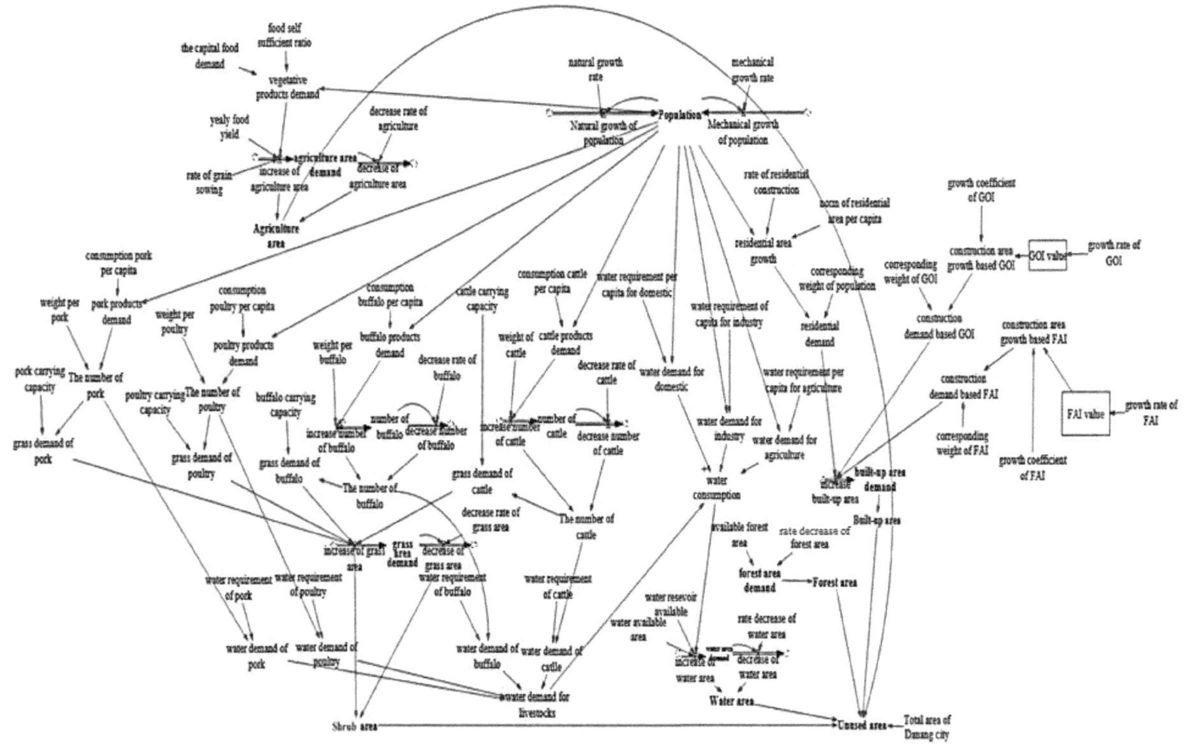

Chapter 4 Data and Methodology

Figure 4.8 The SD model for simulating the demands of land use/cover in Da Nang City

As can be seen from formula **[4.29]**, the demand of cultivated area A_d depends on many indices (P_t, F_c, D_s, Y_a, R_s), where the total population index and per capita food demand index define the total food demand; whereas the yearly food yield per unit area and rate of grain sowing define the food production capacity of cultivated land. Thus, under the setting of the food self-sufficiency ratios, the regional land demand for agriculture was primarily obtained from the total food demand and the food production capacity of cultivated land (Yang Long-fei et al., 2010).

(3) Shrub area demand

In this study region, livestock are generally grazed in the shrub area instead of special grassland. Thus, demanding of shrub area can be simulated based upon the calculation of grassland. The demand of grassland is calculated by dividing the number of grazed livestock using the livestock carrying capacity of the grassland, as follows (Wang et al., 2011):

$$S = \frac{N}{L} \quad [4.30]$$

where S is the area of grass land; N represents the number of livestock; and L is the livestock carrying capacity of the grassland.

(3.1) Number of grazed livestock—**N**

Consumption of livestock product can be estimated based on the population size. From which, we can compute the number of standard heads of grazed livestock by diving the consumption of livestock product using standard livestock units (Wang et al., 2011).

(3.2) The livestock carrying capacity of the grassland—**L**

The livestock carrying capacity of the grassland can be calculated based on four indices: the grass production per unit area of grassland, the grassland utilization rate, the number of grazing days, and the number of grazing days, as follows (Wang et al., 2011):

$$L = \frac{B \cdot E}{D \cdot F} \quad [4.31]$$

where B is the grass production per unit area of grassland; E is the grassland utilization rate; D the number of grazing days; and F is the number of grazing days.

(4) Residential and industrial area demand

According to Wang et al. (2011), the demand of residential and industrial area can be calculated from population, GOI, and FAI of construction factors, which are mutually influenced and restricted to each other. The residential and industrial land can be obtained according to the formula

$$U = U_1 R_1 + U_2 R_2 + U_3 R_3 \quad [4.32]$$

where U is the area of residential and industrial land; U_1, U_2, U_3 represent the area of urban construction predicted as a function of (respectively) population size, GOI, and FAI of construction; and R_1, R_2, R_3 represent the corresponding weights of population, GOI, and FAI of construction, respectively

(4.1) Calculate construction area based on population size—U_1

According to Shao et al. (2006), construction demanding area can be obtained from formula

$$U_1 = \frac{A}{a_0} \quad [4.33]$$

where A is the total residential area and a_0 is the rate of residential construction.

Here A is the normalization of residential area per capita (m²/person).

$$a_0 = \frac{\text{construction area (m}^2\text{)}}{\text{urban area (m}^2\text{)}} \quad [4.34]$$

(4.2) Calculate construction area-based GOI—U_2

$$U_2 = q \cdot t \quad [4.35]$$

where q is the GOI (bill VND [Vietnamese Dong]) and t the growth coefficient of GOI (ha/bill VND).

(4.3) Calculate construction area-based FAI of construction—U_3

$$U_3 = Q \cdot T \quad \text{[4.36]}$$

where Q is FAI (bill VND) and T the growth coefficient of FAI (ha/bill VND).

(4.4) Calculate the corresponding weights **R₁, R₂, R₃**

Grey's correlation analysis can be used to calculate the corresponding weights by quantitatively comparing correlations among factors in system. In this approach, the closeness of correlation is distinguished by the degree of similarity of the geometrical shapes of different time series. Thus, the more similar the curves are, the closer the correlation is. The calculation steps of urban area using grey's correlation analysis are given as follows (Men and Zhao, 2010):

(a) Establish the reference and comparison sequences. First, residential and industrial demand is determined as reference sequence by the following equation:

$$X_0 = \{x_0(1), x_0(2), \ldots, x_0(n)\} \quad \text{[4.37]}$$

where n represents the number of indices

Then, the comparison sequence of related factors is determined as

$$X_i = \{x_i(1), x_i(2), \ldots, x_i(n)\} \text{ (with } i = 1, 2, \ldots, m) \quad \text{[4.38]}$$

where i is the number of comparison sequence and m the comparison objects.

(b) Calculate the initial value of each sequence. Each object has its own unit of measurement. Thus the following formula is used to eliminate the impact of the units of measurement among the sequences of number:

$$X' = \frac{X_i}{x_i(1)} = \{x'_i(1), x'_i(2), \ldots, x'_i(n)\} \quad [4.39]$$

(with $i = 1, 2, \ldots, m$)

(c) Calculate the evaluation of maximum and minimum difference:

$$M = \max_i \max_k \Delta_i(k), \quad m = \min_i \min_k \Delta_i(k) \quad [4.40]$$

where $\Delta_i(k) = |x'_0(k), x'_i(k)|$ (with $k = 1, 2, \ldots, n; i = 1, 2, \ldots, m$)

(d) Evaluate the correlation coefficient:

$$\gamma_{0i}(k) = \frac{m + \xi M}{\Delta_i(k) + \xi M'} \quad [4.41]$$

(with $k = 1, 2, \ldots, n; i = 1, 2, \ldots, m$)

$\xi \in (0, 1)$ is the resolution coefficient, generally, $\xi = 0.5$.

The mean of each correlation coefficient sequence is calculated based on eq. **[4.41]**:

$$\bar{\gamma}_{0i} = \frac{1}{n} \sum_{k=1}^{n} \gamma_{0i}(k) \quad [4.42]$$

(with $i = 1, 2, \ldots, m$)

(e) Calculate the stability formula which is given by

$$S(\gamma_{0i}) = \sqrt{\frac{1}{n} \sum_{k=1}^{n} (\gamma_{0i} - \bar{\gamma}_{0i})^2} \quad [4.43]$$

(with $i = 1, 2, \ldots, m$)

(f) Evaluate the grey similarity correlation degree:

$$R_{0i} = \frac{\gamma_{0i}}{1 + S(\gamma_{0i})} \quad [4.44]$$

(with $i = 1, 2, \ldots, m$)

The degrees of correlation R_i among the influences of population, GOI and FAI of construction, and the area of residential and industrial demanding area range from 0 to 1. These values are used as corresponding weights to calculate residential and industrial area demand in formula **[4.32]**. All correlations are computed by the aid of MATLAB 7.0.

(5) Water area demand

In order to simulate water area, the water demand for all needs is firstly examined. The future water demand includes the purposes of agricultural, industrial, domestic activities, and livestock activities. The method of demand forecasting of water is based on the method of Lawgali (2008) as follows:

$$W = W_A + W_I + W_D + W_L \quad \text{[4.45]}$$

where W is the total water demand; W_A, W_I, W_D, W_L represent the water demand for the purposes of agricultural, industrial, domestic use, and livestock, respectively.

Here

W_A, W_I, W_D = f (population, water requirement per capita for agricultural, industrial, domestic use, respectively)

W_L = f (number of livestock, water requirement per livestock)

(6) Forest area demand

Generally, the forest area demand can be determined based on the assumption of forest products demand as the approach described by Brooks et al. (1995). According to Kangas and Baudin (2003), this approach has many advantages because it involves all aspects, including consumption, production, imports, and exports. It is solved by the following system of equations:

$$Q^D{}_D = f(P_d, P_m, D^D) \quad \text{[4.46]}$$

$$Q^M = f(P_d, P_m, D^M) \quad \text{[4.47]}$$

$$Q^D{}_S = f(P_d, P_x, S^D) \quad \text{[4.48]}$$

$$Q^X = f(P_d, P_x, S^X) \quad \text{[4.49]}$$

where $Q^D{}_D$ is the demand for domestically produced goods, Q^M is the import demand, $Q^S{}_D$ is the supply to domestic markets ($Q^S{}_D = Q^D{}_D$), Q^X is the supply to export markets, P_d is the price in domestic markets, P_m the import price, P_x the export price, D^D the demand shifters for the domestic market, D^M the demand shifters for import demand, S^D supply shifters for the domestic market, S^X the supply shifters for the export market. However, due to the unavailability and complexity of these data, the decreased rate of forest area obtained from *Statistical Year Books* is chosen to calculate the demand of forest area as alternative approach for this study. Detailed information could be seen in **Figure 4.8**.

(7) Unused area

After defining the demands of agriculture, forest, urban, shrub, and water area, it is possible to estimate the unused area by the following equation:

$$U_s = T - A_d - U - F - S - W \quad [4.50]$$

where U_s represents the unused area, T the total area of Da Nang City (excluding area of Paracel Islands, T = 96,817.2 ha), A_d the agricultural area, U the urban area, F, the forest area, S the shrub area, W, the water area.

4.7.1.3 SD model calibration and validation

Before using the results of the SD model as the input of Dyna-CLUE, it is necessary to assess whether the SD model predicts the demand of LULC correctly (Pontius et al., 2004). In this case, calibration and validation are also required. Calibration is the process of "estimation and adjustment of the model parameters and constraints to improve the agreement between model output and a data set," while model validation is "a demonstration that a model within its domain of applicability possesses a satisfactory range of accuracy consistent with the intended application of the model" (Rykiel, 1996).

From the data of initial year 1996, population, economic factors, and LULC types each year in Da Nang City are calculated based on formulas mentioned earlier. In this study, historical statistics obtained from *Statistical Yearbook* of Da Nang City are used to calibrate the

SD model, and data obtained from classified LULC maps in 2003 and 2009 are employed to validate the results of SD model.

4.7.2 Spatial model

The CLUE (conversion of land use and its effects) modeling framework was first created by Veldkamp and Fresco (1996). The empirical model is used to define the processes in changing spatial pattern and estimate possible future changes of LULC. This modeling level was specifically developed through the spatially explicit analysis between LULC and its driving factors under different scenarios (Verburg and Overmars, 2007).

Originally, the CLUE model was applied at national levels, for example, Costa Rica (Veldkamp and Fresco, 1996), Ecuador (de Koning et al., 1999), and China (Verburg et al., 2000) and supranational levels, for example, Central America (Kok and Winograd, 2002), with coarse spatial resolutions varying from 7 × 7 km to 32 × 32 km to identify the critical areas of LULC changes. Consequently, this could lead to large biases in LULC definition because of the decrease or increase in class proportion with respect to pixel size (Verburg et al., 2002). Because of the increasing requirement in impacts assessment of LULC change through landscape pattern, high spatial resolution represented by homogeneous spatial unit is more suitable. Moreover, it is needed to know exactly where the allocations of LULC changes are (Verburg and Overmars, 2007). Hence, the later versions of CLUE model, the CLUE-S model and Dyna-CLUE model, were developed by Peter Verburg and colleagues at Wageningen University (Verburg and Overmars, 2009; Verburg et al., 1999, 2002). These models have been applied to the regional extent with spatial resolution ranging from 20 × 20 m to 1,000 × 1,000 m, in which each pixel is used as one type of LULC (Verburg and Overmars, 2007).

In this study, Dyna-CLUE is chosen for modeling the changes of LULC in Da Nang City. The following sections describe in detail the structure and functioning of Dyna-CLUE model, through which the processes of setting up the model are presented.

4.7.2.1 Dyna-CLUE model structure

The Dyna-CLUE model is an upgraded version of the CLUE-S methodology, in which the spatial allocation of LULC demands are defined as individual grid cells (Verburg, 2010). In Dyna-CLUE model approach, "the top-down allocation of land use/cover change is combined with a bottom-up determination of conversions for specific land use transitions to grid cells." This method is particularly suitable for LULC types where the demand is mutually affected by driving factors.

As shown in **Figure 4.9**, first, analysis starts at the regional level in determining LULC, which is considered or separated as two groups: those demand driven and those that are not aggregate. As a result, the net change of the demand-driven LULC corresponds with the overall change in the area of no-aggregate group. Afterward, the LULC demands are allocated to individual grid cells at the local level through iteratively comparing the allocated area of the individual LULC types with the demanded areas for a given simulation year until getting a satisfactory model solution (Verburg and Overmars, 2009). **Figure 4.10** presents the flowchart of allocation procedure in Dyna-CLUE model, which determines location (*i*) of LULC type (lu) at time (*t*) with the highest total probability ($Ptot_{i,t,lu}$). The total probability is computed as the sum of the location suitability ($Ploc_{i,t,lu}$), neighborhood suitability ($Pnbh_{i,t,lu}$), conversion elasticity ($elas_{lu}$), and competitive advantage ($comp_{t,lu}$) as follows (Verburg and Overmars, 2009):

$$Ptot_{i,t,lu} = Ploc_{i,t,lu} + Pnbh_{i,t,lu} + elas_{lu} + comp_{t,lu} \quad [4.51]$$

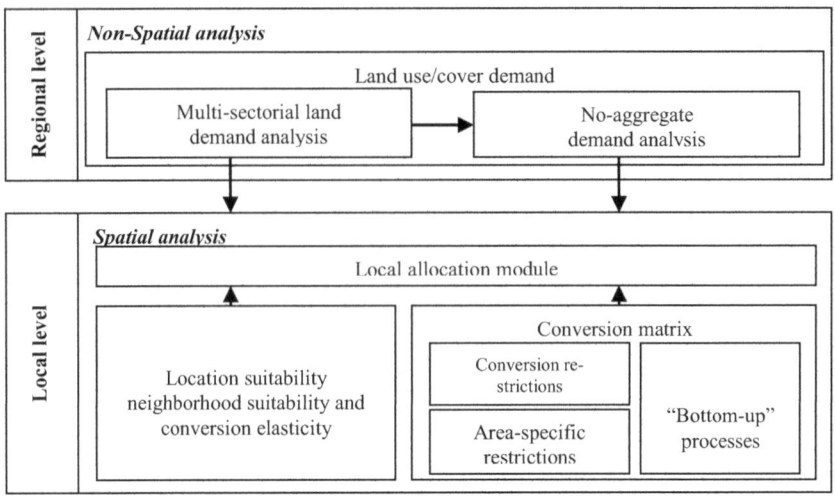

Figure 4.9 Framework of the Dyna-CLUE model
Source: Adapted from Verburg and Overmars (2009)

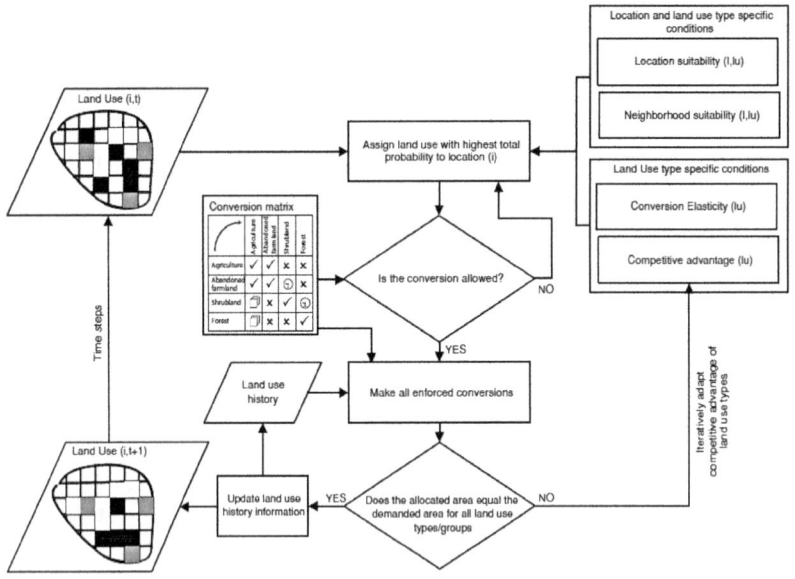

Figure 4.10 Flowchart of the Dyna-CLUE model
Source: Verburg and Overmars (2009)

According to Verburg and Overmars (2009), location suitability ($Ploc_{i,t,lu}$) and neighborhood suitability ($Pnbh_{i,t,lu}$) are obtained based on empirical methods as well as process and expert knowledge, and the dynamic analysis of neighborhood interactions. The conversion elasticity ($elas_{lu}$) measures the expense of one LULC type to another. This parameter is assigned to those locations where the LULC type is found at time t. In contrast to this, the competitive advantage ($comp_{t,lu}$) is iteratively applied to all LULC types during procedure. Based on conversion matrix, the maximization of the total probability ($Ptot_{i,t,lu}$) is controlled at each individual location.

4.7.2.2 Dyna-CLUE model setting

(1) Location suitability - $Ploc_{i,t,lu}$

As pointed out by Lambin et al. (2001), LULC changes result from a set of explanatory factors, such as socioeconomic and biophysical drivers as well as the place based, and human environment conditions. In Dyna-CLUE, LULC conversion involves a change from one cover type to another which takes place at locations that have the highest "preference" of suitability at the moment in time. The preference of a location is generally determined by the explanatory factors that are chosen from the knowledge of the user about the dominant factors caused by the change of LULC in the study area. The preference is calculated as follows (Verburg et al., 2008):

$$R_{k,i} = a_k X_{1,i} + b_k X_{2,i} + \cdots + n_k X_{n,i} \qquad [4.52]$$

where $R_{k,i}$ is the preference to devote location i with land-use type k; $X_{1,2}$ is the biophysical or socioeconomical characteristic of location i; and a_k, b_k, n_k the relative impact of these characteristics on the preference for land-use type k.

However, the preference $R_{k,i}$ cannot be computed directly. Thus, the relative probabilities in finding the difference of LULC types at that location upon biophysical and socioeconomic factors are calculated as the alternative. A logistic model (binary logistic regression) is presented as follows (Verburg et al., 2005):

$$\log\left(\frac{P_i}{1-P_i}\right) = \beta_0 + \sum_{j=0}^{n} \beta_j X_{j,i} \quad [4.53]$$

where P_i is the probability of a grid cell for the occurrence of the considered land-use type on location i; $X_{j,i}$ is the j location factor affecting the suitability of land-use type i; β_n the regression values, obtained from the binary logistic regression model.

The coefficient (β_n) is estimated by logistic regression procedure of SPSS Statistics package 20, where each type of LULC is the dependent variable, and the expected driving factors are independent variables. For selecting the relevant factors from the list of expected driving factors, a stepwise regression of logistic regression model is set up correctly. Variables without significant contribution to the change of LULC types are excluded from the final regression formula (Verburg et al., 1999). In addition, it is needed to evaluate the goodness of fit model. However, the least squares regression (R^2), which is commonly used for measuring the model fit, is not suitable for logistic regression (Verburg et al., 2005). Instead, the relative operating characteristic (ROC) method is therefore chosen for this purpose (Pontius and Schneider, 2001). More details on this method and its utility are presented in model validation.

(2) Neighborhood suitability - **Pnbh**$_{i,t,lu}$

The conversion of LULC type can be exerted partly by the neighborhood of a location relative to the occurrence of this LULC type through the enrichment factor (F), which is given as follows (Verburg et al., 2005):

$$F_{i,k,d} = \frac{n_{k,d,i}/n_{d,i}}{N_k/N} \quad [4.54]$$

where $F_{i,k,d}$ characterizes the enrichment of neighborhood d of location i with land-use type k; $n_{k,d,i}$ is the number of cells of land-use type k in the neighborhood with size d of cell i; $n_{d,i}$ is the total number of cells in the neighborhood; N_k is the number of cells with land-use type k in the whole raster; N the total number of cells in the raster.

In Dyna-CLUE model, the relations between the probabilities P of a location i and the enrichment factors are computed as a logit model. It is similar to the logit model of socioeconomic and biophysical location factors:

$$\log\left(\frac{P_i}{1-P_i}\right) = \beta_0 + \sum_{j=0}^{n}\beta_j F_{j,i} \quad [4.55]$$

The coefficient (β_n) is calculated from the enrichment factor.

(3) Conversion elasticity - **elas**$_{lu}$

Conversion elasticity, known as one of the specific coefficients of Dyna-CLUE model, is used to determine the resistance of each LULC type to the conversions (Khoury, 2012). This coefficient is specified by the user upon the expert knowledge or observed manner of each LULC type in the recent past and ranges from 0 (easy conversion) to 1 (irreversible change) (Verburg, 2010). In other words, the closer the value of conversion elasticity comes to 0, the easier the LULC conversion is; the closer the value of conversion elasticity comes to 1, the harder the LULC conversion is (Khoury, 2012). Verburg (2010) explained the possible values of the conversion elasticity as follows:

> 0: All changes of LULC type are permitted.
>
> > 0 > 1: LULC type is permitted to convert, where the higher the value indicates the more difficult in converting LULC type given in a special location. Generally, this setting relates to the high conversion costs of LULC types.
>
> 1: LULC type can never change.

(4) Competitive advantage - **comp**$_{t,lu}$

During the iterative procedure, competitive advantage is defined for all kinds of land use. This value is increased in case allocated area is smaller than the demanded area. Conversely, it is decreased when the allocated area goes beyond the demanded area. If the demand of a certain LULC type increases, the value of the competitive advantage also increases; whereas, it gets lower value in case the demand of one land-use type decreases. In case of LULC types, there is only a value of competitive advantage which is set for the whole group. This is because the demands of areas are not specified for any individual LULC type within the group (Verburg, 2010).

(5) Conversion matrix

In Dyna-CLUE model, a conversion matrix is defined to indicate the converted capability of LULC types and their temporal dynamic of characteristics (Verburg, 2010). This matrix is created from the number of LULC types available in the study area, where rows and columns denote the present and potential future LULC types, respectively. At each corresponding cell of matrix, the value "1" is assigned if the LULC type can be converted, if not, it is assigned as value "0" (Khoury, 2012). An example of conversion matrix with three land-use types would be found in **Table 4.7**.

Land use/cover	Forest	Agriculture	Grassland
Forest	1	1	1
Agriculture	0	1	1
Grassland	0	1	1

Table 4.7 Example of conversion matrix with three land-use types
Source: Author's calculation

4.7.3 Accuracy assessment of model

For accuracy assessment, we applied three different approaches. First, logistic regression model is assessed with the ROC method. Second, we performed a visual comparison based on two pairs of maps: reference maps of year 1996 and 2003, reference map of year 1996, and simulated map of year 2003. Finally, simulation results were precisely evaluated with the corresponding values from a statistical database.

Rykiel (1996) asserted that any land-use change model system of specific region must be calibrated to improve its goodness of fit. Typically, land-use change model is calibrated upon the historical data. Hence, this process needs two LULC maps: one for the start of simulation period (t_0) and one for the simulation period (t_1). The simulated land-use map at (t_1) is then compared with actual/reference LULC map at (t_1). For validation, the simulated land-use map at (t_2) is then compared with actual/reference LULC map at (t_2). As can be seen, both calibration and validation processes do the same activities in comparing simulated LULC map and actual/reference LULC map at the same period. However, these processes are different in other purposes. Calibration looks for opportunity to improve its accuracy by changing model's parameters, while validation is used for independently evaluating the quality of simulated LULC maps.

4.7.3.1 Relative operating characteristic

As mentioned earlier, it is necessary to evaluate the goodness of fit of logistic regression model prediction. For this purpose, the ROC method is chosen as the quantitative measurements (Verburg et al., 2005). An ROC curve is plotted by the true-positive rate (TPR). TPR defines the proportion of correct positive results occurring among all positive samples available during the test, whereas false-positive rate defines the occurrence of the incorrect positive proportion among all negative samples available in the test. These results could be summarized based on a contingency table. As shown in **Table 4.8**, the columns indicate the occurrence of certain categories (event) and the rows indicate the output of model prediction (diagnosis). The occurrence of a certain LULC type is positive and the non-occurrence is negative. Pontius and Schneider (2001) asserted that "the entries are the number (or proportion) of cells that fall into each category combination." Consequently, the correct proportion is calculated as $(A + D)/(A + B + C + D)$.

Diagnosis	Event		
	Positive	Negative	Total
Positive	A	B	$A + B$
Negative	C	D	$C + D$
Total	$A + C$	$B + D$	$A + B + C + D$

Table 4.8 Two-by-two contingency table
Source: Pontius and Schneider (2001)

Here A represents true positive (TP); B is false positive (FP); C is false negative; and D is true negative.

Cells A and D are the ways that an event agrees with the prediction (positive or negative), while the cells B and C are the ways of disagreement of event to prediction (positive or negative). The TP proportion ($A/A + C$) and the FP proportion ($B/B + D$) are obtained on the vertical and horizontal axes, respectively (Engelsman, 2002). Based on the results of each comparison in the sequence, the ROC curve is constructed by the area under the curve (AUC) which is in a coordinate system with the FPR on the x-axis and the TPR on the y-axis. The ROC curve starts at the point (FP = 0, TP = 0) and ends at the point (FP = 1, TP = 1) (Koch et al., 2012). AUC is computed by trapezoidal approximation as follows (Pontius and Schneider, 2001):

$$\text{Area under the curve} = \sum_{i=1}^{n}[x_{i+1} - x_i][y_i + y_{i+1} - {y_i}/{2}] \quad [4.56]$$

where, x_i is the FPR for scenarios i; y_i the TPR for scenarios i; and n the number of suitability groups.

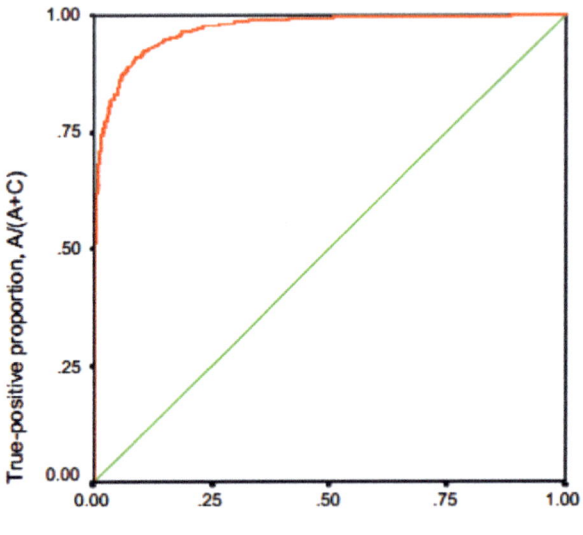

Figure 4.11 Example of ROC curve = 0.970, area under the curve (forest)
Source: Engelsman (2002)

The value of AUC typically ranges from 0.5 to 1 as shown in Figure **4.11**. If this area is equal to 1 (the TPR is 1 and FPR is 0), then the discrimination of logistic regression is perfect. On the other hand, if the ROC curve area is 0.5 (TPR and FPR are equal), then the logistic regression model does not fully predict the changes better than any random approach (Orekan, 2007).

We performed separately ROC analyses for each LULC type. The higher the ROC value is, the better the fit of logistic regression is. The spatial distribution of LULC system within the study area can be determined by the selected driving factors at high ROC value.

4.7.3.2 Visual comparison

According to Pontius and Chen (2006), it is necessary to examine the simulation maps by visual comparison, which is the quickest way to have a glance at spatial pattern. So that the user could decide to invest more time to improve the model or not. Pontius Jr et al. (2004) proposed some effective techniques in validating the spatially explicit of LULC change models, such as three-way map comparison, error budget, multiple resolution comparison, and null resolution. Accordingly, we carried out three-map comparison as visual approach, between the pair of LULC maps extracted from remote satellite data in 1996 and 2003, which we considered as the actual or reference LULC maps. On the one hand, the second pair of maps is between the actual/reference map of year 1996 and the simulation map of year 2003. This was done by the aid of Map Comparison Kit (MCK) without area restriction (Visser and de Nijs, 2006).

4.7.3.3 Model output validation

In recent years, land-use change models have been increasingly used to analyze dynamic change of LULC system, by which spatial policy making could be supported (van Vliet et al., 2011). In this circumstance, it is important to comprehensively assess the accuracy of simulated maps for scientific use as well as policy analysis. Together with visual examination, simulated maps are comprehensively assessed how the model predicts correct location of LULC types.

Validation of land-use change model is typically based on pixel-by-pixel comparison between simulated LULC map and reference LULC map. As mentioned in Section **4.4.2**, kappa coefficient of agreement is well known as a common method in a long time. However, some authors recently argued that kappa has not been the appropriate measure for accuracy any longer (van Vliet et al., 2011). Alternatively, Pontius Jr et al. (2004) presented a validation technique used to determine the agreement of land change model between two pairs of maps, which are achieved over the combination of three maps: reference maps of from time t_1 to time t_2, simulated map of time t_2. The first comparison is based on the reference map of time t_1 and the reference map of time t_2. Continuously, the second comparison between predicted map of time t_2 and the reference map of time t_2 is calculated. To evaluate the performance of the simulation model, the first comparison is examined with the second comparison upon the observed indicators, including disagreement due to quantity, disagreement due to location, agreement due to location, agreement due to quantity, and agreement due to chance. Then, all three maps are checked until the simulation result is more accurate and get the no-change model.. However, van Vliet et al. (2011) asserted that the given statistics do not include a reference level. Hence, it is not possible to know the absolute value of model's accuracy. Afterward, alternative approaches in assessing accuracy of land-use change model were developed by Chen and Pontius (2010) and Hagen-Zanker and Lajoie (2008). However, these methods are still indirect measures. Therefore, van Vliet et al. (2011) introduced a direct measure based on $K_{simulation}$ and its compositions ($K_{transition}$, $K_{transloc}$). This approach is chosen in accessing accuracy of land-use change model within the study and expressed as follows:

(1) $$K_{\text{Simulation}} = \frac{p_o - p_{e(Transition)}}{1 - p_{e(Transition)}} \quad [4.57]$$

where $K_{simulation}$ is the coefficient of agreement between the simulated land-use transition and the actual land-use transition. Values of $K_{simulation}$ range from -1 to 1, as follows: $K_{simulation} = 1$, perfect agreement; $K_{simulation} = 0$, the agreement as good as expected result; $K_{simulation} < 0$, the agreement less good as expected result.

(2) $$K_{\text{Transition}} = \frac{p_{Max(Transition)} - p_{e(Transition)}}{1 - p_{e(Transition)}} \quad [4.58]$$

where $K_{Transition}$ is the agreement in quantity of land-use transition. Values of $K_{Transition}$ range from 0 to 1 as follows: $K_{Transition} = 1$, the sizes of class transition in simulation are exactly in agreement with the sizes of class transition in reality; $K_{Transition} = 0$, there are no class transition appeared in simulated map and reality map as well.

(3) $$K_{Transloc} = \frac{P_o - P_{e(Transition)}}{P_{Max(Transition)} - P_{e(Transition)}}$$ [4.59]

where $K_{Transloc}$ is the degree to which transition agrees in their allocation. Values of $K_{Transloc}$ range from -1 to 1 as follows: $K_{Transloc} = 0$, the agreement in allocation can be expected by chance; $K_{Transition} = 1$, high possible agreement in allocation; $K_{Transition} < 0$, worse agreement in allocation.

Here

(3.1) P_o is the observed fraction of agreement:

$$P_o = \sum_{i=1}^{c} p\,(a = i \wedge s = i)$$ [4.60]

(3.2) $P_{e(Transition)}$ is the expected fraction of agreement:

$$P_{e(Transition)} = \sum_{c=1}^{j} p\,(o = j) \cdot \sum_{c=1}^{j} p\,(a = i|o = j) \cdot p\,(s = i|o = j)$$ [4.61]

(3.3) $P_{Max(transition)}$ is the maximum accuracy:

$$P_{Max(Transition)} = \sum_{c=1}^{j} p\,(o = j) \cdot \sum_{c=1}^{j} \min(p\,(a = i|o = j), p(s = i|o = j))$$ [4.62]

where i represents the land-use classes ($i = 1,2,\ldots, c$); $(a = i \wedge s = i)$ represents the cells on diagonal that have the same land use in both maps; a the cell in map A (actual map); s the cell in map S (simulated map).

All comparisons were computed by the aid of MCK (http://www.riks.nl/mck/). More details of land-use change model's accuracy measures could be found at van Vliet et al. (2011).

The process of calibration and validation in this study is presented in **Figure 4.12**.

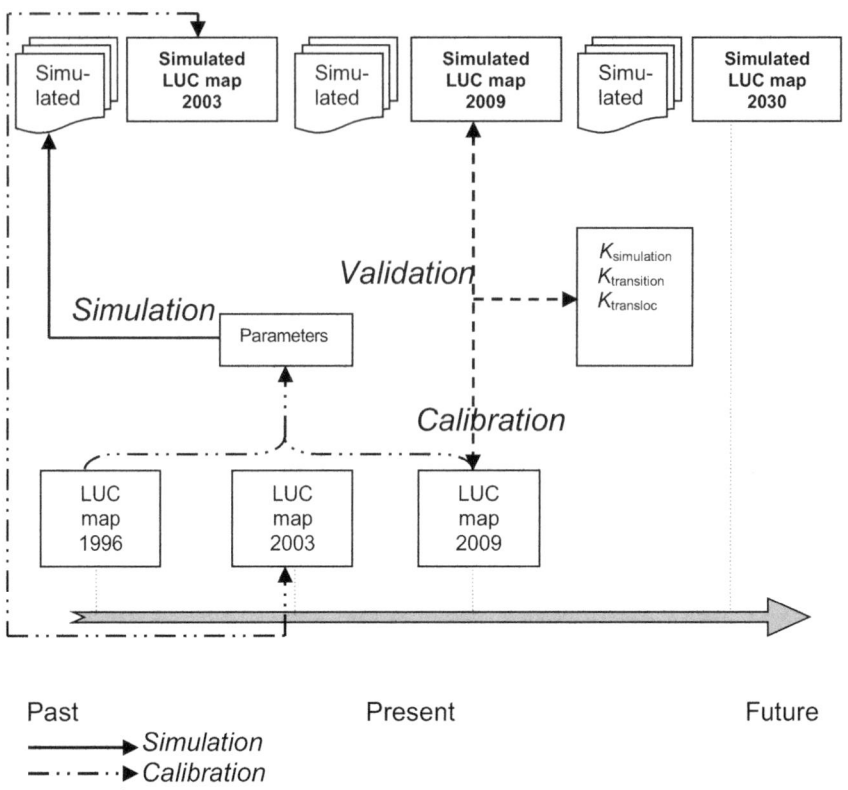

Figure 4.12 Flowchart of calibration and validation process
Source: Adapted from Estoque and Murayama (2012)

4.8 ANOVA analysis for landscape metrics under scenarios

For further understanding, one-way analysis of variance (ANOVA) was applied to examine if there were significant effects of different LULC scenarios to landscape metrics with the aid of IBM SPSS Statistics Version 20. Accordingly, the test employed on each landscape metric (NP, PD, PROX_MN, AREA_MN, IJI, LPI, LSI) using 22 simulation runs per scenario as independent variables. Since the one-way

ANOVA is often followed up with post hoc multiple comparisons, the Tukey's post hoc test at 0.05 significance level was used.

Chapter 5
Land-Use/Cover Changes

Abstract

This chapter provides an historical view of the land-use/cover (LULC) types within the Da Nang City over the past 30 years by multitemporal images. The first part of this chapter describes the rate of LULC changes and explains the causes. Then it attempts to find out the changes in the structure of landscape through the landscape metrics which will be presented in the second part.

5.1 Spatial-temporal dynamics and evolution of LULC changes

The accuracy of land-use/land-cover (LULC) maps in 1979, 1996, 2003, and 2009 was evaluated by means of overall accuracy and various kappa coefficients. From each LULC map, a total of 300 stratified random pixels was set up and then checked with reference data. The overall accuracies of Landsat multispectral scanner (MSS) 1979, Landsat thematic mapper (TM) 1996, Landsat enhanced thematic mapper plus (ETM$^+$) 2003, and advanced space-borne thermal emission and reflection radiometer (ASTER) 2009 were 81.74%, 80.33%, 84.44%, and 89.00%, respectively. **Table 5.1** shows five variations of the kappa index of agreement (K_{no}, $K_{allocation}$, $K_{quantity}$, K_{histo}, and $K_{standard}$) for each land-use map from 1979 to 2009.

In general, the results show that kappa values of all LULC maps are over 0.6. Based on the work of Pontius (2000), a kappa value, which is higher than 0.5, can be considered "satisfactory" in comparison with reference data. In addition, Landis and Koch (1977) characterized the agreement of comparison between classified map and reference data as follows: values from 0.4 to 0.75 are fair to good, and values over 0.75 are good to excellent. Based on these criteria, LULC maps derived from remote satellite imagery can be used for further studying. As shown in **Table 5.1**, the traditional kappa ($K_{standard}$) of ASTER has a higher accuracy compared to others. This could be explained by the better spatial, spectral, and radiometric resolution of ASTER data. The result indicates that the LULC maps have high values of expected overall agreement (K_{no}), high values of predicted quantity ($K_{quantity}$), and low but positive values of predicted allocation ($K_{allocation}$). More details about the observed agreement and disagreement of the quantity and spatial allocation of the categories in LULC maps can be found in **Appendix 1**.

$K_{information}$	**1979**	**1996**	**2003**	**2009**
K_{no}	0.68	0.77	0.79	0.87
$K_{allocation}$	0.67	0.81	0.87	0.86
$K_{quantity}$	0.84	0.8	0.75	0.93
K_{histo}	0.89	0.83	0.85	0.94
$K_{standard}$	0.60	0.67	0.74	0.81

Table 5.1 Kappa scores obtained from the assessment of four different land-use maps
Source: Author's calculation

For classification, a number of training pixels were set for each individual image. The number of pixels for Landsat 1979, Landsat 1996, Landsat 2003, and ASTER 2009 was 11,701, 16,389, 11,927, and 10,693, respectively. Based on supervised classification method using maximum likelihood algorithm, six LULC types were derived from classification maps of years 1979, 1996, 2003, and 2009. The spatial distributions of the LULC classes for four periods of time are shown in **Figure 5.1**. The classification statistics are summarized in **Table 5.2**.

A more thorough insight into a quantitative assessment of the accuracy for entire LULC products derived from remote sensing images was also compared with statistical data (**Figure 5.2**). According to article 13 of Vietnamese Law on Land 2003, land use could be classified into new categories: agricultural land, nonagricultural land, and unused land based on the purpose (Vietnam Laws, 2003).

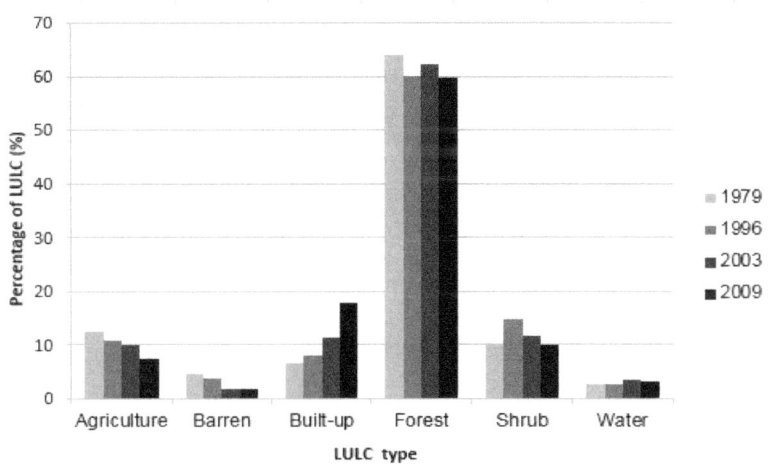

Figure 5.1 Percentage of land use/land cover extracted from remote sensing data
Source: Author's calculation

Unit: ha

LULC class	1979		1996		2003		2009	
	Area (ha)	(%)	Area (ha)	(%)	Area (ha)	(%)	Area (ha)	(%)
Agriculture	12,048.0	12.4	10,416.7	10.8	8,118.1	8.4	7,294.7	7.5
Barren	4,312.2	4.5	3,680.9	3.8	2,487.2	2.6	1,708.9	1.8
Urban	6,315.3	6.5	7,791.5	8.0	11,630.0	12.0	17,298.5	17.9
Forest	61,972.0	64.0	58,126.7	60.0	59,467.1	61.4	57,936.2	59.8
Shrub	9,785.2	10.1	14,253.2	14.7	12,335.9	12.7	9,575.8	9.9
Water	2,384.6	2.5	2,548.3	2.6	2,779.0	2.9	3,003.6	3.1
Total	96,817.2	100	96,817.2	100.0	96,817.2	100	96,817.7	100

Table 5.2 Land use/cover in Da Nang City from 1979 to 2009
Source: Author's calculation

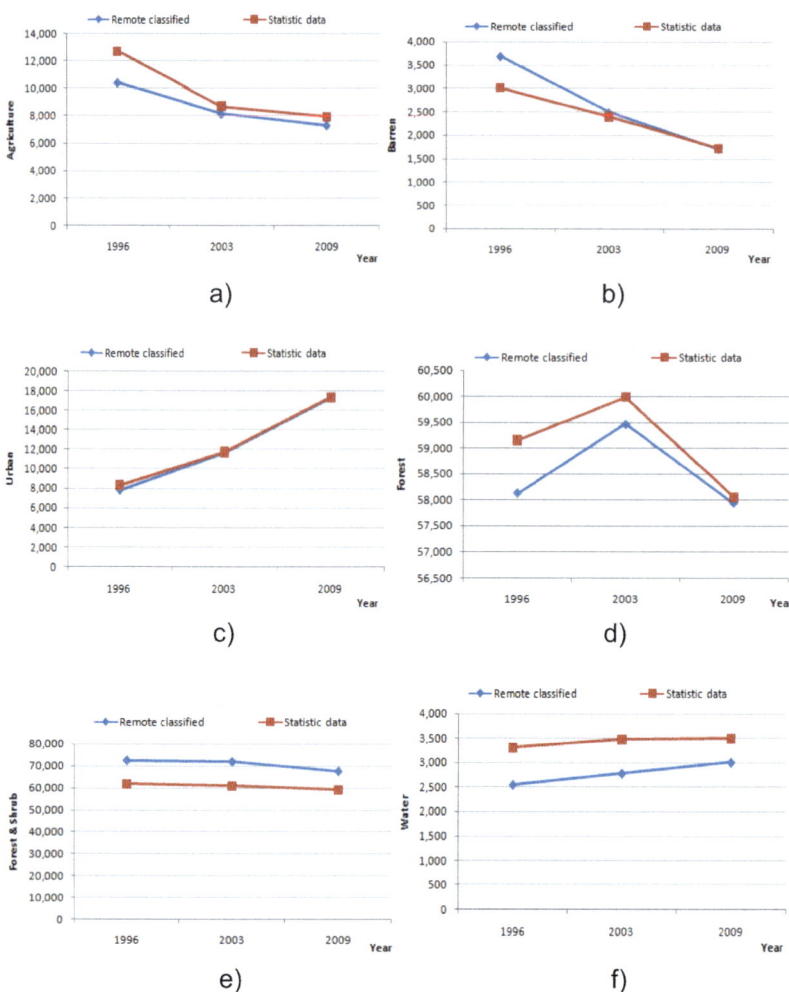

Figure 5.2 Trends of land use/cover from multitemporal images and statistic data: (a) Agriculture; (b) Barren; (c) Urban; (d) Forest; (e) Forest and shrub; and (f) Water
Source: Author's calculation

Agricultural land category comprises land for planting annual crops (rice, cultivation, pastoral, and other annual crops), land for planting perennial crops, forest land, land for aquaculture, land for salt production, and other agricultural land as stipulated by the government. Nonagriculture land category comprises residential land, land for construction, land used for national defense and security purposes, business purposes, public purposes, religious establishments, and other nonagricultural land as stipulated by the government. In which, forest land is defined as the purpose of land used rather than land cover, including "(1) protected forest, for the preservation of water resources, the prevention of erosion, natural disasters, climatic risks, and the overall protection of environment; (2) special use of forest to conserve nature, plant and animal species, to research, and protect historic, cultural, and tourist sites; (3) production forest, for supplying timber and other forest products, and associated with the other types of forest to protect environment" (Ducourtieux and Castella, 2006). This classification system is quite different in comparison with LULC classification scheme for use with remotely sensed data developed by Anderson et al. (1976b). In this circumstance, there is no discrimination between forest and shrub class. Consequently, **Figure 5.2e** is used to observe the trend of shrub. As mentioned earlier, due to the quality of images, Landsat TM 1996 was chosen instead of 1997. Nevertheless, there was no historic data about the state of LULC in this year. Therefore, LULC types extracted from Landsat TM 1996 were compared with statistic data in 1997. Although there were little differences in level, the trends of LULC obtained from satellite imagery were similar to those in statistic data.

Figure 5.1 shows that the dominant LULC classes in spatial distribution pattern were forest and urban. Accordingly, forest area was counted as 64%, 60%, 61.4%, and 59.8% of the total coverage in 1979, 1996, 2003, and 2009, respectively; meanwhile, urban area occupied 6.5%, 8.0%, 12%, and 17.9% of the total coverage in 1979, 1996, 2003, and 2009. During the period from 1979 to 2009, the surface water body covered about 2.5%, 2.6%, 2.9%, and 3.1% of the total region in the study. The results are also shown that from 1979 to 2009 LULC units under shrub, agriculture, and barren decreased from 10.1% to 9.9%, 12.4% to 7.5%, and 4.5% to 1.8%, respectively (**Table 5.2**).

Chapter 5 Land-Use/Cover Changes

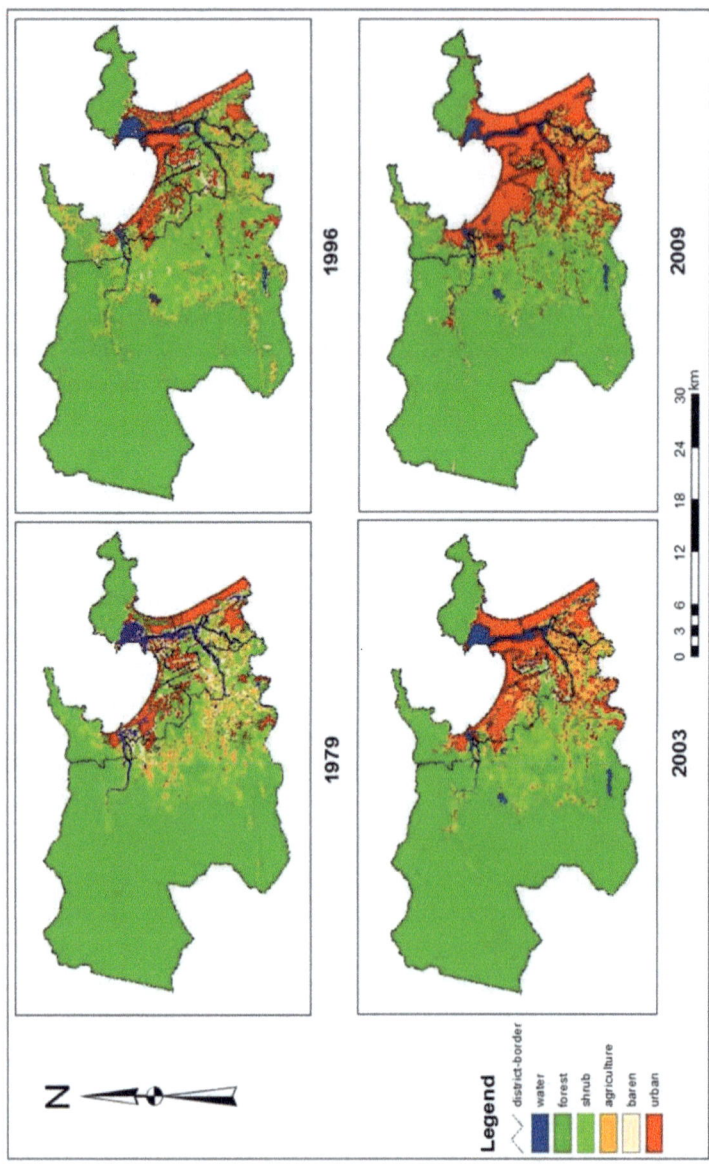

Figure 5.3 Classified land use/cover maps from multi-temporal images
Source: Author's calculation

Figure 5.3 presents the LULC maps of study area generated from multitemporal images for all four years 1979, 1996, 2003, and 2009. LULC areas were specified by multiplying the number of pixels and the spatial resolution of remote data (i.e., 30 m), in which the pixel numbers were determined after applying post-classification analysis. The changes of LULC were measured by the difference of pixel numbers between two dates afterward. Based on post-classification comparison, the from-to-change matrices of LULC in Da Nang City were created in four intervals, 1979–1996, 1996–2003, 2003–2009, and 1979–2009 to provide a further comprehensive analyses in losing and gaining among the six LULC classes (**Table 5.3**). In cross-tabulation, conversion values of classes were arranged in descending order while unchanged pixels were located along the major diagonal of the matrix.

5.1.1 Urban

Urban areas faced the most dramatic change. They increased from 6,314.85 ha in 1979 to 17,298.54 ha in 2009 (**Table 5.2**), thus representing an increase of 140% of total land-use area. The expansion of urban area in Da Nang City is confirmed by the regional statistics. In the first period from 1979 to 1996, urban area grew up to just 1,476.2 ha, representing 13.4% of net increase of urban area. However, only in seven years (1996–2003), after separation from Quang Nam Province and becoming a centrally governed city, the urban area expanded 3,838.5 ha more, which was 35% of net increase of urban area. Within the subsequent six years, from 2003 to 2009, the urban area incessantly increased and gained 5,668.5 ha, which contributed 51.6% to net increase of urban area, experienced a remarkable change of the urban area with a rapid scale. The swift expansion of urban area in the last two periods is the result of rapid economic development. As shown in **Figure 5.4**, gross domestic product (GDP) of Da Nang City increased steadily from 1990 to 2009, with an annual growth of GDP of 10.3% (higher than nation's annual growth of GDP 7.2%). In addition, the increase of population in Da Nang City could be seen as another reason for urban expansion, in which population increases from 679.7 thousand people in 1997 to 890.5 thousand people in 2009, representing an increase of 31%.

Chapter 5 Land-Use/Cover Changes

1996	1979						
	Agriculture	Barren	Urban	Forest	Shrub	Water	1996 total
Agriculture	2,910.96	1,062.45	202.32	3,865.05	2,238.21	125.1	10,416.69
Barren	657.81	481.5	573.84	986.49	832.23	142.56	3,680.91
Urban	486.54	834.48	4,280.67	1,408.77	577.62	189	7,791.48
Forest	2,797.47	711.99	324.81	52,197.03	1,878.3	118.62	58,126.77
Shrub	5,016.06	984.69	655.65	3,294.27	4,084.56	201.69	14,253.21
Water	179.19	237.06	97.02	220.41	174.24	1,607.58	2,548.26
1979 total	12,048.03	4,312.17	6,314.85	61,972.02	9,785.16	2,384.55	
Change 1979–1996	−1,631.34	−631.26	1,476.63	−3,845.25	4,468.05	163.71	

(a) 1979–1996

2003	1996						
	Agriculture	Barren	Urban	Forest	Shrub	Water	2003 total
Agriculture	2,244.51	282.87	575.01	2,165.76	2,782.44	61.2	8,118.09
Barren	325.98	532.08	414.09	360.45	803.7	44.91	2,487.15
Urban	1,127.07	985.5	5,867.1	1,090.71	2,187.63	310.86	11,629.98
Forest	4,389.66	538.29	120.78	51,701.94	2,610.18	34.29	59,466.78
Shrub	2,235.96	1,169.46	578.43	2,572.11	5,698.53	74.79	12,335.94
Water	80.91	166.23	221.67	137.25	154.44	1,989.45	2,778.84
1996 total	10,416.69	3,680.91	7,791.48	58,126.77	14,253.21	2,548.26	
Change 1996–2003	−2,298.6	−1,193.76	3,838.5	1,340.01	−1,917.27	230.58	

(b) 1996–2003

Chapter 5 Land-Use/Cover Changes

2009	2003 Agriculture	Barren	Urban	Forest	Shrub	Water	2009 total
Agriculture	1,858.68	177.66	711	2,880.63	1,645.38	15.03	7,294.68
Barren	86.76	121.86	148.14	860.58	464.04	24.93	1,708.92
Urban	3,188.7	1,188.27	9,025.29	739.35	2,673.81	458.55	17,298.54
Forest	1,036.17	231.93	414.99	52,503.66	3,556.26	95.85	57,935.79
Shrub	1,833.21	656.01	808.56	2,364.21	3,851.46	51.3	9,575.82
Water	108.27	105.48	460.89	46.71	138.33	2,104.29	3,003.57
2003 total	8,118.09	2,487.15	11,629.98	59,466.78	12,335.94	2,778.84	
Change 2003–2009	−823.41	−778.23	5,668.56	−1,530.99	−2,760.12	224.73	

(c) 2003–2009

2009	1979 Agriculture	Barren	Urban	Forest	Shrub	Water	2009 total
Agriculture	1,779.21	991.26	110.79	2,394.99	1,950.3	61.83	7,294.68
Barren	353.07	78.3	91.8	933.93	240.48	8.73	1,708.92
Urban	2,975.04	1,933.56	5,096.7	3,898.26	2,789.37	581.04	17,298.54
Forest	3,787.38	227.52	221.58	51,584.22	1,928.79	89.37	57,935.79
Shrub	2,895.48	747.45	430.47	2,834.19	2,589.48	67.68	9,575.82
Water	257.85	334.08	182.97	326.43	286.74	1,575.9	3,003.57
1979 total	12,048.03	4,312.17	6,314.85	61,972.02	9,785.16	2,384.55	
Change 1979–2009	−4,753.35	−2,603.25	10,983.69	−4,036.23	−209.34	619.02	

(d) 1979–2009

Table 5.3 Land-use/cover transformation matrices
Source: Author's calculation

Chapter 5 Land-Use/Cover Changes

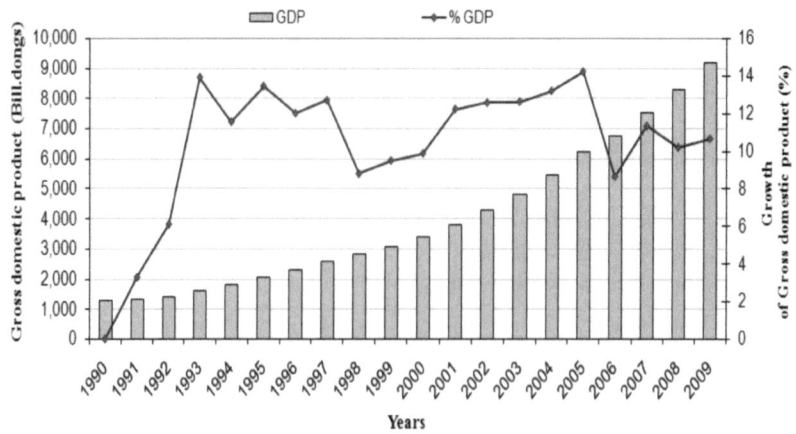

Figure 5.4 Gross domestic product (GDP) and its growth in Da Nang City from 1990 to 2009

Source: Statistical Year Books

Time	Unit	District						
		CL	HC	HV	LC	NHS	ST	TK
1979	Area (ha)	316.3	653.8	866.5	1,607.9	16,745.0	685,08	286.3
	(%)	9.1	30.0	1.2	19.6	42.2	11.0	30.4
1996	Area (ha)	484.9	1,051.7	1,492.3	1,709.6	1,890.4	839.43	535.3
	(%)	14.0	48.4	2.1	20.8	47.7	13.4	56.7
2003	Area (ha)	1,145.9	1,248.0	2,248.0	2,123.91	2,228.9	1,185.0	725.2
	(%)	33.0	57.3	3.1	25.9	56.2	19.0	77.0
2009	Area (ha)	1,910.3	1,595.3	5,350.3	3,287.16	2,753.3	1,569.4	835.3
	(%)	55.1	73.4	7.5	40.0	69.4	25.0	88.4

Note: CL, Cam Le; HC, Hai Chau; HV, Hoa Vang; LC, Lien Chieu; NHS, Ngu Hanh Son; ST, Son Tra; TK, Thanh Khe

Table 5.4 Measuring the changes of urban area in different districts

Source: Author's calculation

Further comparison with the classified LULC maps derived from multitemporal images is shown in **Figure 5.3**, in which, the urban areas are displayed in red color. The spatial distribution and extent of urban area varied differently among the administrative districts within Da Nang City which is clearly presented in **Table 5.4**. In terms of percentage, the most intensive occurrence of urban area was in Thanh Khe district (88.4% of its administrative area), followed by Hai Chau district (73.4%), Ngu Hanh Son district (69.4%), Cam Le district (55.1%), and Lien Chieu district (40.0%) over the past 30 years. As a city located close to the eastern seaboard, habitants of Da Nang City tended to live near the coast. In the period from 1979 to 1996, urban area distributed scattered in Ngu Hanh Son (42.2%), Thanh Khe (30.4%), Hai Chau (30%), Lien Chieu (19.6%), and a part of Son Tra districts (11%). From 1996 to 2003, this area expanded and concentrated in these districts. As observed from **Figure 5.3**, the expansion of urban area tends to vary on the mainland instead of along the coastal line.

Cross-tabulation shows that the increase of urban area gained from the conversions of forest, agriculture, shrub, and barren to urban. Of the 10,983.69 ha of total growth in urban area from 1979 to 2009, 33.5% was converted from forest, 26.1% from agriculture, 21.5% from shrub, and 16.8% from barren. From 1979 to 2009, 3,898.26 ha of forest were converted to urban, while 221.58 ha of urban were converted to forest at the same time. The later change may not be reasonable and looks like the result of classification errors. According to Anderson et al. (1976a), park, garden, recreation, and roads belong to urban LULC classification scheme levels IV and V. However, when the trees in these places grew up, the pixels associated with tree canopies may be classified as forest. Similarly, these commission errors could be found also in the change of urban to agriculture or urban to shrub.

5.1.2 Agriculture

Table 5.2 shows that the agricultural area had an area of 12,048.03 ha in 1979, 10,416.7 ha in 1996, 8,118.1 ha in 2003, and 7,294.7 ha in 2009, representing by 12.4%, 10.8%, 8.4%, and 7.5%, respectively. From 1979 to 2009, agricultural area strongly decreased by 4,753.35 ha (**Table 5.3d**), representing a net decrease of 39.5%, the change of agricultural area altered considerably in different periods of time. Within a span of 17 years, from 1979 to 1996, the agricultural area reduced to 1,631.34 ha, thus representing 13.5%, whereas from 1996 to 2003, within just seven years, the agricultural area reduced by 2,298.6 ha, thus representing 19.1%, and from 2003 to 2009, within six years, agricultural area reduced by 823.41 ha, which represented 6.8%. The loss of agriculture from 1979 to 2009 was mainly caused by the encroachment of urban areas and forestation. According to **Table 5.3d**, the agricultural area gained only 110.79 ha from urban areas, while it lost 2,975.04 ha to urban areas, representing 60.3% of total decrease in agricultural land use. Likewise, 1,392.39 ha of agriculture were converted to forest, representing 29.3% of total decrease in agricultural land use.

As mentioned earlier, the decrease in agricultural area could be the result of the rapid increase of urban area. Moreover, this trend was followed by the oriental economic structure as the overall long-term programming in developing economics and social of Da Nang City, in which the descending order of sectors was services, industry, and agriculture (**Figure 5.5**). The loss of agriculture to forest was the result of changes from crop land to orchard or artificial forest (e.g., *Acacia mangium*, *Acacia auriculiformis*, and *Eucalyptus camaldulensis*). It has been noticed that the change from urban to agriculture was likely to be due to the classification errors. In classified LULC maps, these errors could be omission or commission errors.

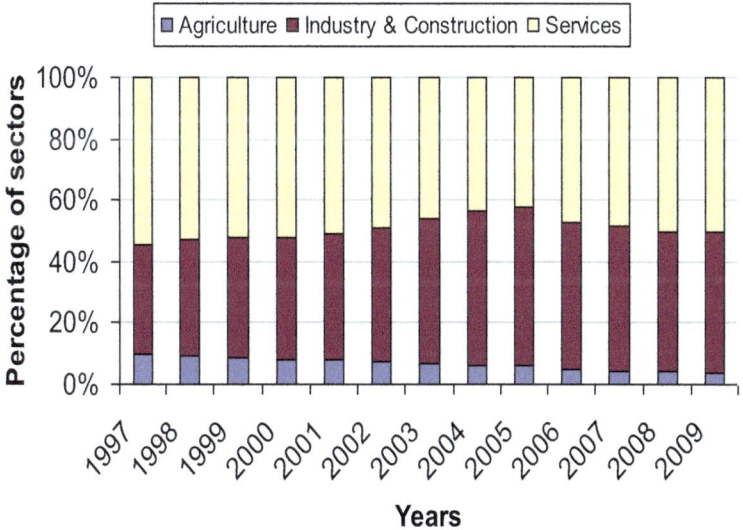

Figure 5.5 Development of the economic structure in Da Nang City from 1997 to 2009
Source: Statistical Year Books

5.1.3 Forest

Table 5.2 shows that forest area decreased in general over the study period. However, this area fluctuated variously in different periods. In quantitative terms, the forest area was detected as 61,972 ha in 1979, 58,126.7 ha in 1996, 59,467.1 ha in 2003, and 57,936.2 ha in 2009, thus representing 64%, 60%, 61.4%, and 59.8% of total area of Da Nang City, respectively. Until 2009, 83.2% (51,584.22 ha) of forests in 1979 that still remained were unchanged (**Table 5.3d**). Results showed that the forest area lost 10,387.8 ha of its 1979 area to other classes, in which 37.5% (3,898.26 ha) converted to urban, 27.3% (2,834.19 ha) to shrub, and 23.1% (2,394.99 ha) to agriculture. The results also indicated that the gain of forest area mainly came from agriculture and shrub. From 1979 to 2009, 6,254.64 ha were converted to forest, in which 60.5% (3,787.38 ha) from agriculture and 30.8% (1,928.79 ha) from shrub. The observed trends of decreasing and increasing of forest area in different periods of time in Da Nang City could be clarified by the following reasons. During the first period from 1979 to 1996, like other provinces in Vietnam, deforestation was mainly caused by the increasing demand of land for agriculture and timber products. Consequently, the *close the natural forest gate* policy to restrict the overexploitation was promulgated by government in 1990. To continue supplying materials for timbers and paper industry, forestry productions were exploited from forest plantation (Van Loi, 2008). Therefore, forest cover area had been slightly increased in the second period from 1996 to 2003 by reforestation programs. However, in the third period from 2003 to 2009, forest area decreased once again (1.6% of total area in Da Nang City) due to the rapid urbanization.

5.1.4 Shrub

The area of shrub cover class during the four periods is shown in **Table 5.2**. Shrub area occupied 9,785.2 ha in 1979, 14,253.2 ha in 1996, 12,335.9 ha in 2003, and 9,575.8 ha in 2009, which represented 10.1%, 14.7%, 12.7%, and 9.9%, respectively. At the end of study period (2009), shrub area decreased by 209.34 ha. Of the 9,575.82 ha of total area in shrub land use, 2,589.48 ha shrub was still unchanged in 2009. As can be seen from statistics, the changes of shrub area were different through periods of times. The reasons that caused the increase and decrease in area of shrub class might be similar with the reasons mentioned in the changes of forest area.

5.1.5 Barren

In the same way, 2,603.25 ha of barren area consistently decreased from 1979 to 2009, which represented that barren lost 60.4% of its 1979 area by 2009 (**Table 5.2**). Based on **Table 5.3d**, only 78.3 ha of barren remained unchanged from 1979 to 2009. Barren lost 44.8% (1,933.56 ha) to urban, 23% (991.26 ha) to agriculture, and 17.3% (747.45 ha) to shrub in the same period. Meanwhile, 933.93, 353.07, and 240.48 ha of barren areas were obtained from forest, agriculture, and shrub. It is noted that the conversion between agriculture and barren might be influenced by acquisition of remotely sensed image in different seasons. It can be asserted that some agriculture plots had been harvested and fallowed during the time for operating of remote satellite.

5.1.6 Water

Water had been an area of 2,384.55 ha in 1979, 2,548.26 ha in 1996, 2,778.84 ha in 2003, and 3,003.57 ha in 2009 (**Table 5.3**). Note that water area in Da Nang City continuously increased from 1979 to 2009. It showed that the water area gained 26% of its 1979 area by 2009. **Table 5.3d** shows that 1,388.07 ha of land to water gained from other classes and lost 808.65 ha of its 1979 area to other classes. About 1,388.07 ha belonged to water class, 24.1% (334.08 ha) came from barren, 23.5% (326.43 ha) from forest, 21% (286.74 ha) from shrub, and 18.6% (257.85 ha) from agriculture. Around 808.65 ha of water area was lost from 1979 to 2009, 72% (581.04 ha) transformed to urban area. The decrease of water pixels could be the result of the different resolution of the sensors used in this study, which caused consequently the omission errors. Besides, the seasonal changes in remotely sensed data may affect the accuracy of water class.

The increase of water in the study period resulted from construction of new reservoirs to collect water in the latter part of the 1980s. Besides the rivers and streams system, Da Nang has 30 reservoirs and lakes with capacity of 3.3 million m^3 of water supplied for 4,580 ha cultivated land. However, these reservoirs and lakes are not distributed equally; most of them are located within Hai Chau and Thanh Khe districts; in contrast to this, there are not many in Son Tra, Ngu Hanh Son, and Lien Chieu; the two largest reservoirs are in Hoa Vang district, namely Dong Nghe and Hoa Trung (Thang, 2009). In the orientation of land-use planning of Da Nang City, increasing water area is an important task to supply water not only for cultivated land but also for the demand of industry as well as residential area and conserving the ecological environment.

5.2 Landscape pattern analysis at class level

Class	PLAND (%)	NP (#)	LPI (%)	AREA_MN (ha)	PD (#/100 ha)	PROX_MN (m)	LSI (#)	IJI (%)
1979								
Agriculture	7.0	1,240	2.7	10.0	0.7	491.2	50.8	71.1
Urban	3.7	682	1.0	9.2	0.4	67.1	41.2	62.5
Forestry	36.0	2,180	29.4	28.4	1.3	2,670.1	26.2	84.0
2009								
Agriculture	3.6	3,051	0.3	2.1	1.7	24.2	60.2	50.0
Urban	10.1	1,771	4.6	10.2	1.0	1,728.6	25.0	79.3
Forestry	33.2	1,554	29.5	38.0	0.9	17,985.4	24.8	82.3

Table 5.5 Metrics of landscape structure at the class level
Source: Author's calculation
Note: PLAND, percentage of landscape; NP, number of patches; LPI, largest patch index; AREA_MN, mean patch area index; PD, patch density; PROX_MN, mean proximity index; LSI, landscape shape index; IJI, interspersion and juxtaposition index.

In order to have a more comprehensive analysis and focusing on spatial changes of classification maps of the years 1979 and 2009, the three representative classes (agriculture, urban, and forest) were chosen to compute spatial landscape matrices. These landscape metric indices were calculated and summarized in **Table 5.5**, through which a comprehensive overall picture of landscape structure (including area, shape, isolation and proximity, and contagion/interspersion) could be revealed.

The dramatic changes of LULC stimulated by intensive development of economics in Da Nang City resulted in the intrinsic change of landscape structure from 1979 to 2009. **Table 5.5** shows the relevant landscape metrics at class level for the three main classes: agriculture, urban, and forestry. In Da Nang City, forestry area is the most dominant class of landscape due to its largest percentage of total area. This could be identified by the largest patch index (LPI), a specific measure used for observing the dominance of a land-cover type. A comparison with agriculture and urban area shows that the LPI of forest area is highest at rates of 29.4% and 29.5% in 1979 and 2009, respectively. During the whole period from 1979 to 2009, the statistic for the forestry class showed that the percentage of landscape (PLAND) index decreased from 36% to 33.2%, the number of patches (NP) decreased from 2,180 to 1,554, and the patch density (PD) index decreased softly from 1.3 per 100 ha to 0.9 per 100 ha. In contrast to this, the mean patch area index (AREA_MN) increased from 28.4 to 38.0 ha, which was supported by the increasing of the mean proximity index (PROX_MN) from 2,670.1 to 17,985.4 m. It can be assumed that forested patches increasingly occupied the neighborhood, defined by a search radius of 300 m. It indicates that those forested patches were more contiguous in the domain of spatial distribution. As can be seen, the 1979 forest class had a high interspersion and juxtaposition index (IJI) (84.0%). This value indicated that the patches were well interspersed in the landscape. Or in short, these forest patches were adjacent to each other equally. In 2009, this index reduced slightly to 82.3%, which characterized a misproportion in the distribution of patch-type adjacencies. However, such changes could be generally negligible. The IJI index of forest patches was still high over 80%. In addition, the landscape shape index (LSI) asserted also a slight decrease from 26.2 in 1979 to 24.8 in 2009; this might suggest a less dispersed in spatial distribution of forest patches.

In regard to agricultural area during the period from 1979 to 2009, **Table 5.5** shows the decrease of this class by the PLAND index, from 7.0% to 3.6%. However, the results also show that NP increased from 1,240 to 3,051, and the PD index increased over twofold from 0.7 per 100 ha to 1.7 per 100 ha. In contrast to this, the AREA_MN decreased from 10.0 to 2.1 ha and the LPI lessened drastically from 2.7% to 0.3%. Also, the PROX_MN decreased strongly from 491.2 to 24.2 m. The combination of these values reveals that the agriculture patches in 2009 were smaller and more fragmented than the agriculture patches in 1979. As shown in **Table 5.5**, the 1979 agricultural class has a higher IJI than the 2009 agricultural class (i.e., 18.1%). Those values indicate the spatial intermixing of agriculture patches in the landscape. Furthermore, the LSI supported this view by the increase from 50.8 to 60.2 within the 30-year study period, emphasizing a higher complexity of this class.

As mentioned earlier, urban area increased promptly from 6,315.3 ha in 1979 to 17,298.5 ha in 2009. Consequently, the spatial distribution of urban areas showed the significant increasing of the PLAND index from 3.7% to 10.1%. Likewise, the LPI increased from

1.0% in 1979 to 4.6% in 2009, reflecting the encroachment of urban area in Da Nang City. It is further supported by the NP index increasing drastically from 682 to 1,771. The AREA_MN of urban area increased from 9.2 to 10.2 ha, whereas PD increased from 0.4 per 100 ha to 1.0 per 100 ha. The agglomeration of new urban areas evidenced the rapid expansion of urban areas in the landscape of Da Nang City during the span of 30 years. It can be seen from **Table 5.5**, the PROX_MN of urban area increased substantially from 67.1 to 1,728.6 m and the IJI heightened 16.2 after 30 years. The first index showed a more uniform landscape configuration, in which urban patches became closer and less isolation. The next one presented that the urban patches were adjacent to each other and tended to take more clumped than before because of converting from other classes. The reduction of LSI from 41.2 to 25 illustrated a less complexity of this class.

5.3 Discussions and conclusions

By using Landsat and ASTER satellite images, this chapter presented the analysis of LULC and landscape change in the Da Nang region over the past 30 years (1979–2009). For detecting LULC changes, post-classification approach was applied. The results show the conspicuous changes of LULC, and thus the substantial impact on landscape pattern. In general, a total of 35,689.79 ha or 37% of the total land has undergone change. The analysis indicates a notable decrease of agriculture, forest, barren, and shrub due to the expansion of urban.

The speed and transformation trends of LULC varied in different research periods. Before separating from Quang Nam Province (1979–1996), the LULC in Da Nang City changed gradually. However, after becoming an independent municipality, the LULC changed with rapid speed, especially urban area. Within 13 years (1996–2009), urban area grew up to 86.6%. Spatially, it was shown that most of the urban area occurred in Thanh Khe, Hai Chau, Ngu Hanh Son, and Cam Le districts. This could be caused by strong focus of economic development. From the increase in urban area, agriculture and forest had a high rate of change, with a decreasing trend. In the meantime, key landscape indices were performed for three main classes, namely, urban, agriculture, and forest for further understanding in spatial distribution. Based on the analysis of landscape metrics, the different changes in landscape of Da Nang City were defined. The dynamic change of landscape indices at agriculture class revealed the breakup of the area into smaller patches. However, except agriculture, patches of forestry and urban areas tended to have a uniform landscape configuration.

The study explored the changes of LULC and spatial distribution of landscape in Da Nang City. This would help the decision maker and local authority have an overview in this area; it can integrate strategies into LULC planning that could be considered. However, this study has its own limitation. According to the results, it has been found that the NP of all classes changed dramatically over the past 30 years. Besides the fragmentation of patches due to the transformation of classes, such an increase is probably due to the fact that ASTER image of 2009 with higher resolution could count small patches, compared to Landsat MSS image of 1979.

Chapter 6
Modeling Land Use/Cover Changes

Abstract

This chapter deals with the simulation of land-use/cover (LULC) types in Da Nang City over periods of time (1996–2030). The first section presents the demand of LULC types for each year at the regional level as three specific scenarios based on system dynamic modeling framework. These nonspatial scenarios are then used as one of the inputs of dynamic conversion of land use and its effects (Dyna-CLUE). Regarding the parameters of Dyna-CLUE model, the relative settings are addressed in following sections. The results of running Dyna-CLUE model are explored through the allocation of LULC types within Da Nang City. The validations of models are assessed as well. The final section presents the effects of different scenarios to landscape structure within the study area.

6.1 Demands of land-use/cover types

6.1.1 Demands of land-use/cover types from 1996 to 2009

As stated earlier, the demands of land-use/cover (LULC) types are simulated using system dynamic (SD) model under various parameters (**Section 4.7.1.2**). The results were examined and calibrated based on social-economic data from 1996 to 2009. **Figure 6.1** shows the comparison between actual and predicted values of population, gross output industry (GOI), and fixed-assets investment (FAI) construction from 1996 to 2009. **Figure 6.2** illustrates the comparison between actual values of LULC areas and their predicted values.

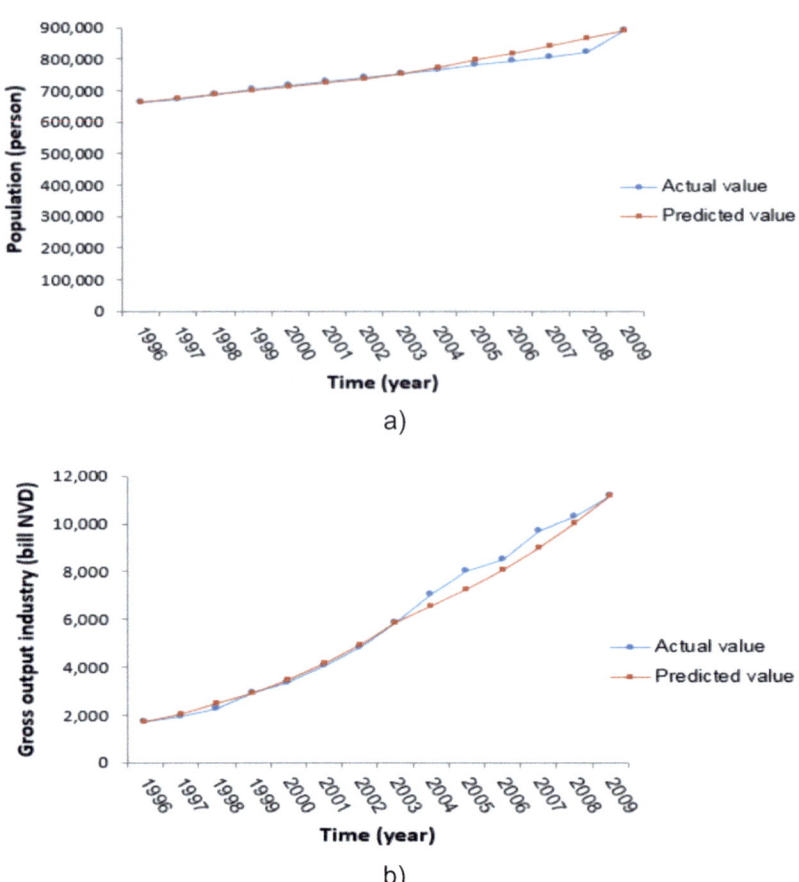

Chapter 6 Modeling Land Use/Cover Changes

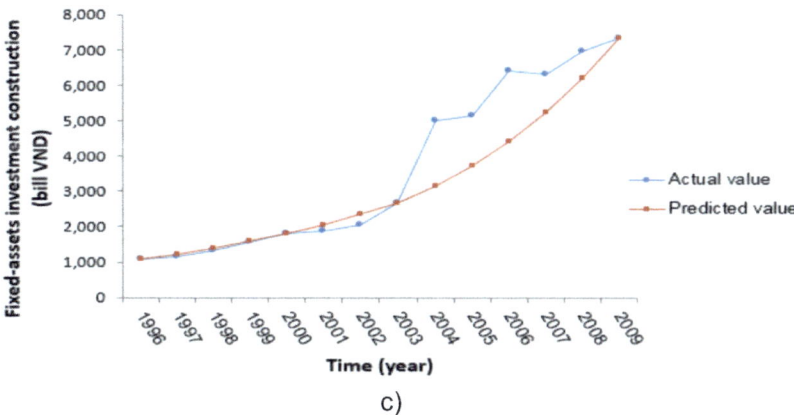

c)

Figure 6.1 Comparison between actual and predicted values of (a) population, (b) gross output industry, and (c) fixed-assets investment construction

Source: Author's calculation

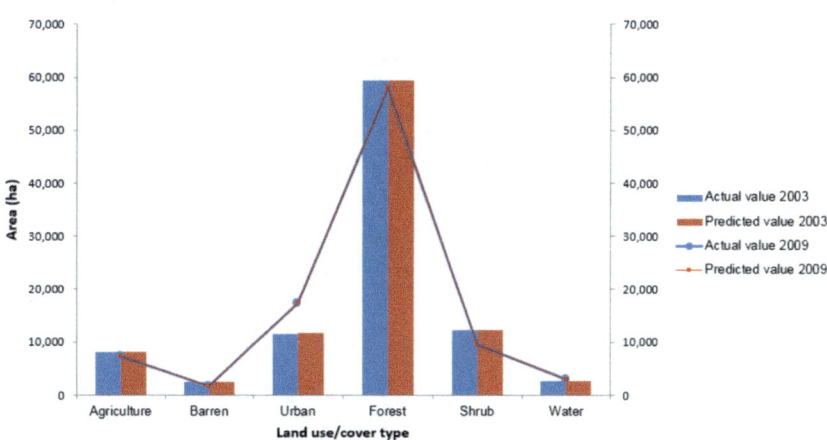

Figure 6.2 Comparison between actual and predicted values of land-use/cover area

Source: Author's calculation

115

Type	Year	Reference	Simulation	Error (%)
Population (person)	2003	752,438	752,438	0.000
	2009	890,490	890,489	0.000
GOI (bill VND)	2003	5,874.59	5,875.16	-0.009
	2009	11,179.48	11,173.3	0.055
FAI (bill VND)	2003	2,673.38	2,673.53	-0.006
	2009	7,341.6	7,345.89	-0.058
Agriculture (ha)	2003	8,118.1	8,118.85	-0.009
	2009	7,294.7	7,293.1	0.022
Barren (ha)	2003	2,487.2	2,457.83	1.181
	2009	1,708.9	1,723.53	-0.856
Urban (ha)	2003	11,630	11,658.2	-0.242
	2009	17,298.5	17,284.9	0.079
Forest (ha)	2003	59,467.1	59,465.8	0.002
	2009	57,936.2	57,942.6	-0.011
Shrub (ha)	2003	12,335.9	12,364.9	-0.235
	2009	9,575.26	9,568.29	0.073
Water (ha)	2003	2,779.0	2,751.62	0.985
	2009	3,003.6	3,004.78	-0.039

Table 6.1 SD model results and validations

Note: GOI, gross output industry; FAI, fixed-assets investment; VND, Vietnamese Dong.
Source: Author's calculation

A quantitative analysis of the predicted parameter's accuracy in 2003 and 2009 was completed and is presented in **Table 6.1**. It indicates that the relative errors of simulation results in SD model are just around 1%, compared with actual data. Hence, this model is reliable and can be used to forecast the future demand of LULC types.

6.1.2 Demands of land-use/cover types from 2009 to 2030

Parameter (%)	Scenario A	Scenario B	Scenario C
Natural growth rate	2.00	1.19	1.19
Mechanical growth rate	0.85	2.8	1.18
GOI rate	20.77	26.43	26.43
FAI rate	18.4	12.20	10.00

Table 6.2 Parameter settings for scenarios
Note: GOI, gross output industry; FAI, fixed-assets investment

Based on the SD model (presented in **Figure 4.7**), it is assumed that the scenarios would be distinguished by the change of four main parameters: natural growth rate, mechanical growth rate, GOI rate, and FAI construction rate, while the other parameters in the model are maintained. These parameters were selected because they directly influence the changes of population and economic factors. In the next 22 years from the year 2009, the designated main parameters are attained from land-use planning guideline and general plan of socioeconomic development of Da Nang City by 2020 (**Table 6.2**).

In this section, three different scenarios are presented. The first scenario is the baseline scenario called *development as usual*, in which the simulation is based on the maintainable parameters obtained from historical statistics of Da Nang City (1996–2009). The second one is *aggressive development*, which may speed up the growth rate of economic factors without considering environmental conditions. The last one is *optimal development*, in which both economic and environmental factors are noticed. The conditions of scenarios are presented as follows:

6.1.2.1 Scenario A

As shown in **Table 6.2**, the demand of LULC in this scenario is particularly based on the growth rate of the development between 1996 and 2009. It is assumed that the increase of population in Da Nang City is mainly due to the growth of natural rate (2% per year). Being one of five centrally controlled municipalities in Vietnam in the early of year 1997, Da Nang city has moved into "a period of massive infrastructure building." Besides, with the adopted Law on Foreign Direct Investment, Da Nang City has attracted various invested projects (Nguyen, 2003). Consequently, the rate of GOI and FAI construction during this period is high. In scenario A, these rates are applied for simulating the demand of LULC area. It is also assumed that the water area (3,003.79 ha in 2009) remained constant during the whole period of running the SD model.

6.1.2.2 Scenario B

In scenario B, the simulation is made upon the assumption that the natural growth rate is 1.19% per year, while the mechanical growth rate is 2.8% per year. In addition, the rate of GOI and FAI construction is 26.43% and 12.20%, respectively. These rates are collected from the general orientation of socioeconomic development in Da

Nang City by 2020. In this scenario, the socioeconomic condition of Da Nang City is supposed to be in a remarkable state; the infrastructure has been completed; and the policy on investment encouragement in Da Nang City is good as well. Hence, the mechanical growth rate is higher than in scenario A because of large-scale immigration to Da Nang City for finding jobs. Together with the increase of mechanical growth rate, the GOI rate of this scenario also increases to 26.43% per year. Out of the "period of massive infrastructure building," the fixed-asset investment construction of this scenario decreases to 12.20% per year. Similarly, the water area in this scenario also remains constant during the whole period of running the SD model.

6.1.2.3 Scenario C

In the third scenario, the supposed conditions of the model are almost the same as those in the second scenario. However, the mechanical growth and FAI construction are lower at 1.18% per year and 10.0% per year, respectively. Importantly, this scenario focuses more on sustainable development according to the long-term planning in Da Nang City. Accordingly, LULC types in Da Nang City must be considered more as protecting, sparely utilizing, and reasonably converting, by which the socioeconomic component of city could be promoted to develop as a sustainable and stable strategy. In the long term, the spatial pattern of city would be extended to the South, the West, and the Northwest through developing the satellite towns. Restricting the conversion of agricultural area (especially, rice area) to other purposes is needed, in order to satisfy the society's demand for agricultural products, supply the raw material for industry, and settle agricultural labors. Additionally, caring and protecting the actual forest area, and intensifying the afforestation play an important role in maintaining the ecological environment. Hence, it requires keeping the forest cover above 60% when compared with the total area in Da Nang City. In this scenario, the water area in 2009 also remained constant during the whole period of running the SD model.

Temporal simulation of LULC system in Da Nang City is presented in **Table 6.3**. Details about the predicted results of LULC area in Da Nang City based on three scenarios could be found in **Appendix 2**.

Unit: ha

Year	Scenario	Agriculture	Barren	Urban	Forest	Shrub	Water
2010	1	7,054.52	1,959.5	17,934.5	57,647.27	9,218.1	3,003.79
	2	6,826.37	1,538.11	18,582.8	57,686.9	9,179.71	3,003.79
	3	7,161.46	1,538	18,087.4	57,936.2	90,90.83	3,003.79
2020	1	6,094.01	0	24,406.01	55,183.5	8,130.37	3,003.79
	2	5,287.91	536.3	24,847.4	55,253.8	7,888.48	3,003.79
	3	6,671.99	536.19	21,734.28	57,936.2	6,935.23	3,003.79
2030	1	4,089.62	0	30,884.66	52,675.6	6,164.01	3,003.79
	2	1,195.72	0	34,451.24	52,810.2	5,356.73	3,003.79
	3	5,297.7	110.55	27,092.77	57,936.2	3,376.67	3,003.79

Table 6.3 Temporal simulation of land-use/cover system in Da Nang City
Source: Author's calculation

6.2 Driving factors for allocation

As stated in **Section 2.1.4**, projecting the future changes of LULC types requires critical driving forces. According to the conditions of available data as well as the local features of the study area, seven factors were chosen to analyze the allocation of LULC in Da Nang City, including extrinsic driving factors (urban rate and mean density of population) and intrinsic driving factors (slope, elevation, distance to road, distance to urban, and distance to water).

Each factor was prepared as a grid map with a cell size of 30 m × 30 m (**Figure 6.3**). The two first factors (urban rate and mean density of population) were calculated based on the collected data in the *Yearly Statistics Book* of Da Nang City, while the rest of the factors were computed with the grid cell as the basic unit. The elevation and slope factors were extracted from the digital elevation model of the study area by the tool in ArcGIS 10.1. The distance to urban, road, and water is Euclidean distances that were also generated upon the application of ArcGIS 10.1 package software. It is assumed that these driving factors contribute to the change of LULC in the study area from 1996 to 2009 and will continue to do so over the next decades.

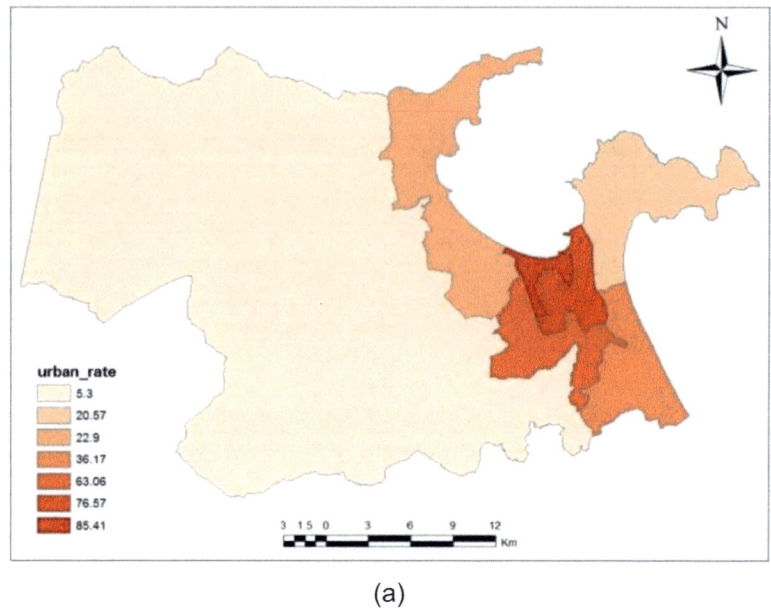

(a)

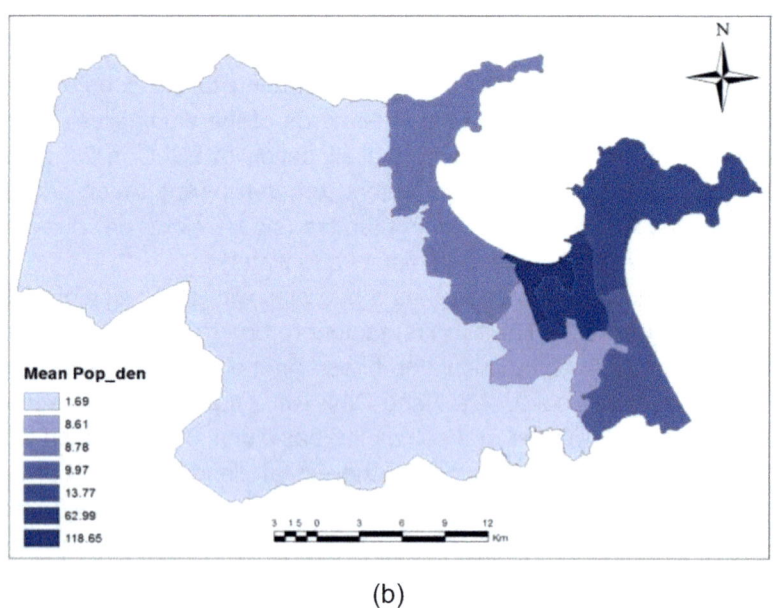

(b)

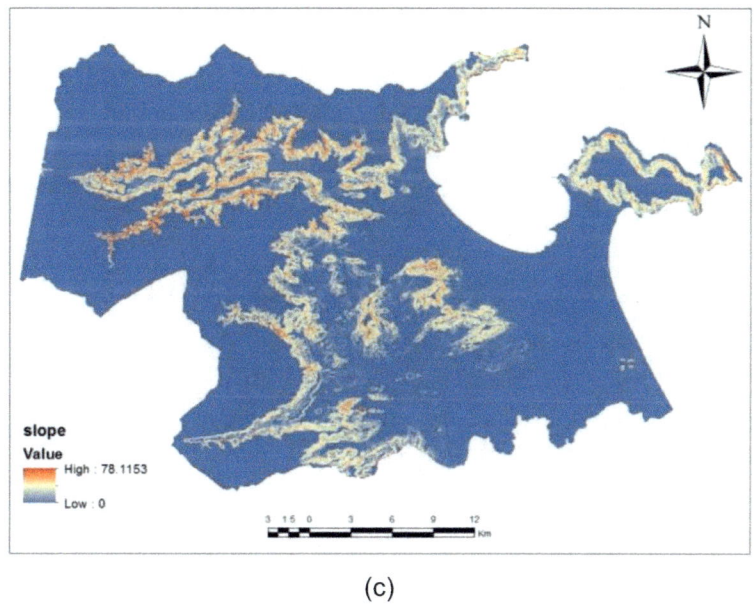

(c)

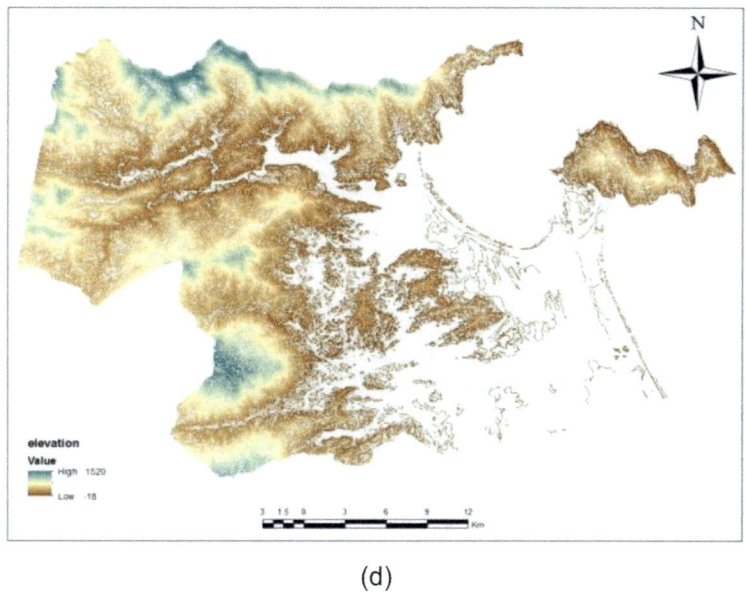

(d)

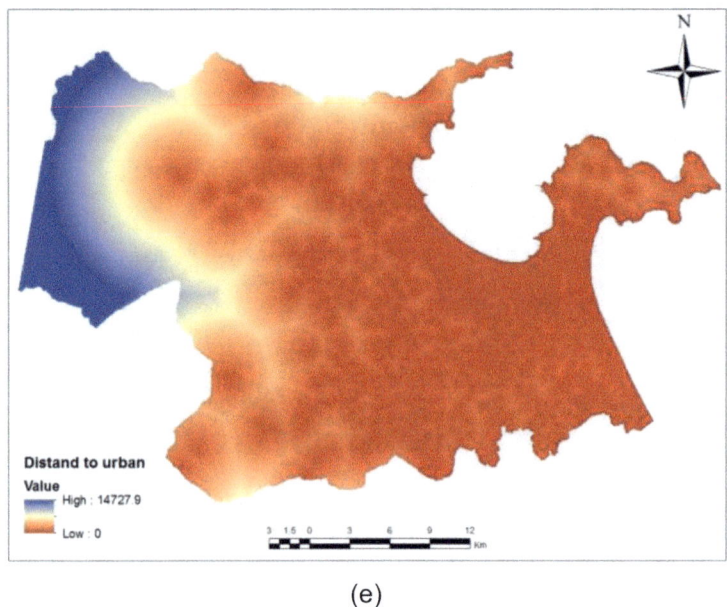

(e)

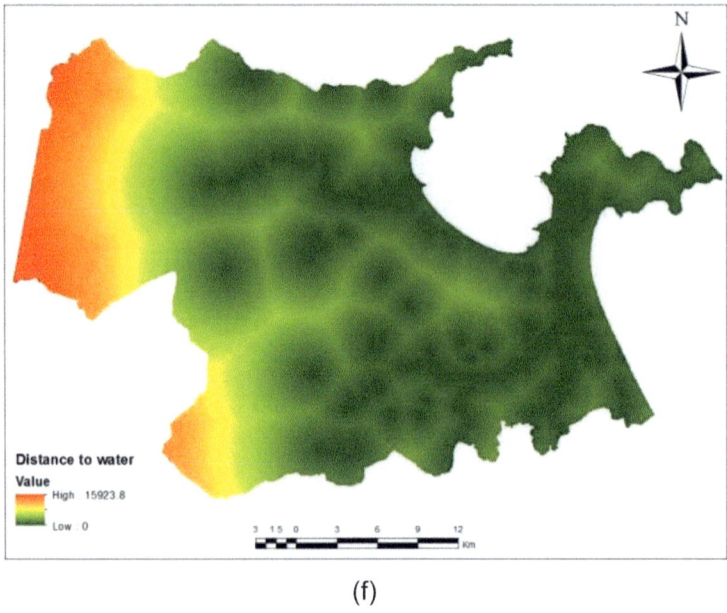

(f)

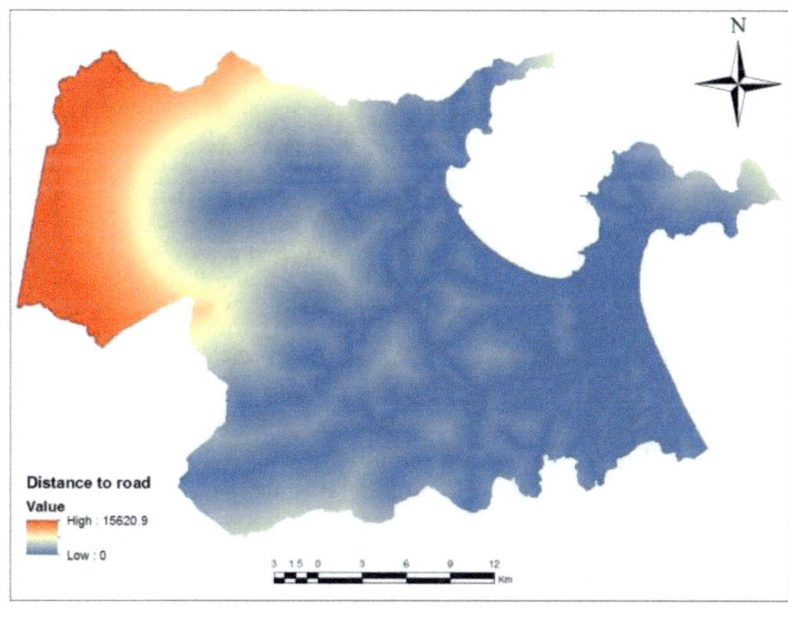

(g)

Figure 6.3 Driving factors: (a) urban rate, (b) mean density of population, (c) slope, (d) elevation; (e) distance to urban, (f) distance to water, and (g) distance to road.

Source: Author's calculation

6.3 Logistic regression analysis

Land use/cover Driving factors	Agriculture	Barren	Urban	Forest	Shrub	Water
Urban rate	-0.01492	-0.00465	0.00645	0.01980	-0.01848	-0.00637
Mean density of population	0.01099	-0.00867	-0.01170	-0.01485	0.02097	-0.00949
Slope	-0.00953	0.00556	-0.00103	0.01690	-0.01731	0.00650
Elevation	-0.00026	-0.00047	0.00036	0.00040	-0.00054	0.00045
Distance to road	-0.00034	-0.00015	-0.00023	0.00052	-0.00030	-0.00008
Distance to urban	-0.00013	-0.00088	-0.02925	0.00118	-0.00097	0.00017
Distance to water	-0.00005	-0.00007	0.00005	0.00018	-0.00005	-0.01899
Constant	0.94382	1.05483	2.63099	-2.41997	1.41003	3.18663
ROC	0.697	0.780	0.990	0.913	0.780	0.998

Table 6.4 Logistic regression of land-use/cover type
Note: ROC, relative operating characteristic.
Source: Author's calculation

To examine the relation between LULC types and their potential driving factors, multivariate logistic regression model was conducted for LULC map in 1996 (the initial year of running dynamic conversion of land use and its effects [Dyna-CLUE] model). In this study, all the driving factors were chosen to assess the appropriateness of a special grid cell to be exerted to a certain LULC type. The logistic regression analysis was run with the statistic software IBM SPSS package 20, where LULC types were set as dependent variables, while driving factors were set as independent variables that influence spatial patterns. The regression confidence degree that was used in the analysis is set to 98% ($\alpha = 0.02$). The results of logistic regression are presented in **Table 6.4**. More detail can be found in **Appendix 3**.

In this regression, seven variables are considered as driving factors. Each variable has its own effect on the spatial pattern of each land-use type. The coefficient β in logistic regression results is used to explain this correlation. Larger positive β value reveals stronger positive correlation between driving factors and LULC type, whereas larger negative β value reveals stronger negative correlation (Priyanto, 2010). **Table 6.4** shows the explanation as to how driving factors affect the probable changes of LULC types in Da Nang City.

Regarding agricultural area, the finding shows that the mean density population is the biggest positive determinant in allocation of this type of land use compared to other driving factors. It has the coefficient β value at 0.01099 and exponential β value at 1.011 (**Appendix 3, Table A3.3**), which means that the increase of 1 unit mean density population variable will influence 0.01099 unit of agricultural area to change with the probability value at 1.009 (or, in other words, 1 unit influence of mean density population has 91.99 probability of changing agricultural area). Other driving factors and other LULC types could be interpreted in the same way. Urban rate has a strong negative effect on allocation of agricultural area (-0.01492). The distance to water is shown to be the factor that has the lowest negative significance in the change of agricultural area (-0.00005).

Similar to agricultural area, barren area also has seven driving factors. However, only slope factor has a positive impact on the occurrence of this kind of land cover (0.00556). Urban rate is considered as the factor that has the largest negative effect to the change of barren area (-0.00465). The results of logistic regression model are reasonable. Most of the barren areas in Da Nang City are distributed in high-slope positions that could be examined from image interpretation. In addition, barren area is seen as the expansive source of any kind of LULC type, especially urban area closely related with the urban rate factor.

According to logistic regression for urban area, some driving factors were classified as positive variables, including urban rate, elevation, and distance to water. On the other hand, four factors (mean density of population, slope, distance to road, and distance to urban) were considered as negative variables. The correlation of each driving factor with the probability change of urban area in this research is reasonable. As observed from remote satellite images, residential areas in Da Nang City tend to expand along the coastal line and river banks. Moreover, people prefer to concentrate their housing in central areas rather than in satellite towns. This could be explained by the psychology of most Vietnamese people liked to be in the existing central area where the public facilities and health facilities are obtained easier. Another interesting finding is that the elevation factor has a positive effect on the increase of urban area. It means that urban area tends to expand in the higher elevation. Most of the existing urban built-up areas in Da Nang City have been located plentifully along the coastal line. In this case, new urban areas must be expanded inland where the elevation is higher. In addition, this could help avoid sea level rise. Another reason is that lower areas are given priority for agriculture and aquaculture activities.

The model for forest area has just one negative factor (mean density of population), and six positive factors in contributing the allocation (urban rate, slope, elevation, distance to road, distance to urban, and distance to water). The results denote that the increase in population and their demands are the main reasons for the loss of forest areas. In contrast to forest land, mean density of population is the positive factor in predicting the presence of shrub; all the rest of the factors are negative.

Related to water area, urban rate, mean density of population, distance to road, and distance to water are the dependent factors that have negative values in logistic regression model. The others have positive effects to the change of water area. The negative relationships with the urban rate and mean density of population reveal that the increase of population may threaten the area of water because of the expansion of urban area.

The allocation of LULC types is well explained by the selected driving factors that have the high ROC test statistic. In this study, ROC values of logistic regression models range from 0.70 to 0.99, depending on the types of LULC. Based on the consideration of Pontius and Schneider (2001), ROC values over 0.7 and less than 0.8 are acceptable, while ROC values over 0.8 are excellent. It can be concluded that the results of the logistic regression model are capable of explaining the spatial variation occurring in the different LULC types within the Da Nang City. The analytical results of the logistic regression model in **Table 6.4** denoted that the allocations of all LULC types are jointly determined by biophysical elements (slope, elevation, etc.) and socioeconomic elements (urban rate, mean density of population). These values could be used as input of the Dyna-CLUE model. More details about ROC curves are presented in **Appendix 4**.

6.4 Elasticity coefficients

The codes of allowing changes and behavior of LULC types in the study area were specified by running the Dyna-CLUE model various times with sets of conversion elasticity specified by the user. After each run, the simulated maps in 2003 and 2009 were converted from ASCII files to grid maps. These maps were assessed the accuracies with reference data in the same year, afterward. It was found that the most reliable simulation results were generated from the following set of elasticity coefficients (**Table 6.5**).

Land use/cover type	Elasticity
Agriculture	0.4
Barren	0.2
Urban	1
Forest	0.9
Shrub	0.6
Water	1

Table 6.5 Elasticity coefficient of land-use/cover type
Source: Author's calculation

Elasticity coefficient of urban is set the maximum value as 1 because it is assumed to have the highest conversion cost compared with other LULC types. Water is set to 1 because it is considered to have maintained the same size and location during the simulation period. Barren area is believed as the most spatially dynamic land use; thus, its elasticity is set to 0.2. During the last two decades, urban areas in Da Nang City have mainly expanded at the expense of agriculture. Hence, its elasticity is supposed to be 0.4. Shrub also could be considered the second source for expanding urban area. Consequently, its elasticity coefficient is assigned at 0.6. Once an area is covered by forest, it is difficult to convert into other kinds of LULC; therefore, its elasticity coefficient is chosen as 0.9. The value of 0.9 denotes that in the condition of net negative change of forest cover, the reforestation plays an important role in compensating the loss of forest area. These values would be used as one of the main parameters in the Dyna-CLUE model. More details could be found in **Appendix 5**.

6.5 Conversion matrix

The conversion matrix is also generated to determine what the future land use is likely to be. Similar to the way in specifying elasticity coefficients, the conversion matrix was examined based on the knowledge about the changes of LULC types within the study area. After running the Dyna-CLUE model in various times, the LULC conversion matrix is determined in **Table 6.6**. In this matrix, the left side (column) is the current LULC types, and the right side (row) is the converted LULC types. If a conversion is supposed possible, then the value is set equal to 1; if not, the value is set equal to 0. Of the six LULC types used, changes are permitted for the following types: agriculture, barren, urban, forest, and shrub. As stated earlier, the size and location of water area is considered to fix at the temporal and spatial scales during the simulation period.

Land-use/ cover type	Agriculture	Barren	Urban	Forest	Shrub	Water
Agriculture	1	1	1	1	1	1
Barren	1	1	1	1	1	1
Urban	0	0	1	0	0	1
Forest	1	1	1	1	1	1
Shrub	1	1	1	1	1	1
Water	0	0	0	0	0	1

Table 6.6 Conversion matrix of land-use/cover type
Source: Author's calculation

6.6 Validation output from the Dyna-CLUE model

6.6.1 Visual comparison

As stated before (Section **4.7.3.2**), visual comparison is the quickest way to access the spatial patterns of models. Consequently, the visual changes of LULC are computed through the following pairs of maps: reference maps of year 1996 and 2003, reference map of year 1996, and simulation map of year 2003. The left-hand side of **Figure 6.4** shows that there is a visual similarity between Dyna-CLUE's simulated map of year 2003 and the reference map of year 2003.

Chapter 6 Modeling Land Use/Cover Changes

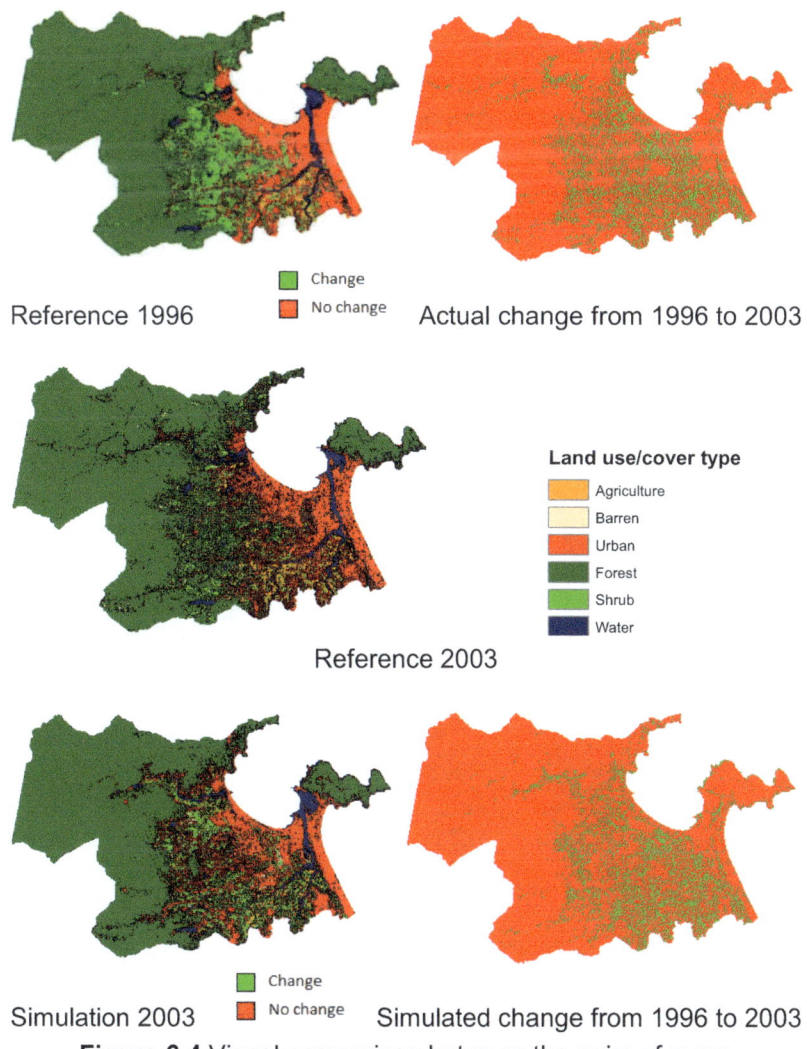

Figure 6.4 Visual comparison between the pairs of maps
Source: Author's calculation

Closer comparisons among the three maps are presented on the right-hand side of **Figure 6.4**. The map on the upper right position of **Figure 6.4** reveals the actual changes based on the reference data, while the map on the bottom right supposes the changes of LULC types in Da Nang City based on predictions of the Dyna-CLUE model. The areas of changes are displayed in green color while non-green color denotes the static characteristic of LULC over the space and time. These pairs of maps show some similarities between the actual and the simulation changes even though there are some differences. The simulated changes from 1996 to 2003 compared to actual changes in the same period show that the most concentrated conversions were in the southeast of Da Nang City.

The earlier findings demonstrate the capability of the Dyna-CLUE model in predicting approximately the LULC changes in Da Nang City. Upon this consideration, statistical techniques of comparison are applied to detect the complex patterns of change that are missed by the human eyes (Pontius Jr et al., 2004).

6.6.2 Agreement components

The model creates a total of 35 simulated maps from the run of each scenario. In this case, to assess the accuracy of the model, the simulated land-use maps at runs 7 and 13 were compared to the available land-use maps extracted from remote satellite data in 2003 and 2009, respectively. This would be done according to the validation processing steps mentioned in Section **4.7.3.3**.

Index	2003	2009
$K_{Simulation}$	0.77	0.76
$K_{Transloc}$	0.71	0.68
$K_{Transition}$	0.96	0.93

Table 6.7 Accuracy assessment indices of land-use change modeling
Source: Author's calculation

Table 6.7 shows the indices in assessing the accuracy of model through the variation of agreement indices, including $K_{Simulation}$, $K_{Transloc}$, and $K_{Transition}$. In general, the result indicates that the agreement of simulated and observed land-use maps is more accurate at simulating the quantity than allocation of LULC types. Because allocation of LULC types in the model were determined by the most appropriate of all factors, including quantity of LULC types, driving factors, elasticity, and so on, $K_{Transition}$ index of both predicted maps in 2003 and 2009 is above 90%, whereas $K_{Transloc}$ index is around 70%. According to Pontius and Schneider (2001), the LULC change model which has kappa index over 0.5 is considered satisfactory. Again, Landis and Koch (1977) asserted the characteristic agreement as follows: values of 0.4 or less reveal a poor model, values from 0.4 to 0.75 are fair to good, and values over 0.75 are very good to excellent. The kappa values of this study are considered similar to the results of other literatures, such as the study of Verburg et al. (1999), who obtained an accuracy range of 71–90% in modeling the change of land use in Ecuador by CLUE-S. In other words, the positive values of kappa in this study assert a positive correlation between the simulated maps and the actual maps. As a result, the predefined rules were considered for running the prediction procedure (see **Figure 4.6**).

6.7 Analysis of the changes of scenarios

6.7.1 LULC changes under different scenarios

The results of the Dyna-CLUE model provide pictures of future LULC within the study area following three differing scenarios for the period 2009–2030 which were differentiated by the demands of LULC types. **Figure 6.5** presents LULC of scenario A in Da Nang City from 2009 to 2030, if the policy in the developing economy is maintained. Between 2009 and 2030, scenario B represents the economic growth storyline with a huge increase of urban area in comparison to scenario C, the environmental emphasis storyline (**Figures 6.6 and 6.7**). According to the simulated results, it is documented that LULC patterns created by the Dyna-CLUE model are consistent with those extracted in the historical maps. **Figures 6.5–6.7** demonstrate that remarkably changed areas are frequently discovered in the southeast part of Da Nang City, especially where the areas have high rate of urban and low elevation.

Chapter 6 Modeling Land Use/Cover Changes

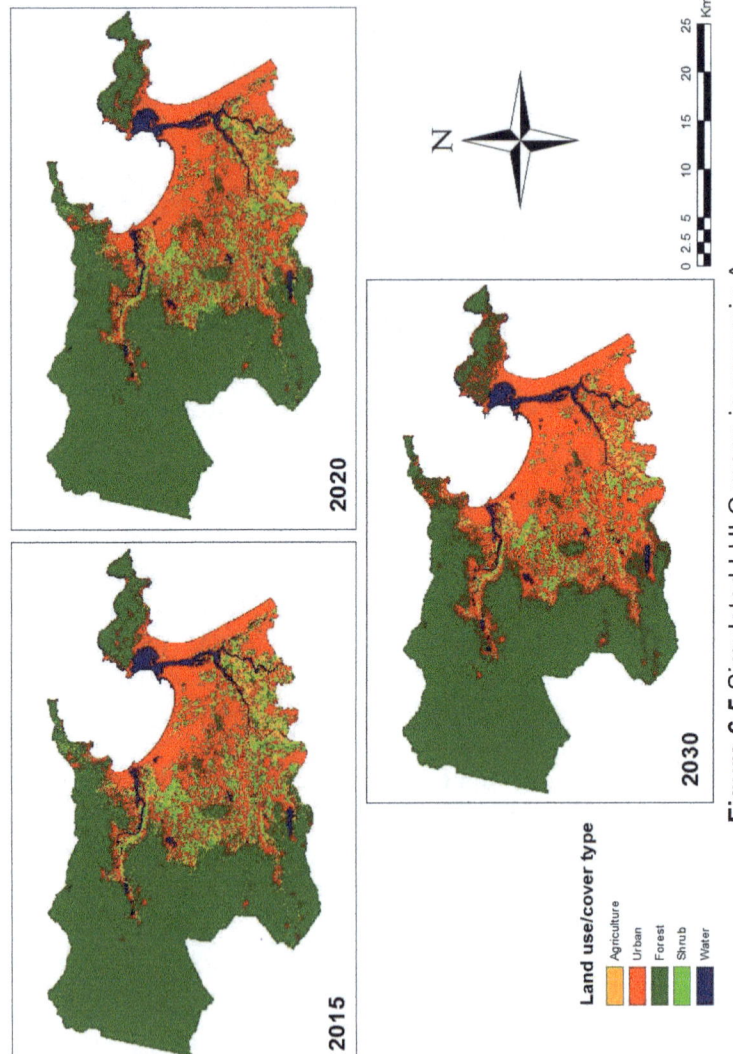

Figure 6.5 Simulated LULC maps in scenario A
Source: Author's calculation

Chapter 6 Modeling Land Use/Cover Changes

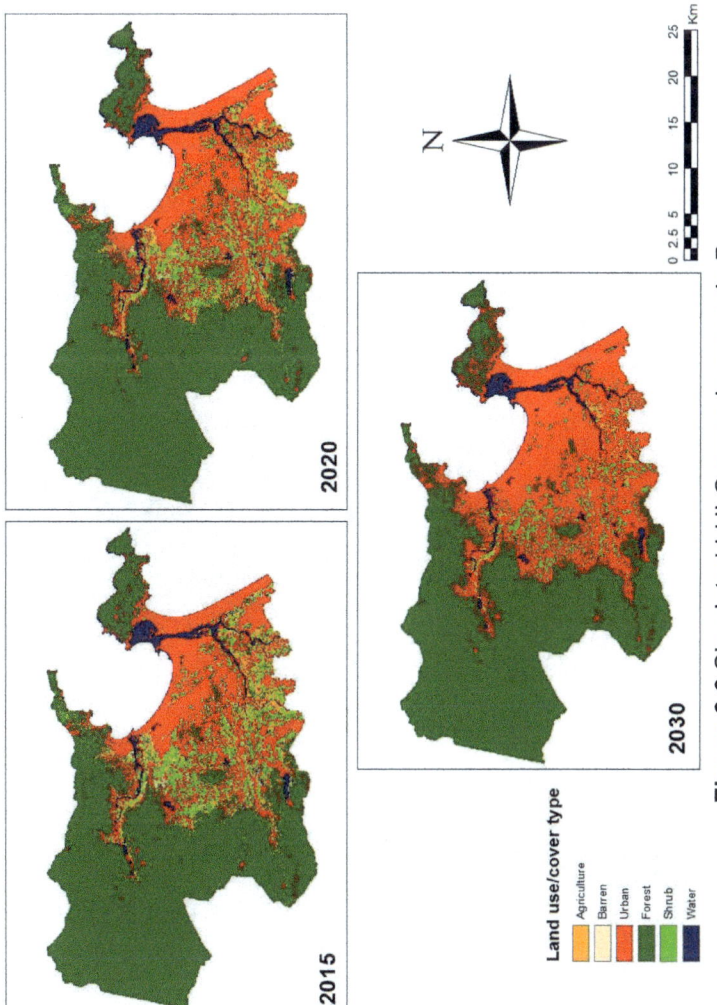

Figure 6.6 Simulated LULC maps in scenario B
Source: Author's calculation

Chapter 6 Modeling Land Use/Cover Changes

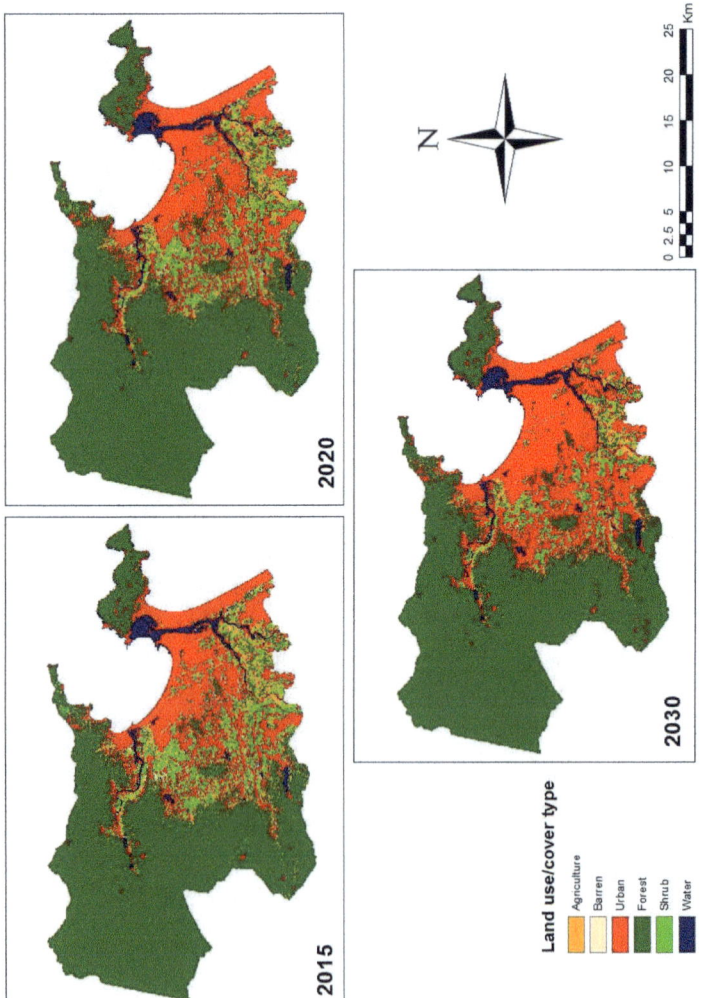

Figure 6.7 Simulated LULC maps in scenario C
Source: Author's calculation

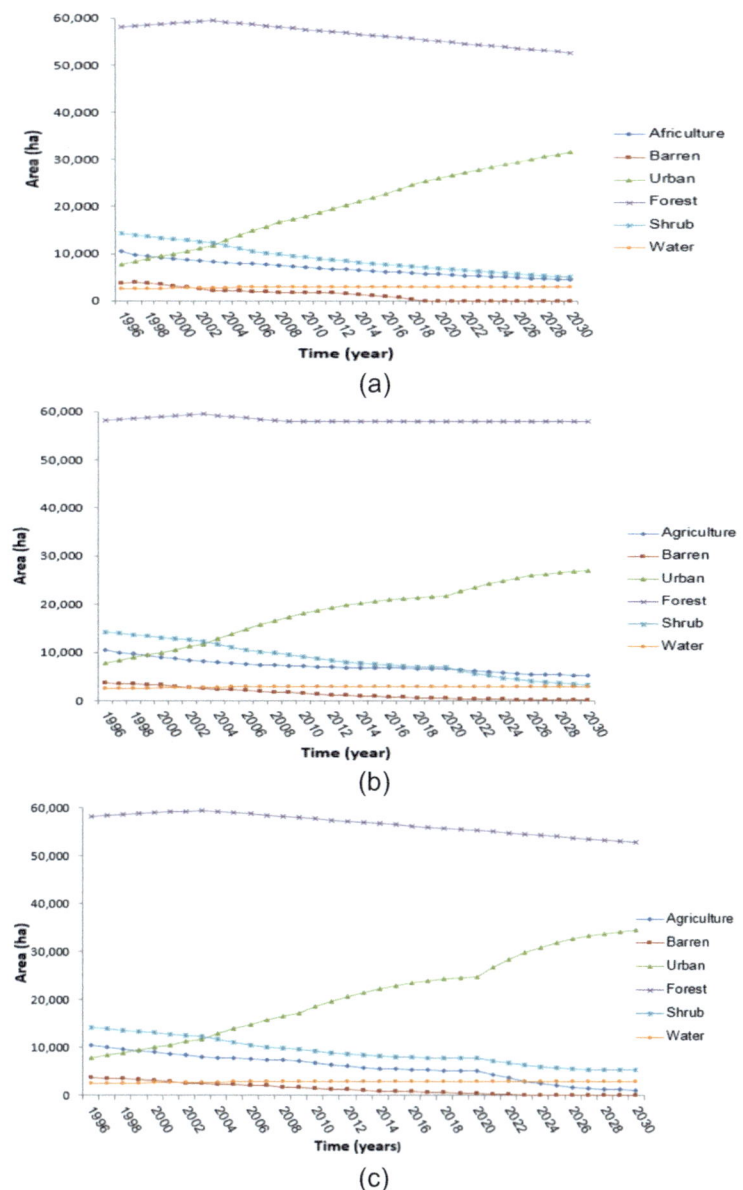

Figure 6.8 Land-use/cover types under different scenarios: (a) Scenario A; (b) Scenario B; and (c) Scenario C
Source: Author's calculation

Chapter 6 Modeling Land Use/Cover Changes

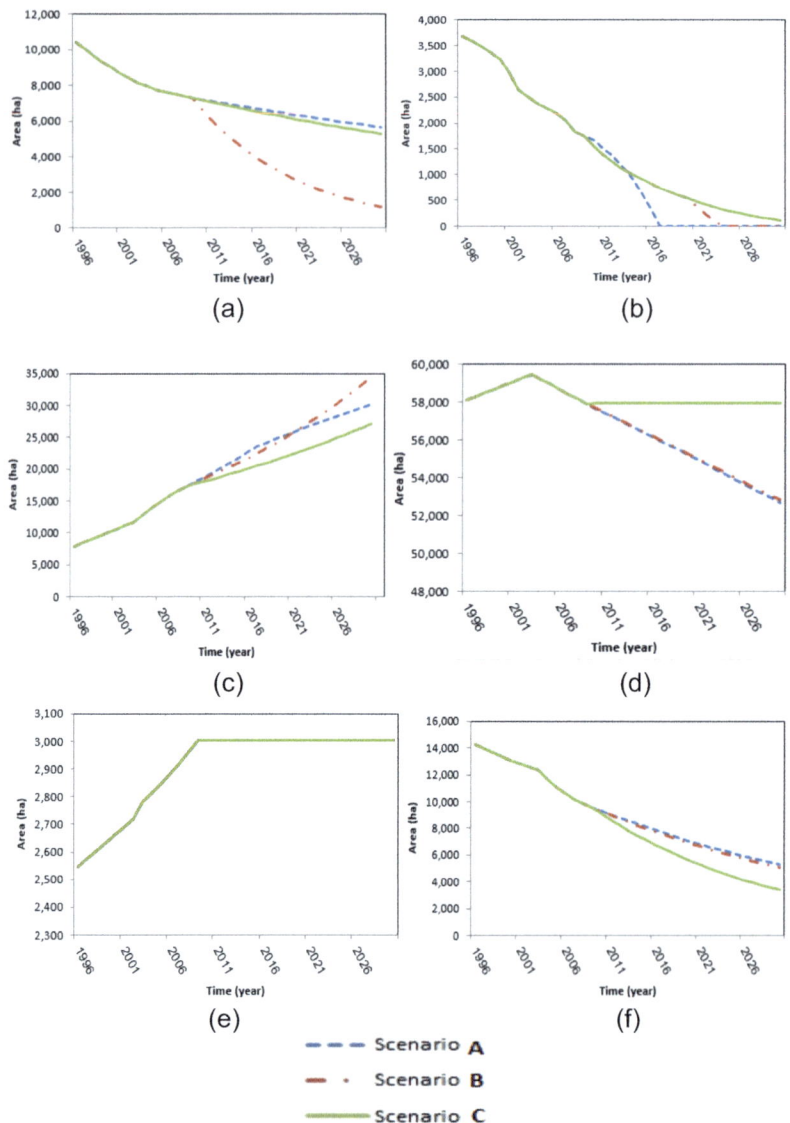

Figure 6.9 Comparisons of land use/cover in three scenarios: (a) Agriculture, (b) Barren, (c) Urban, (d) Forest, (e) Shrub, and (f) Water
Source: Author's calculation

Chapter 6 Modeling Land Use/Cover Changes

Land use/cover	Baseline 2009 Area (ha)	Scenario A Area (ha)	Scenario A Δ Area (ha in %)	Scenario B Area (ha)	Scenario B Δ Area (ha in %)	Scenario C Area (ha)	Scenario C Δ Area (ha in %)
Agriculture	7,294.68	4,089.62	-3,205.06 (43.94)	1,195.72	-6,098.96 (83.61)	5,297.7	-1,996.98 (27.40)
Barren	1,708.92	0	-1,708.92 (100)	0	-1,708.92 (100)	110.55	-1,598.37 (93.53)
Urban	17,298.54	30,884.66	13,586.12 (78.54)	3,4451.24	17,152.7 (99.16)	27,092.77	9,794.23 (56.62)
Forest	57,935.79	52,675.6	-5,269.19 (9.1)	52,810.2	-5,125.59 (8.85)	57,936.2	0.41 (0.00007)
Shrub	9,575.82	6,164.01	-3,411.81 (35.63)	5,356.73	-4,219.09 (44.10)	3,376.67	-6,199.15 (64.74)
Water	3,003.57	3,003.57	0 (0.0)	3,003.57	0 (0.0)	3,003.57	0 (0.0)

Table 6.8 Comparison of land-use/cover changes in 2030 under three scenarios
Source: Author's calculation

The simulation results of each LULC type under different scenarios are presented in **Figures 6.8** and **6.9**. The graphs indicate that only water area does not change during the whole period of running the model. Under the setting conditions of the three scenarios, urban area is the only one which increases at the expense of other LULC types. The urban class expands along the coastal region of Da Nang City in all three scenarios. In comparison, the growth of urban area in scenario C is more sustainable than in the other two scenarios. As shown in **Table 6.8**, the least expansion is 27,092.77 ha in 2030 under scenario C (56.62% net increase compared to baseline 2009), with the environmental success storyline, and the highest one is 34,451.24 ha in 2030 under scenario B (99.16% net increase compared to baseline 2009), with less concern for environment issues. Overall, urban area in Da Nang City is developed by the following space-filling pattern tendency. In this sense, new developments are located around the existing urban areas.

With continuous acceleration of population and economics, the area of agriculture, barren, forest, and shrub will significantly decrease. Barren is considered to be a source for expanding other LULC types, such as urban. As a result, this area decreases strongly in all scenarios. With regard to agriculture, scenario B with the assumption of rapid development shows a decrease by 6,098.96 ha (83.61%) in agricultural area between 2009 and 2030. The agricultural area for scenarios A and C decreases by -3,205.06 ha (43.94%) and 1,996.98 ha (27.40%), respectively. **Figures 6.5** and **6.7** show that good quality agricultural areas in scenarios A and C are kept unchanged. Despite the fact that the remaining agricultural area is small in size, it is the important part contributed to ecosystem in the study area. Forest in scenarios A and B decreases approximately 9% between 2009 and 2030. Meanwhile, scenario C, which is concerned with environmental issues, resulted in maintaining the forest cover over 60% of total area in Da Nang City. Therefore, the forest area in scenario C will be retained at 57,936.2 ha during the whole period of running the model. Finally, the area of shrub in scenario C decreases strongly from 9,575.82 ha in 2009 to 3,376.67 ha in 2030, showing a net decrease of 64.74% after 22 years of simulation.

Consequently, scenario B, assuming rapid development in economics without regulation, resulted in the largest change in barren, urban, and agricultural areas. Scenario C, which is more concerned with environmental issues, resulted in the highest demand for forest area. Scenario A shows the baseline of development within Da Nang City, which could be considered as the average level for comparing scenarios.

6.7.2 LULC changes according to administration boundary

The distribution changes of LULC in 2030 under different scenarios are also summarized in relation to administrative district boundaries (**Table 6.9**). As stated earlier, water area is maintained during the simulated period. Therefore, the area of this land cover is stable in all districts under all scenarios. Scenario B, with the largest changes in urban area, shows the expansion of urban area as largest in Hoa Vang district with 12,208.7 ha (225.3%) in comparison to 2009. The increase of urban area in scenario B in Hoa Vang district is approximately twofold the increase of this kind of land use in scenario C at 7,064.5 ha (130.4%). As presented in **Table 5.4**, urban areas in 2009 were highly concentrated in Thanh Khe, Hai Chau, and Ngu Hanh Son districts with 88.4%, 73.4%, and 69.4%, respectively. Thus, very few new urban areas are distributed in these districts during simulated period. Besides the Hoa Vang district, this dynamic area is also allocated in the Son Tra, Lien

Chieu, and Cam Le districts with 1,105.9 ha (68.9%), 1,545.9 ha (44.6%), and 793.9 ha (38.4%), respectively, under scenario B in 2030. Scenario A results in less change than scenario B. It can be interpreted that the simulated urban areas under all scenarios occur in districts where the urban rate is low, and conversely.

Table 6.9 shows that the agricultural area in scenario B decreases in almost all districts, except Thanh Khe where the agricultural area was too small (0.5 ha in 2009). Although the percentage of change is just around 74.3%, in comparison to other districts, the agricultural area in Hoa Vang has the highest decrease (-3,364.5 ha). Agricultural area in scenario C is forecast to decrease with lower percentage than in scenario B between 2009 and 2030. For example, agricultural area under scenario C is suggested to decrease by 263 ha (32.2%) in Lien Chieu district and 15.5 ha (16.3%) in Son Tra district, while the percentage of these districts in scenario B is 100% and 97.5%, respectively. Similar to urban area, the agricultural areas in scenario A result in less change than in scenario B. As shown in **Table 6.9**, forest with large areas in 2009 were mostly distributed in Hoa Vang, Son Tra, and Lien Chieu districts with 52,450.5, 3,682.4, and 2,744.6 ha, respectively. Scenario A resulted in the largest change in forest area, with the demand for forest area decreasing by 6,286.7 ha in these three districts. Hoa Vang is the district with the greatest transition of forest area, where the area of forest is forecasted to decrease by 5,174.8 ha between 2009 and 2030. Loss of forest areas is the smallest under scenario C. In particular, the forest areas are well retained and not transformed into other LULC types in Cam Le and Hai Chau districts under all scenarios.

Region	LUC 2009	Scenario 2030					
		A		B		C	
	Area (ha)	Δ Area (ha)	Δ Rate (%)	Δ Area (ha)	Δ Rate (%)	Δ Area (ha)	Δ Rate (%)
Cam Le							
Agriculture	532.1	-531.8	-99.9	-532	-100	-492.1	-92.5
Barren	41.6	-41.6	-100	-41.6	-100	-41.6	-100
Urban	2,066.0	668.5	32.4	793.9	38.4	708.6	34.3
Forest	90.5	0	0	0	0	0	0
Shrub	415.4	-95.2	-22.9	-220.4	-53.1	-175.5	-42.2
Water	310.4	0	0	0	0	0	0
Hai Chau							
Agriculture	1.4	0	0	-1.4	-100	0	0
Barren	24.8	-24.8	-100	-24.8	-100	-24.8	-100
Urban	1,689.8	101.1	6	124.8	7.4	123.3	7.3
Forest	2	0	0	0	0	0	0

Region	LUC 2009 Area (ha)	Scenario 2030					
		A		B		C	
		Δ Area (ha)	Δ Rate (%)	Δ Area (ha)	Δ Rate (%)	Δ Area (ha)	Δ Rate (%)
Shrub	158	-76.4	-48.3	-98.7	-62.5	-98.5	-62.3
Water	294.2	0	0	0	0	0	0
Hoa Vang							
Agriculture	4,525.7	-1,138.9	-25.2	-3,364.5	-74.3	-431.9	-9.5
Barren	843.6	-843.6	-100.0	-843.6	-100.0	-738.5	-87.5
Urban	5,419.6	9,581.7	176.8	12,208.7	225.3	7,064.5	130.4
Forest	52,450.5	-5,174.8	-9.9	-5,072.3	-9.7	-1,454.0	-2.8
Shrub	7,506.3	-2,424.5	-32.3	-2,928.3	-39.0	-4,440.1	-59.2
Water	984.9	0	0	0	0	0	0
Lien Chieu							
Agriculture	816.5	-508.5	-62.3	-816.4	-100	-263	-32.2
Barren	31.1	-31.1	-100	-31.1	-100	-27.9	-89.6
Urban	3,468.0	1,171.6	33.8	1,545.9	44.6	774.6	22.3
Forest	2,744.6	-199.3	-7.3	-183.5	-6.7	0	0
Shrub	801.2	-432.7	-54.0	-514.9	-64.3	-663.0	-82.8
Water	316.4	0	0	0	0	0	0
Ngu Hanh Son							
Agriculture	379.8	-95.8	-25.2	-379.8	-100	0	0
Barren	12	-12	-100	-12	-100	-12	-100
Urban	2,968.6	151.3	5.1	473.3	15.9	-122	-4.1
Forest	78.5	-71.3	-90.8	-71.3	-90.8	0	0
Shrub	201.4	27.6	13.7	-10.3	-5.1	133.9	66.5
Water	316.1	0	0	0	0	0	0
Son Tra							
Agriculture	94.9	-41.4	-43.6	-92.5	-97.5	-15.5	-16.3
Barren	19.7	-19.7	-100.0	-19.7	-100.0	-17.3	-87.7
Urban	1,604.3	1,070.7	66.7	1,105.9	68.9	427.8	26.7
Forest	3,682.4	-912.6	-24.8	-886.7	-24.1	-272.9	-7.4
Shrub	135.8	-96.9	-71.4	-106.9	-78.7	-122.0	-89.9
Water	689.2	0	0	0	0	0	0
Thanh Khe							
Agriculture	0.5	0	0	0	0	0	0
Barren	1.4	-1.4	-100	-1.4	-100	-1.4	-100
Urban	872.9	0	0	0	0	0	0
Forest	2.3	-2.0	-88	-2	-88	-1.5	-68
Shrub	41.4	3.4	8.2	3.4	8.2	3.0	7.2
Water	22.1	0	0	0	0	0	0

Table 6.9 Comparison of land-use/cover types in 2030 under three scenarios according to administration boundary

Source: Author's calculation

6.8 Landscape structure of scenarios

6.8.1 At landscape level

In this section, we focus on studying the changes of landscape structure for three different scenarios. Hence, the seven metrics mentioned in **Section 4.6** were used to explore the temporal changes of spatial patterns at landscape level for three scenarios across the entire landscape from 2009 to 2030, including the number of patches (NP), patch density (PD), mean proximity (PROX_MN), mean patch area (AREA_MN), interspersion and juxtaposition (IJI), largest patch index (LPI), largest shape index (LSI). In this case, the percentage of patches (percentage of landscape index, PLAND) metric was not used because it does not exist at landscape level. The analytical metrics are presented in **Figure 6.10**. For the years observed in our analysis, the values of NP, PD, IJI, LPI, and LSI decrease for all scenarios (**Figure 6.10a, b, e, f, and g**). **Figure 6.10c, d** shows that the values of PROX_MN and AREA_MN of all scenarios increase during the simulated period (2009–2030).

In three scenarios, the values of NP substantially decreased from 2009 to 2030 indicating that many dispersive patches within the study area trend toward an increasingly large-grained pattern (**Figure 6.10a**).

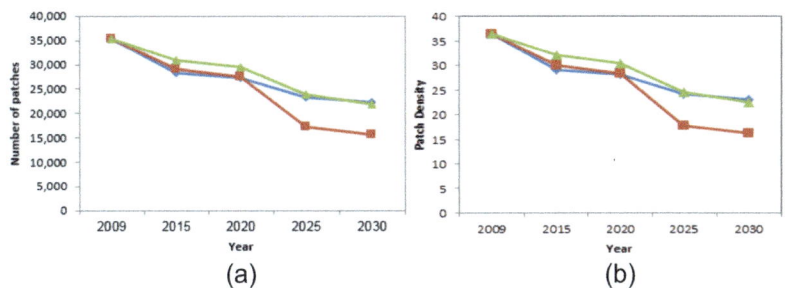

(a)   (b)

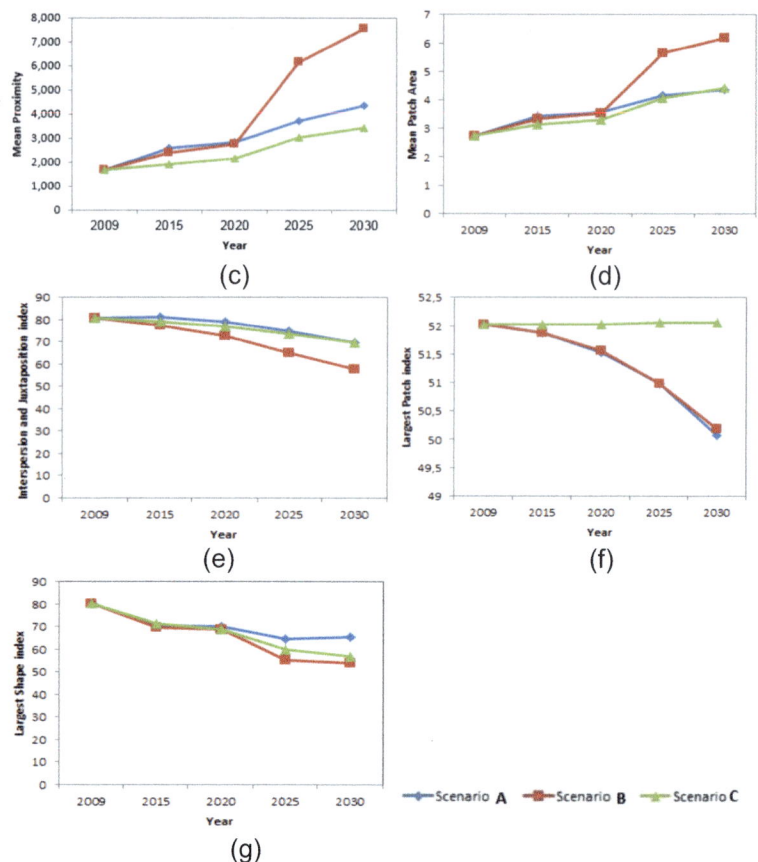

Figure 6.10 Landscape metrics at landscape level under scenarios (a) Number of patches, (b) Patch density, (c) Mean proximity, (d) Mean patch area, (e) Interspersion and juxtaposition index, (f) Largest patch index, and (g) Largest shape index

This is also supported by the decreasing tendency of PD (**Figure 6.10b**), where the values of NP and PD of landscape in scenarios A (the baseline policy) and C (sustainable development) are greater than those for scenario B (economic development). It is illuminating that the landscape in scenario B is less heterogeneous than the landscapes in scenarios A and C. It means that the patches are formed. Many dispersive patches would merge into large ones. Hence, the landscape heterogeneity declined. Again, this judgment could be proved by observing the distribution of urban area (the red color) from simulation scenarios in **Figures 6.5**, **6.6**, and **6.7**, respectively.

Correspondingly, the NP and AREA_MN of all scenarios had a negative relationship, which indicates that there are less patches in a landscape and that the mean patch sizes are larger. Similarly, the PROX_MEAN defined by a search radius of 300 m for all scenarios would continuously increase between 2009 and 2030. It can be assumed that patches in all scenarios would increasingly occupy the neighborhood. **Figure 6.10c** and **d** shows that scenario B has the highest value by 2030, compared to scenarios A and C.

In all scenarios, values of IJI within the study area slightly decrease between 2009 and 2030 (**Figure 6.10e**), indicating that the landscape pattern would shift from a dispersion state to a distributed state, in which scenario B has lower IJI values by 2030 than scenarios A and C. In other words, spatial distribution of various patches in scenario B would become more interconjugated and better connected than patches in other scenarios.

Regarding LPI, the value indicates the degree of control of large patches on the landscape. Our results show that the LPI values of scenarios A and B continuously decrease during the periods 2009–2030. The smaller LPI values by 2030 testify that the largest patch in the landscape of scenarios A and B lose their dominant place, while LPI values in scenario C are nearly constant. It is reflected that the landscape in scenario C is less affected by the changes of LULC types. In general, this finding is reasonable because it reflects the *optimal development* of scenario C as mentioned earlier.

LSI of different scenarios is calculated by deviation between the patch area and the same square area for measuring the complexity of its shape. Our analytical results show that the values of LSI in the trio of scenarios are decreased within the study area. It is demonstrated that the landscape patches become less complex. Among them, scenario B has lower values during the periods 2020–2030 than scenarios A and C through human forward interference.

The aforementioned results reveal that contiguous processes in the three scenarios are strengthened temporally and spatially. The information underlines that spatial pattern within Da Nang City in scenario B would be less heterogeneous compared to scenarios A and C on the one hand. On the other hand, it demonstrates that scenario B affects the landscape more than scenarios A and C through the interference of human activities.

6.8.2 At class level

Similarly, the calculation of seven landscape metrics for the three scenarios was also analyzed at class level. **Figures 6.11–6.16** show the differences of landscape metrics for the agriculture, barren, urban, forest, shrub, and water class under three scenarios. In this case, PLAND was not examined, because it was explained in detail in **Section 6.7**.

In general, the values of NP, PD, PROX_MN, and IJI of agricultural class under all scenarios decrease during the period of simulation (**Figure 6.11a, b,** and **c**). It indicates that agriculture land patches are distributed more isolated by the end of simulation in 2030. In addition, the smaller patches of LPI index also indicate that the largest patches of agriculture in the landscape lost its dominant place. Moreover, the LSI values of agriculture decrease continuously. It reveals that agriculture land patches become regular and less complex after implementing the LULC model. Our results show that the values of NP, PD, PROX_MN, LPI, and LSI of agricultural class in scenario C are greater than those in scenarios A and B. It means that agriculture land patches in scenario C are affected less compared to those in other scenarios. This finding is reasonable with the policy of scenario C in sustainable development; especially agriculture land always comes high on the list of priority preservation.

Among all landscape types, barren land within the study area is a special one, which is considered as the source for expansion of other landscape types. Hence, **Figure 6.12** shows that values of all landscape metrics of this barren land tend to move toward or approximate to 0 at the end of simulation period. As mentioned earlier, scenario C tries to develop in a sustainable way. Consequently, the values of all landscape metrics in this scenario are always higher than in scenarios A and B.

The changes of landscape metrics in urban class from 2009 to 2030 are presented in **Figure 6.13**. Our results show that urban land is the most variable landscape patch type. For instance, NP in scenario A is considered higher after 2009, increasing from approximately 4,500 patches in 2009 to over 8,000 patches in 2030. In addition, values of PD increase greatly from 45 patches per 100 ha to 80 patches per 100 ha. Both PROX_MN and LPI strongly increase which indicates that urban land patches become dominant within the study area during the simulation period. In contrast to agriculture and barren land, values of landscape metrics in scenario C are mostly lower than scenarios A and B.

Forest is the landscape type that also has notable variation. The trends of all landscape metrics at this kind of class are similar to those at the landscape level (**Section 6.8.1**). Since the LULC in Da Nang City is dominated by forest. Because of the requirement in keeping the forest cover above 60% compared with total area in Da Nang City during the simulation periods, almost landscape metrics of forest in scenario C remain as constant, whereas in scenarios A and B they change significantly during 2009–2030 (**Figure 6.14**). At the end of simulation period, NP in Da Nang City of both scenarios A and B decrease almost twofold from 5,000 to 2,500 in value. Meanwhile, PD of forest land patches in these scenarios shows the same trend. This indicates that large and continuous areas of forest land patches in Da Nang City are formed. Correspondingly, AREA_MN of forest patches take on an expanding trend (**Figure 6.14d**). Values of LSI in both scenarios decrease from 400 to 270 which represent the shape of forest land patches in Da Nang City becomes less complex (**Figure 6.14g**).

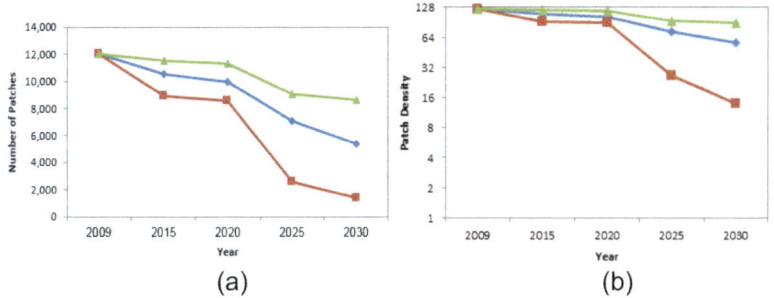

(a)   (b)

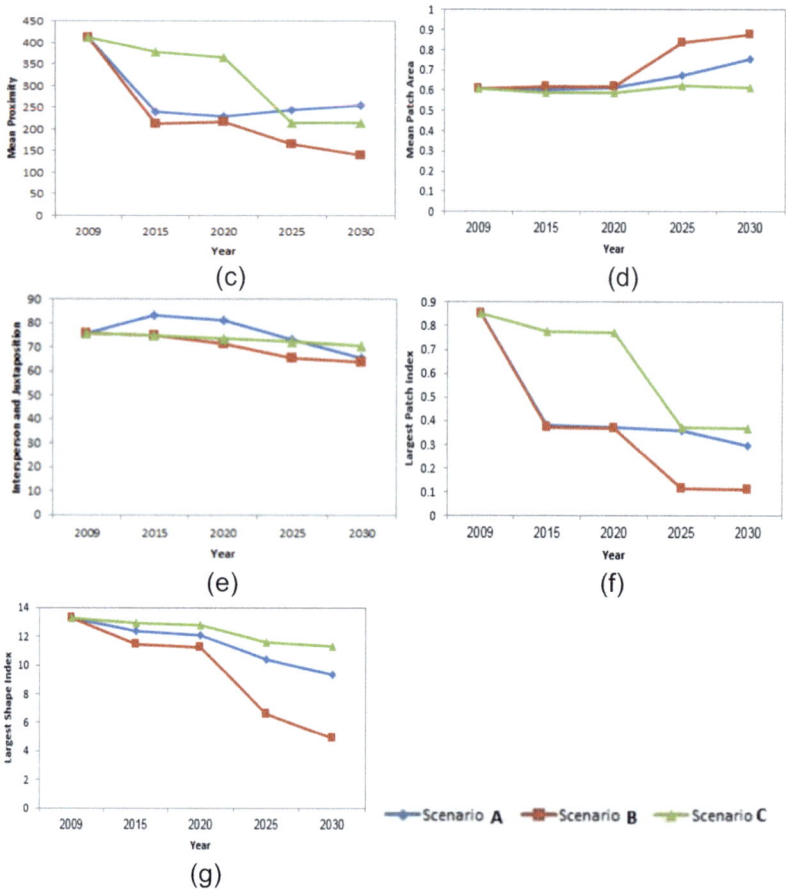

Figure 6.11 Landscape metrics at agriculture class under scenarios (a) Number of patches, (b) Patch density, (c) Mean proximity, (d) Mean patch area, (e) Interspersion and juxtaposition index, (f) Largest patch index, and (g) Largest shape index

Chapter 6 Modeling Land Use/Cover Changes

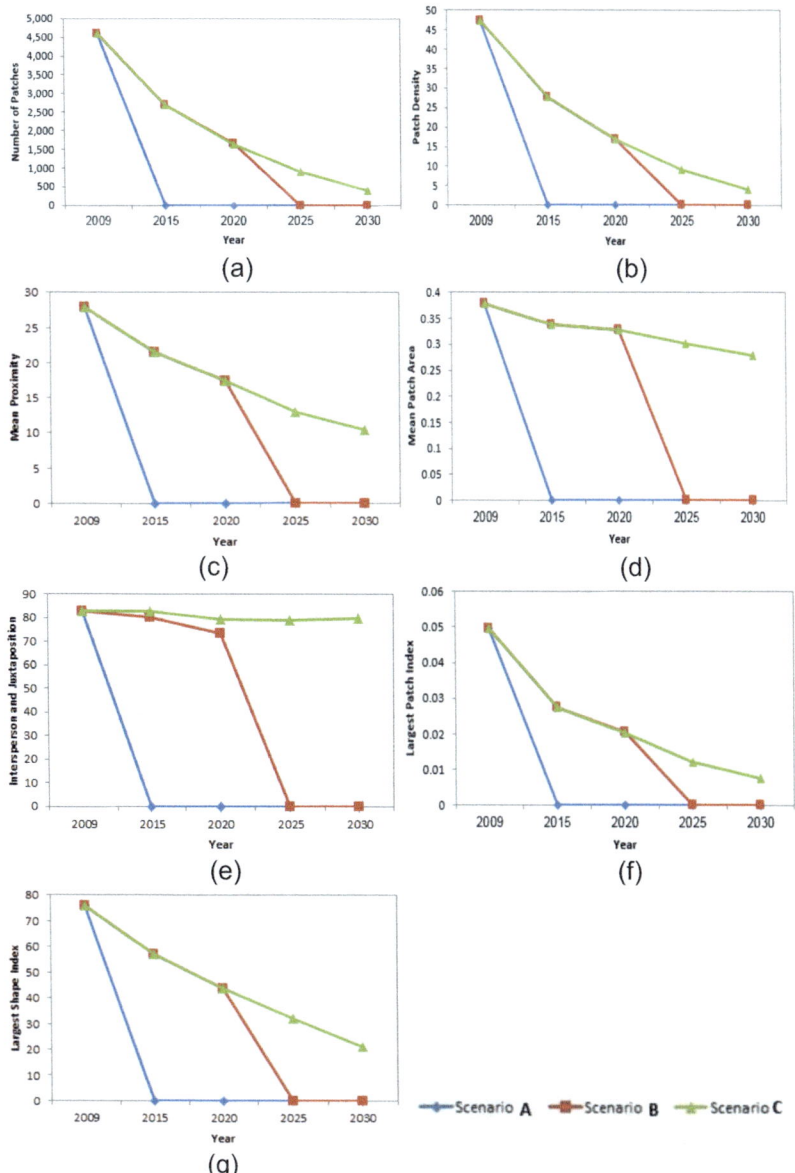

Figure 6.12 Landscape metrics at barren class under scenarios (a) Number of patches, (b) Patch density, (c) Mean proximity, (d) Mean patch area, (e) Interspersion and juxtaposition index, (f) Largest patch index, and (g) Largest shape index

Chapter 6 Modeling Land Use/Cover Changes

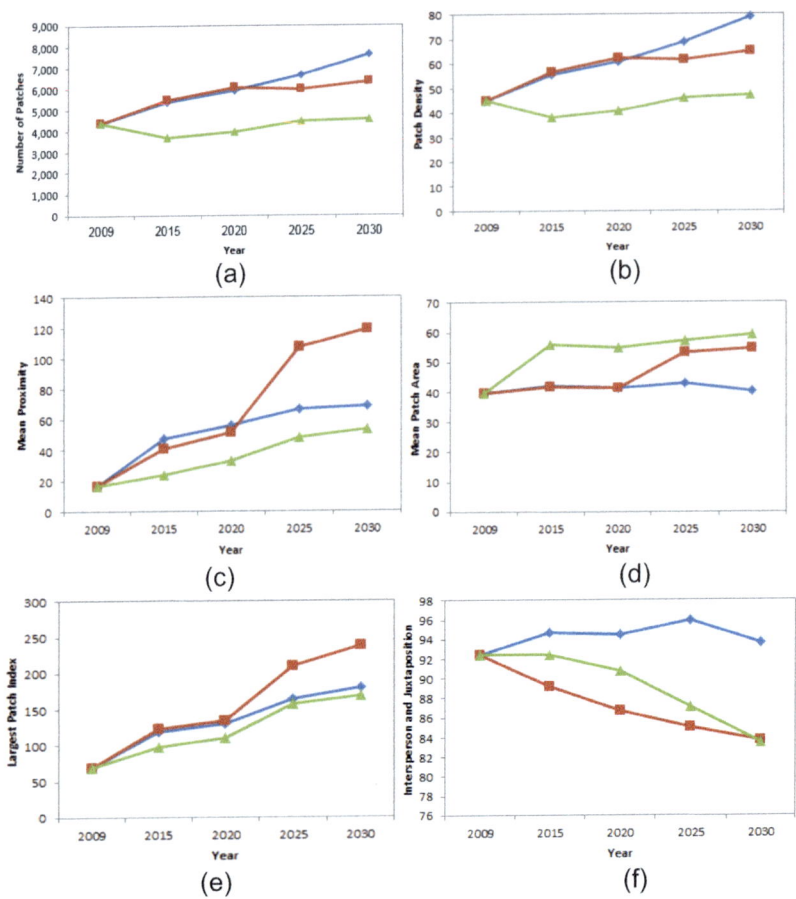

(a) (b) (c) (d) (e) (f)

Chapter 6 Modeling Land Use/Cover Changes

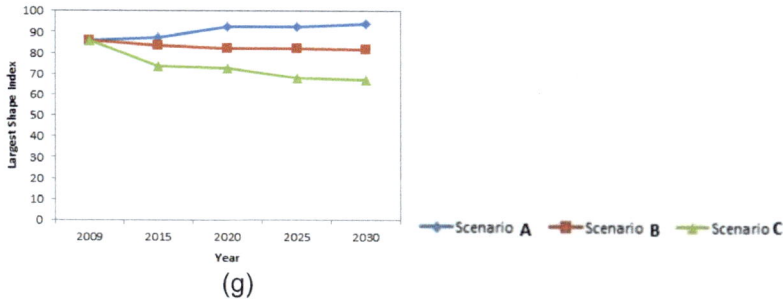

(g)

Figure 6.13 Landscape metrics at urban class under scenarios (a) Number of patches, (b) Patch density, (c) Mean proximity, (d) Mean patch area, (e) Interspersion and juxtaposition index, (f) Largest patch index, and (g) Largest shape index

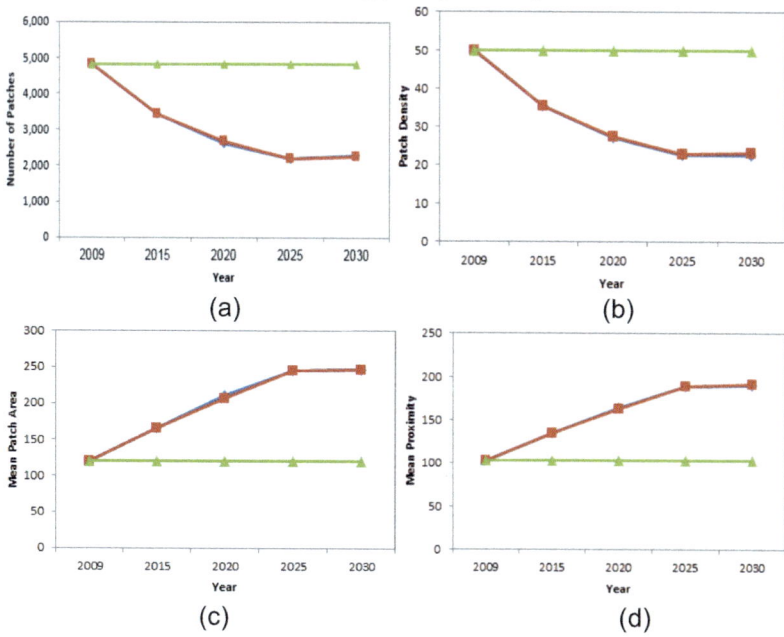

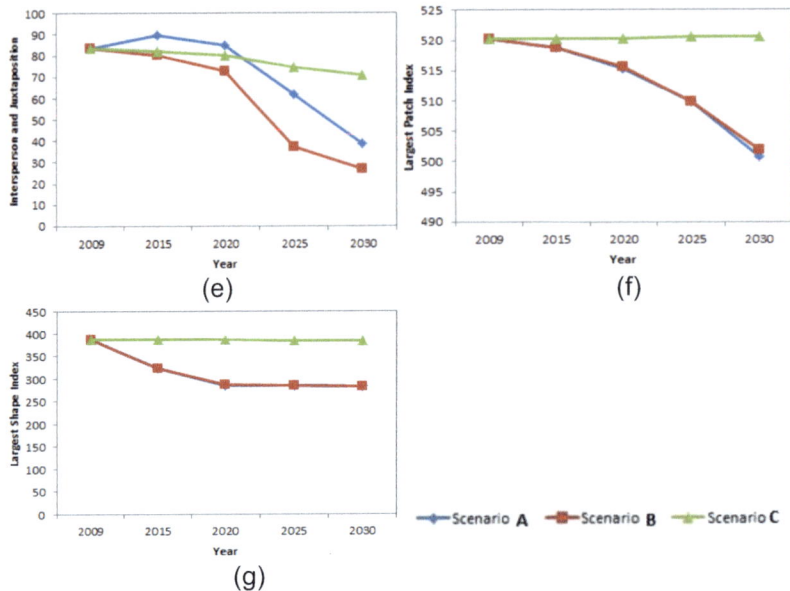

Figure 6.14 Landscape metrics at forest class under scenarios (a) Number of patches, (b) Patch density, (c) Mean proximity, (d) Mean patch area, (e) Interspersion and juxtaposition index, (f) Largest patch index, and (g) Largest shape index

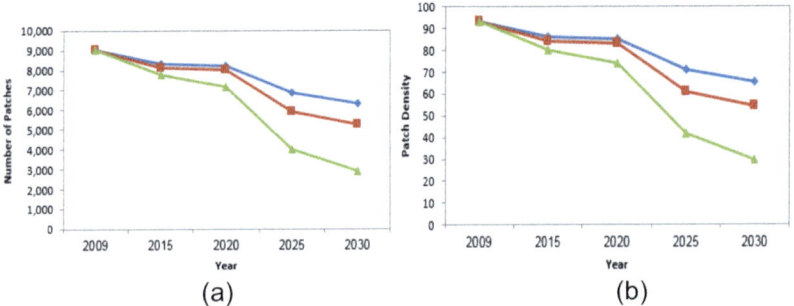

Chapter 6 Modeling Land Use/Cover Changes

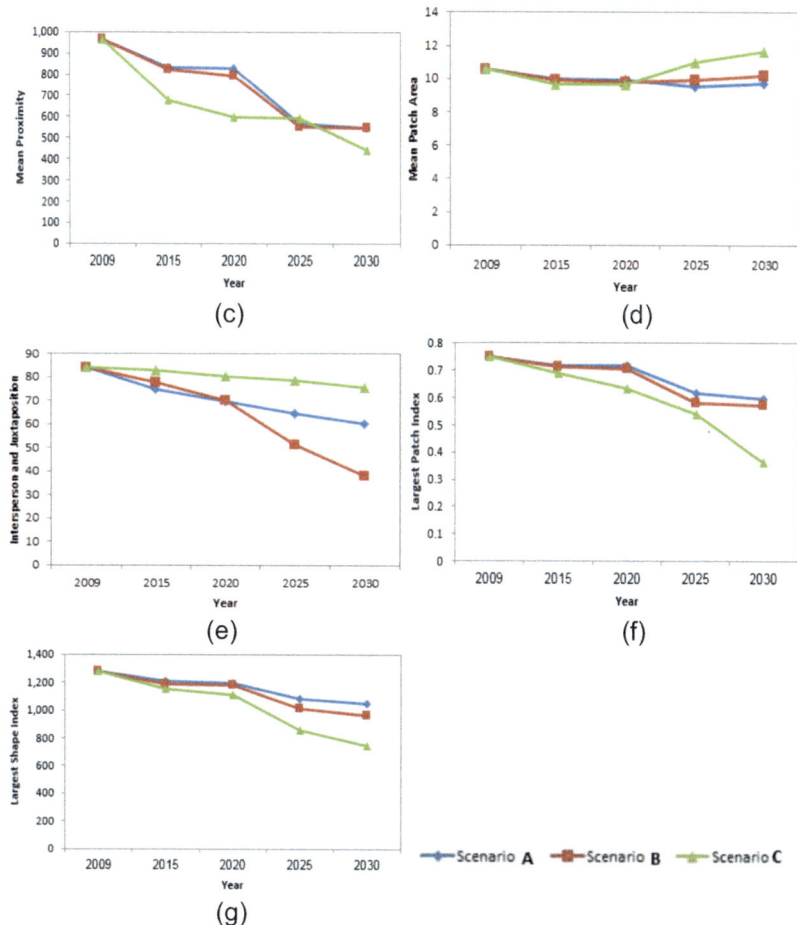

Figure 6.15 Landscape metrics at shrub class under scenarios (a) Number of patches, (b) Patch density, (c) Mean proximity, (d) Mean patch area, (e) Interspersion and juxtaposition index, (f) Largest patch index, and (g) Largest shape index

Chapter 6 Modeling Land Use/Cover Changes

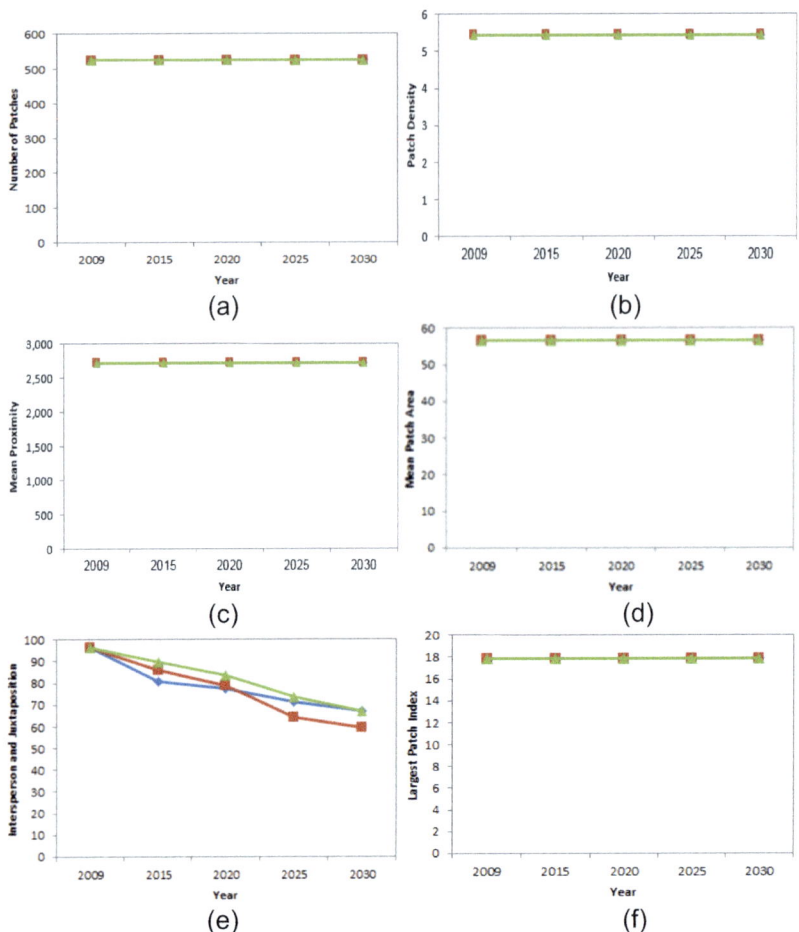

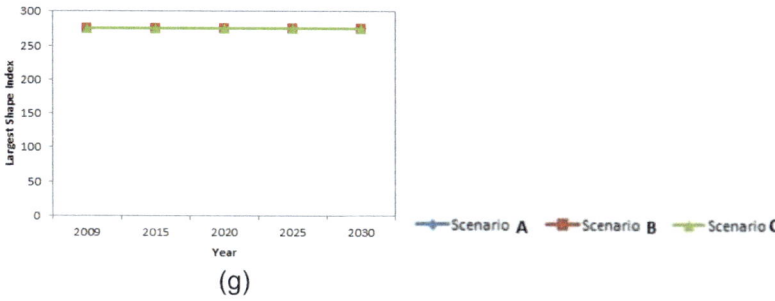

(g)

Figure 6.16 Landscape metrics at water class under scenarios (a) Number of patches, (b) Patch density, (c) Mean proximity, (d) Mean patch area, (e) Interspersion and juxtaposition index, (f) Largest patch index, and (g) Largest shape index

Shrub is another highly variable patch type. During the simulation period, its patches decrease dramatically (**Figure 6.15a**). It happens similarly with PD of shrub land patches. In general, the changes in shrub land, compared to the expansion of urban land, display a contrary degradation process in the region. Those results at the class level suggest that the heterogeneity of shrub significantly decrease from 2009 to 2030.

As noted earlier, water areas would be retained during the simulation period. Hence, most of the landscape metrics of water patches in the three scenarios are stable during the simulation period, except IJI index. As shown in **Figure 6.16e**, the IJI values of water class in all scenarios have the same decreasing tendency. It testifies that water areas are aggregated in a particular area. The changes of this index are caused by the spatial variations of other classes within the study area, in which IJI values of scenario B are lower than those for scenarios A and C.

6.8.3 Effects of land-use scenarios to landscape structure

Level	F-value						
	NP	PD	PROX_MN	AREA_MN	IJI	LPI	LSI
Landscape	2.46*	2.46*	6.57	4.28	7.72	13.37	2.12*
Agriculture	12.85	136.49	9.42	10.75	11.87	10.58	10.58
Barren	4.18	4.18	12.19	22.93	27.66	6.15	10.27
Urban	37.10	37.10	8.14	41.93	31.73	3.29	100.31
Forest	52.30	23.25	33.47	34.27	5.96	13.37	55.38
Shrub	5.83	5.83	2.23	5.68	12.22	4.69	5.83
Water	0.000*	0.000*	0.000*	0.000*	1.5*	0.000*	0.000*

Not significant at the 0.05 level.

Table 6.10 Descriptive values of landscape metrics obtained with one-way ANOVA

Source: Author's calculation

For further understanding, the study would test if there is significant difference in the landscape structure under different modeled scenarios. In this case, we employed the test of variance (one-way analysis of variance [ANOVA]) on each landscape metrics (NP, PD, Prox_MN, Area_MN, JIJ, LPI, LSI), using each of 22 simulation runs (from 2009 to 2030) per scenario as independent value. Tukey's post hoc test was set at $\alpha = 0.05$.

Table 6.10 presents the results of one-way ANOVA in analyzing the effects of different LULC scenarios to landscape structure within the entire study area. At the landscape level, it indicates that the landscape metrics LPI and IJI of all scenarios differ significantly with the changes of LULC during the period of simulation for the entire study area. Meanwhile, the landscape metrics for NP, PD, and LSI do not significantly differ for all scenarios.

At the class level, the analytical results show that the landscape metric NP of forest has the highest significant difference for all scenarios during the simulated period. Continuously, this metric also differs significantly with demand for urban and agriculture classes in the trio of scenarios. Regarding the landscape metric PD, the ANOVA results show that PD at agriculture class differs significantly by the demand of LULC for all scenarios, which is approximately fourfold the number of difference in urban class and sixfold the number of difference in forest class. Again, the landscape metrics of

PROX_MN and LPI under three scenarios are different by the changes of demand in forest class. In the AREA_MN landscape metric, urban class is considered to have the highest significant difference than the other classes. Similar to AREA_MN, the landscape metrics IJI and LSI of urban class in all scenarios have the highest values. The landscape metric LSI, in particular, varies significantly with the demands of LULC for all scenarios throughout the simulation period. The significant difference of this landscape metric is approximately 2-fold the value of forest class, 10-fold the value of agriculture class, and 17-fold the value of shrub class. Because of the stability during the simulated period, all landscape metrics of water class do not significantly differ for all LULC scenarios.

With respect to the spatial configuration of LULC scenarios, main results of landscape metrics, which are obtained by running one-way ANOVA for 22 simulations (from 2009 to 2030), are presented in **Table 6.11**. The results show that the mean values of landscape metrics under three scenarios do not differ significantly, except NP and PROX_MN. As shown in **Table 6.11**, the mean value of landscape metric NP in scenario B is the lowest one, compared to scenarios A and C. It reveals that the spatial configuration in scenario B is less heterogeneous than scenarios A and C. In addition, the value of landscape metric PROX_MN in scenario B is the highest one, which indicates that there are more patches in a search radius of 300 m of scenario B than scenarios A and C. More details could be found in **Appendix 6**.

Landscape metrics	Scenario A		Scenario B		Scenario C	
	Mean	SD	Mean	SD	Mean	SD
NP	27,035.50	4,059.21	24,819.00	6,755.59	28,256.36	4,391.18
PD	27.92	4.19	25.63	7.00	29.19	4.50
PROX_MN	2,996.57	849.70	3,903.40	2,159.67	2,397.63	621.24
AREA_MN	3.65	0.52	4.22	1.30	3.51	0.567
IJI	77.59	3.88	71.54	7.65	76.22	3.50
LPI	51.37	0.61	51.42	0.57	52.04	0.16
LSI	69.51	4.81	65.06	8.73	67.26	7.40

Table 6.11 Obtained landscape metrics of scenarios
Source: Author's calculation

6.9 Discussions and conclusions

6.9.1 Discussions

According to the earlier findings and interpretations, it can be concluded that the integration of SD and Dyna-CLUE models is capable of predicting the future LULC distributions within the study area. However, there are some issues, involved driving factors, scale of input data, and elasticity parameters that should be considered to get a deep understanding of the models.

Priyanto (2010) asserted that the shortage of input data could give an inaccuracy in estimating the changes of LULC based on causative effects of driving factors. Similarly, too many variables without significant effects could not well explain the behavior of LULC changes. In addition, Verburg and Veldkamp (2004) stated that the number of involved driving factors should be selected upon the extent and actual conditions of the research area. Large areas need more variety of driving factors to describe the distribution of LULC over a period of time, whereas small areas, like Da Nang City, need fewer variables. Consequently, seven driving factors, evaluated by measuring the goodness of logistic regression for every LULC type (ROC values from 0.7 to 0.9), are believed to reflect the dynamics of Da Nang City. If the Dyna-CLUE model has more socioeconomic data, such as the preference of society in choosing new urban locations with high business potential, it could improve the capability of the model in simulating LULC behavior. Unfortunately, these data are unavailable. Hence, if the data become available, it should be incorporated in the future work.

As mentioned in Section **4.3.1**, all images used in this study were resampled to scale resolution of 30 m. In the CLUE-S model, this cell size is considered as a large grid-based system (Verburg et al., 2002). If input data are acquired at higher spatial resolution, more detailed information could be revealed; thus, it has the possibility to improve the understanding of dynamic changes within the study area (Cheng, 2003). However, Priyanto (2010) noticed that more capacity and time are required for iteration processes when the model is running with data at a larger resolution.

The elasticity parameters of this study (detailed in **Section 6.4**) are defined based on experiments getting from historical dynamic changes within the study area and arranged from 0.2 to 1. According to Carlson (2004), it is feasible to access more reasonable parameters by trying many times. Hence, it is essential to choose and test other different elasticity values to evaluate the simulation results of the Dyna-CLUE model in our future research.

6.9.2 Conclusions

Understanding the changes of LULC types as well as their future distribution in a particular region plays an important role in helping land-use planners and managers adjust their spatial planning decisions and avoid inappropriate decisions (Pontius and Neeti, 2010). By modeling the changes of LULC, a depicted future of land-use distribution can be empirically tested through developed scenarios. It means that the results of modeling can provide insights into the future occurrence and configuration of LULC. Also, it is necessary to consider the relation among natural, socioeconomic conditions and dynamic transitions of LULC types under different scenarios. Therefore, this study developed scenarios with different mission storylines to simulate the future changes of LULC in Da Nang City by using the Dyna-CLUE model from 2009 to 2030.

First, all three scenarios were calibrated based on observed changes of LULC types in Da Nang City in the 1996–2009 period and this was used to simulate the dynamics in the period 2009–2030. Seven exogenous explanatory variables, including urban rate, mean density of population, slope, elevation, distance to road, distance to urban, and distance to water were analyzed by binary logistic regression model in order to simulate 35 probability maps. The ROC values of logistic regression models, ranged from 0.70 to 0.99 based on the types of LULC, indicate that these driving factors can be used to explain the spatial pattern within the study area.

Second, all scenarios (A, B, and C) give a continuous increase in urban area and a gradual decrease in agriculture, barren, and shrub areas. The change of urban area by 2030 is the highest under scenario B with 17,152.7 ha (99.16%), the lowest under scenario C with 9,794.23 ha (56.62%). Visually, the urban areas mostly occur in the adjacent of existing urban area in the southeast part of Da Nang City, and densely along the coastal zone. Around these parts, urban areas also tend to expand to the western part of this zone. Consequently, the expansion of urban areas causes the conversion of agricultural area and other LULC types. Scenario B results in the most loss of agricultural area 6,098.96 ha (83.61%), while scenario C shows the least loss of agricultural area 1,996.98 ha (27.40%) during the simulated period. Particularly, forest areas decease by 5,269.19 ha (9.1%), 5,125.59 ha (8.85%) under scenarios A and B, respectively; meanwhile, scenario C emphasized the environmental issue, which shows no change in forest (57,936.2 ha) during the simulated period. Overall, urban areas increase the most in Hoa Vang district, by 9,581.7 ha (176.8%), 12,208.7 ha (225.3%), and 7,064.5 ha (130.4%) under scenarios A, B, and C, respectively, while Thanh Khe is shown to have the least change in LULC, compared to other districts.

Finally, one-way ANOVA analysis shows that landscape metrics LPI and IJI at the landscape level under scenarios differ significantly with the changes of LULC during the simulated period within the entire study area. At class level, the results show that the forest class has high differences with landscape metrics NP, PROX_MN, and LPI. Meanwhile, the landscape metrics AREA_MN, IJI, and LSI of urban class are considered to have the highest significant difference than the others. Regarding agriculture, the ANOVA results show that PD at agriculture class level differs significantly by the demand of LULC for all scenarios, which is approximately fourfold the number of difference in urban class level and sixfold the number of difference in forest class level. For analyzing the spatial configuration of LULC under scenarios, one-way ANOVA results also show that the mean value of landscape metrics under scenarios does not differ significantly, except NP and PROX_MN. The value of NP in scenario B is the lowest one, compared to scenarios A and C. It reveals that the spatial configuration in scenario B is less heterogeneous than scenarios A and C. This conclusion is supported by the highest value of PROX_MN in scenario B.

According to the aforementioned analysis, the results of scenario prediction would provide a guide for land-use-planners and decision makers in Da Nang City. In this case, an optimal strategy for sustainable development is chosen; it would be most suitable for planners and decision makers to seek scenario C for the best land-use plan. It is the most plausible plan to constrain the dynamic growth of urban area to protect land resources and promote sustainable strategy.

Chapter 7
Conclusions

Abstract

This chapter provides remarkable conclusions of the research based on the main results and analysis obtained from previous chapters. Hence, an insight about the research objectives is presented. This chapter is also concerned with some certain advisory ideas arising from the results of the research. Furthermore, it will emphasize the probable future works according to this perspective.

7.1 General conclusions

The key objective of this research is to address and simulate the changes of land use/cover (LULC) in Da Nang City. LULC changes are well known as the results of spatial-temporal interactions between biophysical and human activities at various scales (Veldkamp A, 2001; Verburg et al., 2004). The changes of LULC affect the environment of a region in different ways. Therefore, it is necessary to define and simulate the changes of LULC in a spatial-temporal pattern. Through this examination, the causes and consequences as well as ecological impacts could be revealed, in order to support decision makers and land-use planner in making better-informed decisions (Luo et al., 2010).

Based on LULC maps obtained from satellite imagery, the study has explored the potential of system dynamics (SD) and dynamic conversion of land use and its effects (Dyna-CLUE) models in examining the future of LULC changes in Da Nang City under different scenarios. In this thesis, we accomplished these following missions:

- Assessing the change of land use/cover, in particular urban land use under the impacts of urbanization by using time series remotely sensed images from 1979 to 2009

Chapter 7 Conclusions

From satellite imagery, LULC maps of Da Nang City in 1979, 1996, 2003, and 2009 were established. It was found that the changes of LULC within Da Nang City mainly occurred due to the expansion of urban area that had a net increase, 140% of total area of Da Nang City over the past 30 years (1979–2009). In the first 18 years (1979–1996), urban area increased to 13.4%. However, only in seven years (1996–2003), after separation from Quang Nam Province and becoming a centrally governed city, the urban area had a net increase of 35%. Within the six years (2003–2009), the urban area incessantly increased and contributed 51.6% to net increase of urban area. Besides, water area increased with the annual rate of change of 0.87% in the same period. Conversely, barren and agricultural areas consistently lost 60.4% and 39.5% of their 1979 area, respectively. In addition, forest and shrub decreased to 6.5% and 2.1% in the same period, respectively. Given the results shown in this research, urbanization has significantly modified the LULC in Da Nang City during the entire study period. Urban area is markedly distributed in Thanh Khe, Hai Chau, Ngu Hanh Son, and Cam Le districts. Hence, it could cause pressures on coastal plain in the Da Nang City.

- Analyzing patterns of changes in landscape within the study area during the last three decades

To have an intrinsic evaluation about spatial changes of LULC, three representative classes (urban, agriculture, and forest) were chosen to compute spatial landscape matrices, namely, percentage of landscape (PLAND), number of patches (NP), largest patch index (LPI), average size of patches (AREA_MN), patch density (PD), proximity index (PROX_MN), interspersion and juxtaposition index (IJI), and landscape shape index (LSI). These metrics were chosen for analysis based on actual conditions of the study area as well as own background knowledge. As mentioned earlier, urban area grew up rapidly from 1979 to 2009. It was reflected by the increase of LPI. Furthermore, the landscape metrics of urban class showed the increase of NP, AREA_MN, and PD as the evidence of expanded urban during the span of 30 years. Based on these findings, the values of PROX_MN, IJI, and LSI presented in this thesis show that configuration of urban class became more uniform and less complex. Regarding agriculture class, although its NP and PD increased during the period from 1979 to 2009, the relevant landscape metrics (AREA_MN, LPI, and PROX_MN) decreased strongly. The combination of these values revealed that agriculture class in 2009 became more fragmented than in 1979, also, it was supported by the decrease of IJI. Forest class was the most dominant LULC in Da Nang City until 2009; hence, the LPI of forest was the highest, compared to other classes. However, the decrease of NP and PD gave evidence about the change of forest class. In contrast to this, the results showed the increase of AREA_MN and PROX_MN as well, which indicated that forested patches became more contiguous in the domain of spatial distribution. It was supported again by the high value of IJI. From a landscape point of view, it can be documented that the coastal landscape characteristics in Da Nang City were affected strongly after three decades.

- Determining the underlying and proximate causes of land-use/land-cover changes

The findings of this study revealed that the growth of population (31%), the increase of economics, especially annual growth rate of GDP (10.3% from 1990 to 2009), and the focus on development of industry and construction, services sectors were the main causes of LULC changes in Da Nang City over the past 30 years (1979–2009).

- Simulating and locating the changes of land use/cover within the study area during the period 2009 to 2030

Based on targets obtained from strategic development of Da Nang City in the next 20 years, the SD model was applied to predict the demands of LULC changes within Da Nang City under three different scenarios, namely, scenario A *development as usual*, scenario B *aggressive development*, and scenario C *optimal development*. Scenario A is predefined by retaining all conditions, so these conditions are same as those in the historical data. Scenario B corresponds to a vigorous development with the consideration of high investment in industry. Scenario C constrains the development of LULC within the study area by projecting population, as well as protecting the actual forest area, sparely utilizing, and reasonably converting LULC. In further steps of modeling, the three scenarios were used to allocate the spatial pattern with the Dyna-CLUE model. The changes of LULC generated under three scenarios are consistent with those detected from historical maps. It means that the increase of urban area and decrease of agriculture would still be the main tendency of LULC types in Da Nang City. The results show that the urban area has an increase of 99.16% under scenario B, 78.54% under scenario A, and 56.62% under scenario C. Scenario B generates a substantial increase of urban area at the expense of agriculture, and other LULC types, compared to the other two scenarios. Thus, scenario B results in the most loss of agricultural area (83.61%), while scenario C shows the least loss of 27.4%. Particularly, forest area in scenario C is retained during the simulated period. Overall, the changes of urban area mostly occur in Hoa Vang, Son Tra, and Lien Chieu districts, where the urban rate is low before simulating. Also, these changes of LULC types affect landscape structure in various ways. Of which, urban class is considered to have the highest change at AREA_MN, IJI, and LSI metrics. As stated earlier, the expansion of urban area causes the decrease of agricultural area. Consequently, the PD metric of agriculture class differs significantly for all scenarios. Meanwhile, NP, PROX_MN, and LPI metrics of forest show a large difference. The analysis also reveals that spatial configuration under scenario B would lead to the least heterogeneous landscape compared to the other two scenarios on the one hand. On the other hand, scenario B shows the evidence of serious interference of human activities on landscape structure. In this sense, scenario C suggests an effective way to develop Da Nang City in the next 20 years.

In general, my thesis exhibited a significant contribution to land-use planning process in Da Nang City by predicting the changes of LULC in a spatial-temporal pattern. Also, it helps local decision makers better comprehend the complexity of LULC system. The simulated results could give anticipative information around coastal region in the future, which could be considered as consultative strategies for land-use planning. The most important contribution of this thesis is that the framework of used models could provide a serviceable and scientific tool for planners at the initial stage of the planning process. Practically, the study of my thesis can be applied not only in Da

Nang city but also in other similar regions with rapid urbanization in Vietnam.

7.2 Future works

Generally, the results within this thesis indicate that the integration of the SD model and Dyna-CLUE model has the capability to explain LULC behavior by using significant factors as a complete process. According to Pijanowski et al. (2000), the use of the cause-effect relationship created from driving factors and LULC change in the CLUE model could prevent spurious interpretation and subjective human intervention. However, further improvements of this research could be implemented.

The study was completely done as a process for supporting land-use planning from initial data. Due to the conditions of research, available data used for analysis are different at acquisition sources and spatial resolution. This would cause some inaccuracies in interpreting data. Thus, if one kind of higher spatial resolution data could be accessed (e.g., Vietnamese first satellite VNREDSat-1, 07/05/2013), it would overcome this restriction. Consequently, more information explored from the specific region could enhance the understanding of the real situation.

As can be seen from historical data, the transportation network significantly influences the urbanization process. Currently, the actual road network was used as one of the critical driving factors in the Dyna-CLUE model. In addition, constraint factors such as the price of an area or an area in good condition for business were not included in the model. Hence, if future transportation network information and related data could be identified and inserted into the model, it may improve the simulated outcomes.

In **Section 6.9.1**, it is discussed that LULC conversion elasticity was defined based on empirical assessment. In this sense, it is possible to investigate the elasticity from local planners or managements. Furthermore, the cooperation could help in various ways, including more relevant data could be easily accessed and used, more practical policy could be established in models, and it is the shortest way to let local planners and managers know and apply the models to their usual works.

References

Agarwal, C., Green, G. M., Grove, J. M., Evans, T. P., and Schweik, C. M., 2002, A Review and Assessment of Land-Use Change Models: Dynamics of Space, Time, and Human Choice, Gen. Tech. Rep. NE-297. Newton Square, PA: U.S. Department of Agriculture, Forest Service, Northeastern Research Station, p. 61.

Ahmed, B., Ahmed, R., and Zhu, X., 2013, Evaluation of model validation techniques in land cover dynamics: ISPRS International Journal of Geo-Information, v. 2, no. 3, pp. 577–597.

Anderson, J. R., Hardy, E. E., Roach, J., and Witmer, R. E., 1976a, A land use/cover classification system for use with remote sensor data: US Geological Survey Professional, Sioux Falls, SD, p. 964.

Anderson, J. R., Hardy, E. E., Roach, J. T., and Witmer, R. E., 1976b, A land use and land cover classification system for use with remote sensor data: Tech.rep., U.S. Geological Survey Professional Paper, p. 964.

Angel, D. P., Attoh, S., Kromm, D., Dehart, J., Slocum, R., and White, S., 1998, The drivers of greenhouse gas emissions: What do we learn from local case studies?: Local Environment: The International Journal of Justice and Sustainability, v. 3, no. 3, pp. 263–277.

Antrop, M., and Van Eetvelde, V., 2000, Holistic aspects of suburban landscapes: visual image interpretation and landscape metrics: Landscape and Urban Planning, v. 50, no. 1–3, pp. 43–58.

Apan, A., Raine, S. R., and Paterson, M.S., 2000, Image analysis techniques for assessing landscape structural change: a case study of the Lockyer Valley catchment, Queensland, in Proceedings 10th Australasian Remote Sensing and Photogrammetry Conference, pp. 438–455.

Bakr, N., Weindorf, D. C., Bahnassy, M. H., Marei, S. M., and El-Badawi, M. M., 2010, Monitoring land cover changes in a newly reclaimed area of Egypt using multi-temporal Landsat data: Applied Geography, v. 30, no. 4, pp. 592–605.

References

Batty, M., Xie, Yichun, and Sun, Z., 1999, Modeling urban dynamics through GIS-based cellular automata: Computers, Environment and Urban Systems, v. 23, pp. 205–233.

Bhatta, B., 2010, Analysis of Urban Growth and Sprawl From Remote Sensing Data, Springer Heidelberg Dordrecht London New York, p. 191.

Braimoh, A. K., and Onishi, T., 2007, Geostatistical techniques for incorporating spatial correlation into land use change models: International Journal of Applied Earth Observation and Geoinformation, v. 9, no. 4, p. 438.

Brooks, D., A. Baudin, and Schwarzbauer, P., 1995, Modelling forest products demand, supply and trade, UN-ECE/FAO Timber and Forest Discussion Papers, ETTS V Working Paper, ECE/TIM/DP/5.

Brown, D. G., Walker, R., Manson, S., and Seto, K., 2004, Modeling land use and land cover change, in Gutman, Garik, Janetos, Anthony C., Justice, Christopher O., Moran, Emilio F., Mustard, John F., Rindfuss, Ronald R., Skole, David, Lee Turner II, Billy, and Cochrane, M. A., eds., Land Change Science: Observing, Monitoring and Understanding Trajectories of Change on the Earth's Surface Springer, p. 482.

Campbell, B. J., 1996, Introduction to Remote Sensing, 2nd Edition, Guilford Press, New York.

Campbell, B. J., 2002, Introduction to Remote Sensing, 3rd Edition, Guilford Press, New York.

Campbell, J. B., 2007, Introduction to Remote Sensing, Guilford Press.

Canty, M. J., and Nielsen, A. A., 2008, Automatic radiometric normalization of multitemporal satellite imagery with the iteratively reweighted MAD transformation: Remote Sensing of Environment, v. 112, no. 3, pp. 1025–1036.

Canty, M. J., Nielsen, A. A., and Schmidt, M., 2004, Automatic radiometric normalization of multitemporal satellite imagery: Remote Sensing of Environment, v. 91, no. 3–4, pp. 441–451.

Caprioli, M., Figorito, B., and Tarantino, E., 2006, Radiometric normalization of Landsat ETM+ data for multitemporal analysis: Proceedings of ISPRS Commission VII Mid-term Symposium on "Remote sensing: From pixels to Process" v. 34, no. Part XXX.

References

Caprioli, M., Figorito, B., and Tarantino, E., 2008, Radiometric calibration methods for change detection analysis of satellite data aimed at environmental risk monitoring, in Proceedings The International Archives of the Photogrammetry, Remote Sensing and Spatial Information Sciences, Beijing, Volume XXXVII. Part 8, pp. 397–402.

Carlson, T. N., 2004, Analysis and prediction of surface runoff in an urbanizing watershed using satellite imagery: Journal of the American Water Resources Association, v. 40, no. 4, pp. 1087–1098.

Caselles, V., and García, M. J. L., 1989, An alternative simple approach to estimate atmospheric correction in multitemporal studies: International Journal of Remote Sensing, v. 10, no. 6, pp. 1127–1134.

Chase, T. N., Pielke Sr, R. A., Kittel, T. G. F., Nemani, R. R., and Running, S. W., 2000, Simulated impacts of historical land cover changes on global climate in northern winter: Climate Dynamics, v. 16, no. 2–3, pp. 93–105.

Chen, H., and Pontius, R. Jr., 2010, Diagnostic tools to evaluate a spatial land change projection along a gradient of an explanatory variable: Landscape Ecology, v. 25, no. 9, pp. 1319–1331.

Chen, X., Vierling, L., and Deering, D., 2005, A simple and effective radiometric correction method to improve landscape change detection across sensors and across time: Remote Sensing of Environment, v. 98, no. 1, pp. 63–79.

Chen, Z., and Wang, J., 2010, Land use and land cover change detection using satellite remote sensing techniques in the mountainous Three Gorges Area, China: International Journal of Remote Sensing, v. 31, no. 6, pp. 1519–1542.

Cheng, J., 2003, Modelling the spatial and temporal land use growth [Doctoral Dissertation: Utrecht University, Utrecht, The Netherlands.

Chorley, R. J., and Haggett, P., 1967, Models in geography.

Chorley, R. J., and Haggett, P., 2013, Integrated Models in Geography, Routledge, Taylor & Francis group.

Colgalton, R. G., and Green, K., 1999, Assessing the Accuracy of Remotely Sensed Data: Principles and Practices, CRC Lewis Publishers.

References

Collier, U., 1997, Local authorities and climate protection in the European union: Putting subsidiarity into practice?: Local Environment: The International Journal of Justice and Sustainability, v. 2, no. 1, pp. 39–57.

Collier, U., and Löfstedt, R. E., 1997, Think globally, act locally?: Local climate change and energy policies in Sweden and the UK: Global Environmental Change, v. 7, no. 1, pp. 25–40.

Committee on Global Change Research, 1999, Global Environmental Change: Research Pathways for the Next Decade, National Academy Press, Washington, DC, 596 p.

Conel, J. E., 1990, Determination of surface reflectance and estimates of atmospheric optical depth and single scattering albedo from Landsat Thematic Mapper data: International Journal of Remote Sensing, v. 11, no. 5, pp. 783–828.

Crocetto, N., and Tarantino, E., 2009, A Class-Oriented Strategy for Features Extraction from Multidate ASTER Imagery: Remote Sensing, v. 1, no. 4, pp. 1171–1189.

Curran, P. J., 1987, Review Article Remote sensing methodologies and geography: International Journal of Remote Sensing, v. 8, no. 9, pp. 1255–1275.

Da Nang's Committee, 2012, Population planning and developing in Da Nang city from 2011 to 2020. Assessed on 12/11/2012 http://dhtp.vn/img/uploads/Van%20ban%20dieu%20hanh/UBND%20TP%20DN/QD5882-UBtp.pdf.

Danang Info, 2012, Danang overview. Accessed on 18/03/2013 http://www.danangcity.gov.vn/portal/page/portal/danang/english/danang_info/ove.

Danang' Statistical Office, 2009, Statistical Yearbook, Danang Publishing House, p. 118.

de Koning, G. H. J., Verburg, P. H., Veldkamp, A., and Fresco, L. O., 1999, Multi-scale modelling of land use change dynamics in Ecuador: Agricultural Systems, v. 61, no. 2, pp. 77–93.

DeAngelo, B. J., and Harvey, L. D. D., 1998, The jurisdictional framework for municipal action to reduce greenhouse gas emissions: Case studies from Canada, the USA and Germany: Local Environment: The International Journal of Justice and Sustainability, v. 3, no. 2, pp. 111–136.

References

Deng, J. S., Wang, K., Hong, Y., and Qi, J. G., 2009, Spatio-temporal dynamics and evolution of land use change and landscape pattern in response to rapid urbanization: Landscape and Urban Planning, v. 92, no. 3–4, pp. 187–198.

Dewan, A. M., and Yamaguchi, Y., 2009, Land use and land cover change in Greater Dhaka, Bangladesh: Using remote sensing to promote sustainable urbanization: Applied Geography, v. 29, no. 3, pp. 390–401.

Dietzel, C., Herold, M., Hemphill, J. J., and Clarke, K. C., 2005, Spatio-temporal dynamics in California's Central Valley: empirical links urban theory: International Journal of Geographic Information Sciences, v. 19, no. 2, pp. 175–195.

Ding, H., Wang, R. C., Wu, J. P., Zhou, B., Shi, Z., and Ding, L. X., 2007, Quantifying land use change in Zhejiang coastal region, China using multi-temporal Landsat TM/ETM+ Images: Pedosphere, v. 17, no. 6, pp. 712–720.

Du, Y., Teillet, P. M., and Cihlar, J., 2002, Radiometric normalization of multitemporal high-resolution satellite images with quality control for land cover change detection: Remote Sensing of Environment, v. 82, no. 1, pp. 123–134.

Ducourtieux, O., and Castella, J. C., 2006, Land reforms and impact on land use in the uplands of Vietnam and Laos: Environmental protection or poverty alleviation?, At the frontier of land issues: Social embeddedness of rights and public policy: Montpellier, France, Assessed 09/07/2012 http://www.mpl.ird.fr/colloque_fon cier/Communications/PDF/Ducourtieux.pdf.

Dunn, C. P., Sharpe, D. M., Guntensbergen, G. R., Stearns, F., and Yang, Z., 1991, Methods for analyzing temporal changes in landscape pattern *in* Turner, M. G., and Gardner, R. H., eds., Quantitative Methods in Landscape Ecology: The Analysis and Interpretation of Landscape Heterogeneity, New York: Springer Verlag, pp. 173–198.

Durlauf, Steven N., and Blume, L. E., 2008, The New Palgrave Dictionary of Economics, Palgrave Macmillan.

Ehlers, M., Jadkowski, M. A., Howard, R. R., and Brostuen, D. E., 1990, Application of SPOT data for regional growth analysis and local planning: Photogrammetric Engineering and Remote Sensing, v. 56, pp. 175–180.

References

Ellis, E., 2010, Land-use and land-cover change. Accessed on 14/03/2013 http://www.eoearth.org/article/Land-use_and_land-cover_change.

Elvidge, C. D., Sutton, P. C., Wagner, T. W., Rhonda Ryzner, J. E. V., Goetz, Scott J., Andrew, J., Smith, C. J., Seto, Karen C., Imhoff, Marc L., Wang, Y. Q., and Cristina Milesi, R. N., 2004, Urbanization Land Change Science: Observing, Monitoring and Understanding Trajectories of Change on the Earth's Surface, Volume Remote Sensing and Digital Image Processing, Kluwer Academic Publishers, pp. 315–328.

Engelsman, W., 2002, Simulating land use changes in an urbanising are in Malaysia: An application of the CLUE-S model in the Selangor river basin [Master Thesis: Wageningen University], 67 p.

Estoque, R. C., and Murayama, Y., 2012, Examining the potential impact of land use/cover changes on the ecosystem services of Baguio city, the Philippines: A scenario-based analysis: Applied Geography, v. 35, no. 1–2, pp. 316–326.

FAO, 1995, Planning for Sustainable Use of Land Resources: Towards a New Approach, Food and Agriculture Organization of the United Nations.

Forman, R. T. T., and Gordon, M., 1986, Landscape Ecology, Wiley, New York.

Forrester, J. W., 1961, Industrial Dynamics, Pegasus Communications.

Fragkias, M., Langanke, T., Boone, C. G., Haase, D., Marcotullio, P. J., Munroe, D., Olah, B., Reenberg, A., Seto, K. C., Simon, D., 2012, Land Teleconnections in an Urbanizing World.

Hagen-Zanker, A., and Lajoie, G., 2008, Neutral models of landscape change as benchmarks in the assessment of model performance: Landscape and Urban Planning, v. 86, no. 3–4, pp. 284–296.

Haines-Young, R. H., 1989, Modelling geographical knowledge, *in* Macmillan, W., ed., Remodelling Geography, Oxford: Basil Blackwell, pp. 22–39.

Haines-Young, R. H., and Petch, J. H., 1986, Physical Geography: Its Nature and Methods, London: Harper & Row, 230 p.

References

Hall, F. G., Strebel, D. E., Nickeson, J. E., and Goetz, S. J., 1991, Radiometric rectification: Toward a common radiometric response among multidate, multisensor images: Remote Sensing of Environment, v. 35, no. 1, pp. 11–27.

Hargis, C., Bissonette, J., and David, J., 1998, The behavior of landscape metrics commonly used in the study of habitat fragmentation: Landscape Ecology, v. 13, no. 3, pp. 167–186.

Harris, P. M., and Ventura, S. J., 1995, The integration of geographic data with remotely sensed imagery to improve classification in an urban area: Photogrammetric Engineering and Remote Sensing, v. 61, pp. 993–998.

Harvey, L. D. D., 1993, Tackling urban CO_2 emissions in Toronto: Environment, v. 35, no. 7, pp. 16–20.

He, C., Okada, N., Zhang, Q., Shi, P., and Zhang, J., 2006, Modeling urban expansion scenarios by coupling cellular automata model and system dynamic model in Beijing, China: Applied Geography, v. 26, no. 3–4, pp. 323–345.

Heo, J., and FitzHugh, T. W., 2000, A standardized radiometric normalization method for change detection using remotely sensed imagery: Photogrammetric Engineering and Remote Sensing, v. 66, no. 2, pp. 173–181.

Herold, M., Couclelis, H., and Clarke, K. C., 2005, The role of spatial metrics in the analysis and modeling of urban land use change: Computers, Environment and Urban Systems, v. 29, no. 4, pp. 369–399.

Hinton, J. C., 1996, GIS and remote sensing integration for environmental applications: International Journal of Geographical Information Systems, v. 10, no. 7, pp. 877–890.

Houghton, R. A., Hackler, J. L., and Lawrence, K. T., 1999, The U.S. carbon budget: Contributions from land-use change: Science, v. 285, no. 5427, pp. 574–578.

Huang, J., Lin, J., and Tu, Z., 2010, Detecting spatiotemporal change of land use and landscape pattern in a coastal gulf region, southeast of China: Environment, Development and Sustainability, v. 12, no. 1, pp. 35–48.

IDS, 2007, Governance Screening for Urban Climate Change Resilience Building and Adaptation Strategies in Asia: Assessment of Danang, Vietnam. Accessed on 09/03/2013 http://www.ids.ac.uk/files/dmfile/DaNang.pdf

Janzen, D. T., Fredeen, A. L., and Wheate, R. D., 2006, Radiometric correction techniques and accuracy assessment for Landsat TM data in remote forested regions: Canadian Journal of Remote Sensing, v. 32, no. 5, pp. 330–340.

Jat, M. K., Garg, P. K., and Khare, D., 2008, Monitoring and modelling of urban sprawl using remote sensing and GIS techniques: International Journal of Applied Earth Observation and Geoinformation, v. 10, no. 1, pp. 26–43.

Jensen, J. R., 2000, Remote Sensing of the Environment: An Earth Resource Perspective, Prentice Hall, NJ, p. 544.

Jensen, J. R., 2005, Introductory Digital Image Processing: A Remote Sensing Perspective, Prentice-Hall, New Jersey, p. 545.

Ji, W., Ma, J., Twibell, R. W., and Underhill, K., 2006, Characterizing urban sprawl using multi-stage remote sensing images and landscape metrics: Computers, Environment and Urban Systems, v. 30, no. 6, pp. 861–879.

Johannsen, C. J., Petersen, G. W., Carter, P. G., and Morgan, M. T., 2003, Remote sensing changing natural resource management: Journal of Soil and Water Conservation, v. 58, no. 2, pp. 42A–45A.

Jokar Arsanjani, J., 2012, Dynamic Land Use/Cover Change Modelling: Geosimulation and Multiagent-Based Modelling, Springer-Verlag Berlin Heidelberg.

Kangas, K., and Baudin, A., 2003, Modelling and projections of forest productions demand, supply and trade in Europe, UN-ECE/FAO Geneva Timber and Forest discussion paper 30.

Kashaigili, J. J., and Majaliwa, A. M., 2010, Integrated assessment of land use and cover changes in the Malagarasi river catchment in Tanzania: Physics and Chemistry of the Earth, Parts A/B/C, v. 35, no. 13–14, pp. 730–741.

Käyhkö, N., Fagerholm, N., Asseid, B. S., and Mzee, A. J., 2011, Dynamic land use and land cover changes and their effect on forest resources in a coastal village of Matemwe, Zanzibar, Tanzania: Land Use Policy, v. 28, no. 1, pp. 26–37.

References

Keleş, S., Sivrikaya, F., Çakir, G., and Köse, S., 2008, Urbanization and forest cover change in regional directorate of Trabzon forestry from 1975 to 2000 using Landsat data: Environmental Monitoring and Assessment, v. 140, no. 1–3, pp. 1–14.

Khoury, A. E., 2012, Modelling land use changes in the South Nation watershed using Dyna-CLUE [Master thesis]: University of Ottawa, p. 104.

Koch, J., Wimmer, F., Schaldach, R., and Onigkeit, J., 2012, An integrated land-use system model for the Jordan River Region, in Appiah-Opoku, S., ed., Environmental Land Use Planning: Intech, pp. 87–116.

Kok, K., and Winograd, M., 2002, Modelling land-use change for Central America, with special reference to the impact of hurricane Mitch: Ecological Modelling, v. 149, no. 1–2, pp. 53–69.

Koomen, E., Stillwell, J., Bakema, A., Scholten, H. J. (Eds.), 2007, Modelling Land-use change: Progress and Applications, P.O. Box 17, 3300 AA Dordrecht, The Netherlands., Springer, GeoJournal Library.

Kyriakidis, P. C., Liu, X., and Goodchild, M. F., 2004, Geostatistical Mapping of Thematic Classification Uncertainty, Remote Sensing and GIS Accuracy Assessment, CRC Press, pp. 145–162.

Lambin, E. F., 2004, Modelling land use change, John Wiley & Sons, Inc., West Sussex, Lon, Environmental modelling: finding simplicity in complexity, p. 342.

Lambin, E. F., Geist, H. J., and Lepers, E., 2003, Dynamics of land use and land cover change in tropical regions: Annual Review of Environment and Resources, v. 28, no. 1, pp. 205–241.

Lambin, E. F., Rounsevell, M. D. A., and Geist, H. J., 2000, Are agricultural land-use models able to predict changes in land-use intensity?: Agriculture, Ecosystems & Environment, v. 82, no. 1–3, pp. 321–331.

References

Lambin, E. F., Turner, B. L., Geist, H. J., Agbola, S. B., Angelsen, A., Bruce, J. W., Coomes, O. T., Dirzo, R., Fischer, G., Folke, C., George, P. S., Homewood, K., Imbernon, J., Leemans, R., Li, X., Moran, E. F., Mortimore, M., Ramakrishnan, P. S., Richards, J. F., Skånes, H., Steffen, W., Stone, G. D., Svedin, U., Veldkamp, T. A., Vogel, C., and Xu, J., 2001, The causes of land-use and land-cover change: moving beyond the myths: Global Environmental Change, v. 11, no. 4, pp. 261–269.

Lambright, W. H., Changnon, S. A., and Harvey, L. D. D., 1996, Urban reactions to the global warning issue: agenda setting in Toronto and Chicago: Climate Change, v. 34, pp. 463–478.

Landis, J. R., and Koch, G. G., 1977, The measurement of observer agreement for categorical data: Biometrics, v. 33, pp. 159–174.

Lawgali, F. F., 2008, Forecasting water demand for agricultural, industrial and domestic use in Libya: International Review of Business Papers, v. 4, no. 5, pp. 231–248.

Lee, C.-L., Huang, S.-L., and Chan, S.-L., 2009, Synthesis and spatial dynamics of socio-economic metabolism and land use change of Taipei Metropolitan Region: Ecological Modelling, v. 220, no. 21, pp. 2940–2959.

Leinenkugel, P., 2010, The combined use of optical and SAR data for large area impervious surface mapping [Msc: Paris-Lodron Salzburg University], 121 p.

Leitao, A. B., and Ahern, J., 2002, Applying landscape ecological concepts and metrics in sustainable landscape planning: Landscape and Urban Planning, v. 59, no. 2, pp. 65–93.

Lin, Y.-P., Hong, N.-M., Wu, P.-J., Wu, C.-F., and Verburg, P. H., 2007, Impacts of land use change scenarios on hydrology and land use patterns in the Wu-Tu watershed in Northern Taiwan: Landscape and Urban Planning, v. 80, no. 1–2, pp. 111–126.

Liu, Y., 2009, Modelling Urban Development with Geographical Information Systems and Cellular Automata, CRC Press, Taylor & Francis group, p. 204.

Lunetta, R. S., and Elvidge, C. D., 1998, Remote Sensing Change Detection: Environmental Monitoring Methods and Applications, Taylor & Francis, London.

References

Luo, G., Yin, C., Chen, X., Xu, W., and Lu, L., 2010, Combining system dynamic model and CLUE-S model to improve land use scenario analyses at regional scale: A case study of Sangong watershed in Xinjiang, China: Ecological Complexity, v. 7, no. 2, pp. 198–207.

Lyons, M. B., Phinn, S. R., and Roelfsema, C. M., 2012, Long term land cover and seagrass mapping using Landsat and object-based image analysis from 1972 to 2010 in the coastal environment of South East Queensland, Australia: ISPRS Journal of Photogrammetry and Remote Sensing, v. 71, pp. 34–46.

McEvoy, D., Gibbs, D. C., and Longhurst, J. W. S., 1999, The prospects for improved energy efficiency in the UK residential sector: Journal of Environmental Planning and Management, v. 42, no. 3, pp. 409–424.

McGarigal, K., Cushman, S. A., and Ene, E., 2012, FRAGSTATS v4: Spatial Pattern Analysis Program for Categorical and Continuous Maps. Computer software program produced by the authors at the University of Massachusetts, Amherst. http://www.umass.edu/landeco/research/fragstats/fragstats.html.

McGarigal, K., Cushman, S. A., Neel, M. C., and Ene, E. 2002, FRAGSTATS: Spatial Pattern Analysis Program for Categorical Maps. Computer software program produced by the authors at the University of Massachusetts, Amherst: http://www.umass.edu/landeco/research/fragstats/fragstats.html.

McGarigal, K., and Marks, B. J., 1995a, FRAGSTATS: Spatial pattern analysis program for quantifying landscape structure.

McGarigal, K., and Marks, B. J., 1995b, Fragstats: Spatial pattern analysis program for quantifying landscape structure U. S. Forest Service General Technical Report, Portland, OR, USA.

Meadows, D. H., 2008, Thinking in Systems: A Primer, Chelsea Green Publishing, White River Junction, Vermont.

Men, Ke-pei, and Zhao, Kai, 2010, Grey correlation between agriculture input factors and regional GDP growth in Anhui Province: Asian Agriculture Research v. 2, no. 4, pp. 31–33.

Mesev, V., 1998, The use of census data in urban image classification: Photogrammetric Engineering and Remote Sensing, v. 64, pp. 431–438.

References

Michalak, W. Z., 1993, GIS in land use change analysis: integration of remotely sensed data into GIS: Applied Geography, v. 13, no. 1, pp. 28–44.

Mondal, S. M., Sharma, N., Kappas, M., and Garg, P. K., 2012, Modeling of spatio-temporal dynamics of land use land cover—a review and assessment: Journal of Geomatics, v. 6, no. 2, pp. 29–39.

Moran, M. S., Jackson, R. D., Slater, P. N., and Teillet, P. M., 1992, Evaluation of simplified procedures for retrieval of land surface reflectance factors from satellite sensor output: Remote Sensing of Environment, v. 41, no. 2–3, pp. 169–184.

Muchoney, D. M., and Strahler, A. H., 2002, Pixel- and site-based calibration and validation methods for evaluating supervised classification of remotely sensed data: Remote Sensing of Environment, v. 81, no. 2–3, pp. 290–299.

Müller, D., 2003, Land use change in the central highlands of Vietnam: A spatial econometric model combining satellite imagery and village survey data [PhD PhD]: Georg-August-University at Göttingen, p. 190.

Mulligan, M., and Wainwright, J., 2004, Modelling and model building, in Wainwright, J., and Mulligan, M., eds., Environmental modelling: finding simplicity in complicity, John Wiley & Sons, Inc., West Sussex, London, p. 432.

Myint, S. W., and Wang, L., 2006, Multicriteria decision approach for land use land cover change using Markov chain analysis and a cellular automata approach: Canadian of Remote Sensing, v. 32, no. 6, pp. 390–404.

Nguyen, X. T., 2003, Danang: policy options for investment and economic development: Accessed on 03/09/2013 http://agro.gov.vn/images/2007/04/Danang%20Policy%20Options%20for%20Investment%20and%20Economic%20Development.pdf.

O'Neill, R. V., Krummel, J. R., Gardner, R. H., Sugihara, G., Jackson, B., DeAngelis, D. L., Milne, B. T., Turner, M. G., Zygmunt, B., Christensen, S. W., Dale, V. H., and Graham, R. L., 1988, Indices of landscape pattern: Landscape Ecology, v. 1, no. 3, pp. 153–162.

O'Neill, R. V., Riitters, K. H., Wickham, J. D., and Jones, K. B., 1999, Landscape pattern metrics and regional assessment: Ecosystem Health, v. 5, no. 4, pp. 225–233.

OECD, 2006, Competitive Cities in the Global Economy: OECD, Paris.

OECD, 2009, Regions at Glance 2009: OECD, Paris.

OECD, 2010, Cities and Climate Change, OECD Publishing, Paris.

Olsen, L. M., Dale, Virginia H., and Foster, Thomas, 2007, Landscape patterns as indicators of ecological change at Fort Benning, Georgia, USA: Landscape and Urban Planning, v. 79, pp. 137–149.

Orekan, V. O. A., 2007, Implementation of the local land use and land cover change model CLUE-s for Central Benin by using socio-economic and remote sensing data [PhD: Rheinischen Friedrich-Wilhelms-Universität Bonn], p. 204.

Parker, D. C., Evans, Tom, and Meretsky, V., 2001, Measuring Emergent Properties of Agent-Based Landcover/Landuse Models using Spatial Metrics, Seventh annual conference of the international society for computational economics.

Peng, H., and Lu, H., 2007, Study on the Impacts of Urban Density on the Travel Demand Using GIS Spatial Analysis: Journal of Transportation Systems Engineering and Information Technology, v. 7, no. 4, pp. 90–95.

People's Committee Danang City, 2010, Planning social-economic developing to 2020.

Pijanowski, B. C., Gage, S. H., Long, D. T., and Cooper, W. C., 2000, A land transformation model for the Saginaw Bay watershed, in Sanderon, J., and Harris, L. D., eds., Landscape Ecology: A Top-Down Approach, Lewis Publishers, p. 246.

Pontius, J. R. G., 2000, Quantification error versus location error in comparison of categorical maps: Photogrammetric Engineering and Remote Sensing, v. 66, no. 8, pp. 1011–1016.

Pontius, J. R. G., 2002, Statistical methods to partition effects of quantity and location during comparison of categorical maps at multiple resolutions: Photogrammetric Engineering and Remote Sensing, v. 68, no. 10, pp. 1041–1049.

Pontius Jr, R. G., Huffaker, D., and Denman, K., 2004, Useful techniques of validation for spatially explicit land-change models: Ecological Modelling, v. 179, no. 4, pp. 445–461.

Pontius Jr., R. G., and Millones, M., 2011, Death to Kappa: birth of quantity disagreement and allocation disagreement for accuracy assessment: International Journal of Remote Sensing, v. 32, no. 15, pp. 4407–4429.

Pontius Jr., R. G., and Neeti, N., 2010, Uncertainty in the difference between maps of future land change scenarios: Sustainability Science, v. 5, no. 1, pp. 39–50.

Pontius, R., and Chen, H., 2006, GEOMOD Modeling. Land-use and cover change modeling. Note on GEOMOD modeling available within IDRISI Andes package. Clark Labs, Clark University, USA, http://clarklabs.org.

Pontius, R. G., and Schneider, L. C., 2001, Land-cover change model validation by an ROC method for the Ipswich watershed, Massachusetts, USA: Agriculture, Ecosystems & Environment, v. 85, no. 1–3, pp. 239–248.

Priyanto, A. T., 2010, The impact of human activities on coastal zones and strategies towards sustainable development: a case study in Pekalongan, Indonesia [Master of science: University of Twente], p. 88.

Quan, B., Chen, J. F., Qiu, H. L., Römkens, M. J. M., Yang, X. Q., Jiang, S. F., and Li, B. C., 2006, Spatial-Temporal Pattern and Driving Forces of Land Use Changes in Xiamen: Pedosphere, v. 16, no. 4, pp. 477–488.

Que, T. T., and Phuc, T. X., 2003, The Doi Moi policy and its impact on the poor. Accessed on 19/07/2012 http://www.socialwatch.org/node/10854

Radzicki, M., and Taylor, R., 2008, Origin of system dynamics: Jay W. Forrester and the history of system dynamics, U.S. Department of Energy's introduction to system dynamics. Accessed on 24/05/2013 http://www.systemdynamics.org/DL-IntroSysDyn/start.htm.

Rafiee, R., Mahiny, A. S., Khorasani, N., Darvishsefat, A. A., and Danekar, A., 2009, Simulating urban growth in Mashad City, Iran through the SLEUTH model (UGM): Cities, v. 26, no. 1, pp. 19–26.

References

Riitters, K. H., O'Neill, R. V., Hunsaker, C. T., Wickham, J. D., Yankee, D. H., Timmins, S. P., Jones, K. B., and Jackson, B. L., 1995, A factor analysis of landscape pattern and structure metrics: Landscape Ecology, v. 10, no. 1, pp. 23–39.

Rogan, J., and Chen, D., 2004, Remote sensing technology for mapping and monitoring land-cover and land-use change: Progress in Planning, v. 61, no. 4, pp. 301–325.

Roy, P. S., and Tomar, S., 2001, Landscape cover dynamics pattern in Meghalaya: International Journal of Remote Sensing, v. 22, no. 18, pp. 3813–3825.

Rykiel, E. J., 1996, Testing ecological models: The meaning of validation: Ecological Modelling, v. 90, no. 3, pp. 229–244.

Sala, O. E., Stuart Chapin, F. III, Armesto, J. J., Berlow, E., Bloomfield, J., Dirzo, R., Huber-Sanwald, E., Huenneke, L. F., Jackson, R. B., Kinzig, A., Leemans, R., Lodge, D. M., Mooney, H. A., Oesterheld, M. n., Poff, N. L., Sykes, M. T., Walker, B. H., Walker, M., and Wall, D. H., 2000, Global biodiversity scenarios for the year 2100: Science, v. 287, no. 5459, pp. 1770–1774.

Schott, J. R., Salvaggio, C., and Volchok, W. J., 1988, Radiometric scene normalization using pseudoinvariant features: Remote Sensing of Environment, v. 26, no. 1, pp. 1–14, IN11, 15–16.

Shalaby, A., and Tateishi, R., 2007, Remote sensing and GIS for mapping and monitoring land cover and land-use changes in the Northwestern coastal zone of Egypt: Applied Geography, v. 27, no. 1, pp. 28–41.

Shao, J. Y., Wang, K., Xiao, X. H., and Zhao, X. M., 2006, A study on prediction methods for urban construction land: Acta Agriculture Universitis Jiangxiensis, v. 28, no. 3, pp. 472–476.

Silva, E., and Wu, N., 2012, Surveying models in urban land studies: Journal of Planning Literature, v. 27, no. 2, pp. 139–152.

Sloke, D. I., 1994, Data on global land cover change: aquisition, assessment and analysis, in Meyer, W. B., and Turner II, B. L., eds., Changes in Land Use and Land Cover: A Global Perspective, Cambridge: Cambridge University Press, pp. 437–471.

References

Song, Conghe, Woodcock, Curtis E., Seto, Karen C., Lenney, Mary Pax, and Macomber, S. A., 2001, Classification and change detection using Landsat tm data when and how to correct atmospheric effects?: Remote Sensing of Environment, v. 75, pp. 230–244.

Stefanov, W. L., Ramsey, M. S., and Christensen, P. R., 2001, Monitoring urban land cover change: An expert system approach to land cover classification of semiarid to arid urban centers: Remote Sensing of Environment, v. 77, no. 2, pp. 173–185.

Thang, L. A., 2009, Studying and assessing the natural resources of Da Nang region for suitable development [Master Thesis: Vietnam National University, University of science], p. 106.

The Statistics Department, 2005, Danang city—30 years construction and development, *in* Statistics, ed., Danang City.

Tolba, M. K., and El-Kholy, O. A., 1992, The World Environment 1972–1992: Two Decades of Challenge, Chapman & Hall, London.

Treitz, P., and Rogan, J., 2004, Remote sensing for mapping and monitoring land-cover and land-use change--an introduction: Progress in Planning, v. 61, no. 4, pp. 269–279.

Treitz, P. M., Howard, P. J., and Gong, P., 1992, Application of satellite and GIS technologies for land-cover and land-use mapping at the rural-urban fringe: A case study: Photogrammetric Engineering and Remote Sensing, v. 58, pp. 439–448.

Turner, B. L., 1994, Local faces, global flows: The role of land use and land cover in global environmental change: Land Degradation and Development, v. 5, no. 2, pp. 71–78.

Turner, B. L. I., Sloke, D., Sanderson, S., Fisher, G., Freso, L., and Leemans, R., 1995, Land use and land cover change, IGBP Report, v. 35, HDP Report, v. 7. Stockholm and Geneva, IGBP and HDP.

Turner, M. G., 1989, Landscape ecology: The effect of pattern on process: Annual Review of Ecology and Systematics, v. 20, no. 1, pp. 171–197.

Turner, M. G., Gardner, R. H., and O'Neill, R. V., 2001, Landscape Ecology in Theory and Practice: Pattern and Process, Springer, New York, p. 401.

References

UN, 2008, State of the World's Cities 2008/2009: Harmonious Cities, United Nations Human Settlements Programme, Nairobi, Kenya.

USGS, 2009, News archive: change in status alert for the ASTER SWIR detector. Accessed on 26/03/2011 https://lpdaac.usgs.gov/about/news_archive/wednesday_july_01_2009.

Van Loi, N., 2008, Use of GIS modelling in assessment of forestry land's potential in Thua Thien Hue province of central Vietnam [PhD thesis: Georg-August Goettingen University], p. 220.

van Vliet, J., Bregt, A. K., and Hagen-Zanker, A., 2011, Revisiting Kappa to account for change in the accuracy assessment of land-use change models: Ecological Modelling, v. 222, no. 8, pp. 1367–1375.

Veldkamp, A., and Fresco, L. O., 1996, CLUE-CR: an integrated multi-scale model to simulate land use change scenarios in Costa Rica: Ecological Modelling, v. 91, pp. 231–248.

Veldkamp A, L. F. F., 2001, Editorial: predicting land use change: Agriculture, Ecosystems and Environment, v. 85, pp. 1–6.

Verburg, P., 2010, The Clue modeling framework. Accessed on 18/10/2012 http://www.ivm.vu.nl/en/Images/Exercises_tcm53-284019.pdf.

Verburg, P., and Overmars, K., 2009, Combining top-down and bottom-up dynamics in land use modeling: exploring the future of abandoned farmlands in Europe with the Dyna-CLUE model: Landscape Ecology, v. 24, no. 9, pp. 1167–1181.

Verburg, P., Schot, P., Dijst, M., and Veldkamp, A., 2004, Land use change modelling: current practice and research priorities: GeoJournal, v. 61, no. 4, pp. 309–324.

Verburg, P., Tom Veldkamp, and Lesschen, J. P., 2008, Exercises for the CLUE-S model. Accessed on 18/09/2012 http://www.feweb.vu.nl/gis/ModellingLand-UseChange/ExerciseClues.pdf.

Verburg, P., Van de Steeg, J., and Schulp, N., 2005, Manual for the CLUE-Kenya application. Accessed on 27/02/2013 http://www.trajectories.org/download/CLUE_manual.pdf

Verburg, P., and Veldkamp, A., 2004, Projecting land use transitions at forest fringes in the Philippines at two spatial scales: Landscape Ecology, v. 19, no. 1, pp. 77–98.

References

Verburg, P. H., Chen, Y., and Veldkamp, T., 2000, Spatial explorations of land use change and grain production in China: Agriculture, Ecosystems & Environment, v. 82, no. 1–3, pp. 333–354.

Verburg, P. H., de Koning, G. H. J., Kok, K., Veldkamp, A., and Bouma, J., 1999, A spatial explicit allocation procedure for modelling the pattern of land use change based upon actual land use: Ecological Modelling, v. 116, no. 1, pp. 45–61.

Verburg, P. H., and Overmars, K. P., 2007, Dynamic simulation of land-use change trajectories with the CLUE-S model, *in* Koomen, E., Stillwell, J., Bakema, A., and Scholten, H. J., eds., Modelling Land-use Change, Springer, pp. 321–355.

Verburg, P. H., Soepboer, W., Veldkamp, A., Limpiada, R., Espaldon, V., and Mastura, S. S. A., 2002, Modeling the spatial dynamics of regional land use: The CLUE-S model: Environmental Management, v. 30, no. 3, pp. 391–405.

Vietnam Laws, 2003, Law on Land: Vietnam Laws Home Page, www.vietnamlaws.com/freelaws/Lw13na26Nov03Land[X2865].pdf.

Visser, H., and de Nijs, T., 2006, The map comparison kit: Environmental Modelling & Software, v. 21, no. 3, pp. 346–358.

Vitousek, P. M., Mooney, H. A., Lubchenco, J., and Melillo, J. M., 1997, Human Domination of Earth's Ecosystems: Science, v. 277, no. 5325, pp. 494–499.

Wang, H., Li, X., Long, H., Qiao, Y., and Li, Y., 2011, Development and application of a simulation model for changes in land-use patterns under drought scenarios: Computers & Geosciences, v. 37, no. 7, pp. 831–843.

Weng, Q., 2002, Land use change analysis in the Zhujiang Delta of China using satellite remote sensing, GIS and stochastic modelling: Journal of Environmental Management, v. 64, no. 3, pp. 273–284.

Weng, Q., 2010, Remote sensing and GIS integration: Theories, methods and applications, The McGraw-Hill Companies, Inc., p. 383.

Wilbanks, T. J., and Kates, R. W., 1999, Global change in local places: How scale matters: Climate Change, v. 43, pp. 601–628.

References

Wilkinson, G. G., 1996, A review of current issues in the integration of GIS and remote sensing data: International Journal of Geographical Information Systems, v. 10, no. 1, pp. 85–101.

Wilson, E. H., Hurd, J. D., Civco, D. L., Prisloe, M. P., and Arnold, C., 2003, Development of a geospatial model to quantify, describe and map urban growth: Remote Sensing of Environment, v. 86, no. 3, pp. 275–285.

Wu, J., Jelinski, D. E., Luck, M., and Tueller, P. T., 2000, Multiscale Analysis of Landscape Heterogeneity: Scale Variance and Pattern Metrics: Geographic Information Sciences, v. 6, no. 1, pp. 6–19.

Wu, Q., Li, H.-Q., Wang, R.-S., Paulussen, J., He, Y., Wang, M., Wang, B.-H., and Wang, Z., 2006, Monitoring and predicting land use change in Beijing using remote sensing and GIS: Landscape and Urban Planning, v. 78, no. 4, pp. 322–333.

Xiao, J., Shen, Y., Ge, J., Tateishi, R., Tang, C., Liang, Y., and Huang, Z., 2006, Evaluating urban expansion and land use change in Shijiazhuang, China, by using GIS and remote sensing: Landscape and Urban Planning, v. 75, no. 1–2, pp. 69–80.

Xinping, Ye, 2008, Characterizing the Spatial Distribution of Giant Pandas in China using MODIS data and landscape metrics. Accessed on 21/02/2013 http://www.itc.nl/library/papers_2008/msc/gem/xingpingye.pdf [Msc thesis], p. 54.

Yang, Long-fei, Zhao, Qiao-gui, and Yang, Zi-sheng, 2010, Prediction on the farmland demand of Yunnan province in 2020 based on food security: Asian Agriculture Research, v. 2, no. 3, pp. 58–61.

Yang, X., and Lo, C. P., 2002, Using a time series of satellite imagery to detect land use and land cover changes in the Atlanta, Georgia metropolitan area: International Journal of Remote Sensing, v. 23, no. 9, pp. 1775–1798.

Yuan, D., and Elvidge, C. D., 1996, Comparison of relative radiometric normalization techniques: ISPRS Journal of Photogrammetry and Remote Sensing, v. 51, no. 3, pp. 117–126.

Zhan, Q., 2003, A hierarchical object-based approach for urban land-use classification from Remote sensing data [PhD Thesis PhD Thesis]: Wageningen University.

References

Zheng, X.-Q., Zhao, L., Xiang, W.-N., Li, N., Lv, L.-N., and Yang, X., 2012, A coupled model for simulating spatio-temporal dynamics of land-use change: A case study in Changqing, Jinan, China: Landscape and Urban Planning, v. 106, no. 1, pp. 51–61.

Appendices

Appendix 1
Accuracy assessment error matrices

LULC 1979

Sample Matrix

Population count	6		Reference or Time2	Reference or Time2	Reference or Time2	Reference or Time2	Reference or Time2	Reference or Time2
			Agri_79	Barren_79	built-up_79	Forest_79	Shrub_79	Water_79
37	Comparison or Time1	Agri_79	17	1	0	12	2	0
14	Comparison or Time1	Barren_79	5	7	4	1	3	0
20	Comparison or Time1	built-up_79	1	0	15	5	1	1
192	Comparison or Time1	Forest_79	5	5	0	165	3	0
30	Comparison or Time1	Shrub_79	9	1	1	9	19	0
7	Comparison or Time1	Water_79	0	0	0	0	2	6

185

Appendices

300		37	14	20	192	30	7
Reference or Time2	Total						
Reference or Time2	Proportion	0.12	0.05	0.07	0.64	0.10	0.02
Minimum1	Proportion	0.12	0.05	0.07	0.25	0.10	0.02
Minimum2	Proportion	0.11	0.05	0.07	0.59	0.10	0.02
Product	Proportion	0.01	0.00	0.01	0.38	0.01	0.00
	Omission or gain intensity	0.54	0.50	0.25	0.14	0.37	0.14
Allocation Information	Perfect	0.61	0.94	1.00			
Allocation Information	Medium	0.49	0.76	0.81			
Allocation Information	No	0.25	0.41	0.44			
		No Quantity information	Medium Quantity information	Perfect Quantity information			
	K_{no}	0.68					
	$K_{allocation}$	0.67					
	$K_{quantity}$	0.84					
	K_{histo}	0.89					
	$K_{standard}$	0.60					
	Chance agreement	25					
	Quantity agreement	16					
	Allocation agreement	35					
	Allocation disagreement	17					
	Quantity disagreement	6					
	Pierce skill score for Boolean case	0.65					
	Figure of merit for Boolean case	0.74					

Source: Author's calculation

Components

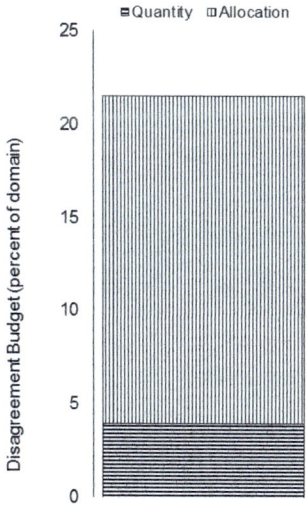

Agreement–Disagreement

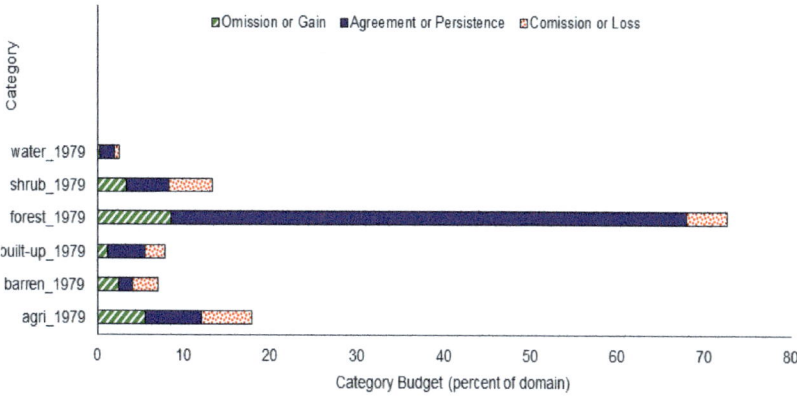

Intensity

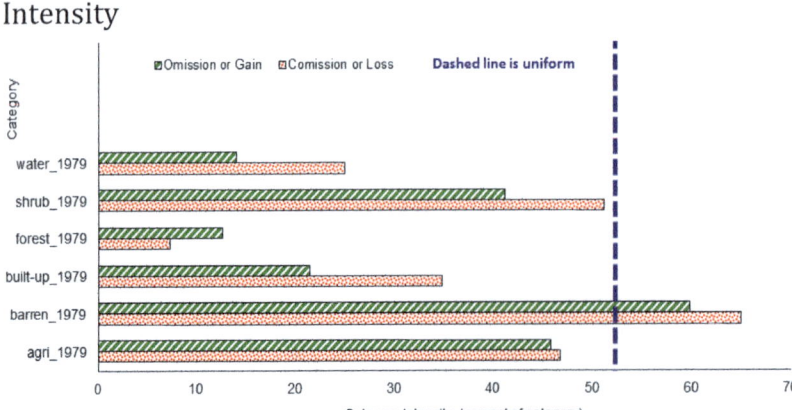

Source: Author's calculation

Appendices

LULC 1996

Sample Matrix

Population count		Reference or Time2 agri_96	Reference or Time2 barren_96	Reference or Time2 built-up_96	Reference or Time2 forest_96	Reference or Time2 shrub_96	Reference or Time2 water_96
32	Comparison or Time1 agri_96	15	0	1	16	0	0
11	Comparison or Time1 barren_96	0	8	1	2	0	0
24	Comparison or Time1 built-up_96	2	0	18	2	0	2
180	Comparison or Time1 forest_96	1	0	9	169	0	1
44	Comparison or Time1 shrub_96	5	1	14	0	24	0
9	Comparison or Time1 water_96	1	0	0	0	0	7
300	Reference or Time2 Total	24	9	43	189	24	10
	Reference or Time2 Proportion	0.08	0.03	0.14	0.63	0.08	0.03
	Minimum1 Proportion	0.08	0.03	0.14	0.17	0.08	0.03
	Minimum2 Proportion	0.08	0.03	0.08	0.60	0.08	0.03
	Product Proportion	0.01	0.00	0.01	0.38	0.01	0.00
	Omission or gain intensity	0.38	0.11	0.58	0.11	0.00	0.30
	Allocation Information Perfect	0.53	0.90	1.00			
	Allocation Information Medium	0.46	0.81	0.89			
	Allocation Information No	0.17	0.41	0.44			

Appendices

Information	No Quantity information	Medium Quantity information	Perfect Quantity information
K_{no}	0.77		
$K_{allocation}$	0.81		
$K_{quantity}$	0.80		
K_{histo}	0.83		
$K_{standard}$	0.67		
Chance agreement	17		
Quantity agreement	25		
Allocation agreement	39		
Quantity disagreement	9		
Pierce skill score for Boolean case	10		
Figure of merit for Boolean case	1.00		
	1.00		

Source: Author's calculation

Components

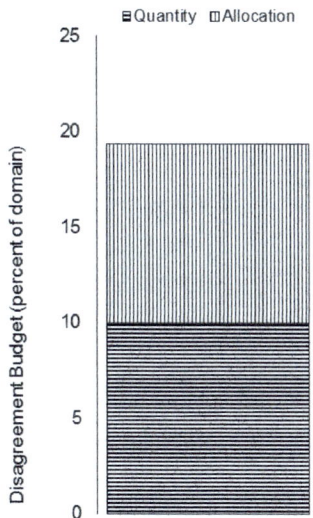

Agreement–Disagreement

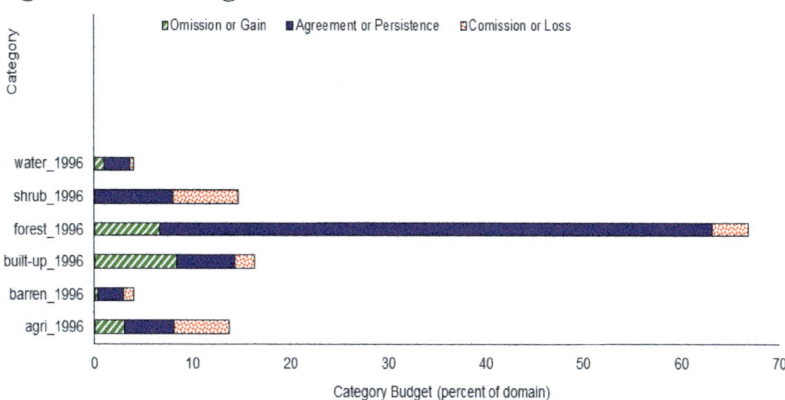

Intensity

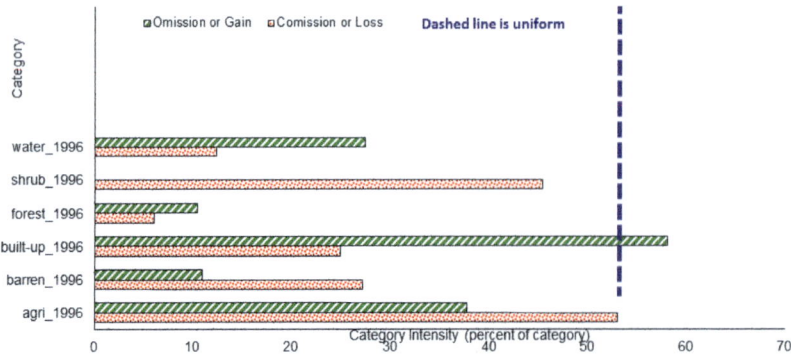

Source: Author's calculation

Appendices

LULC 2003

Sample Matrix

Population count	6		Reference or Time2 agri_03	Reference or Time2 barren_03	Reference or Time2 built-up_03	Reference or Time2 forest_03	Reference or Time2 shrub_03	Reference or Time2 water_03
29	Comparison or Time1	agri_03	21	3	1	4	0	0
5	Comparison or Time1	barren_03	2	3	0	0	0	0
34	Comparison or Time1	built-up_03	9	0	25	0	0	0
187	Comparison or Time1	forest_03	7	8	1	171	0	0
35	Comparison or Time1	shrub_03	7	0	0	0	26	2
10	Comparison or Time1	water_03	0	1	1	1	0	7
300	Reference or Time2	Total	46	15	28	176	26	9
	Reference or Time2	Proportion	0.15	0.05	0.09	0.59	0.09	0.03
	Minimum1	Proportion	0.15	0.05	0.09	0.25	0.09	0.03
	Minimum2	Proportion	0.10	0.02	0.09	0.59	0.09	0.03
	Product	Proportion	0.01	0.00	0.01	0.37	0.01	0.00
		Omission or gain intensity	0.54	0.80	0.11	0.03	0.00	0.22
	Allocation Information	Perfect	0.66	0.91	1.00			
	Allocation Information	Medium	0.61	0.84	0.92			

Appendices

Allocation Information	No Quantity information	0.40 Medium Quantity information	0.39 Perfect Quantity information
	0.25		
K_{no}	0.79		
$K_{allocation}$	0.87		
$K_{quantity}$	0.75		
K_{histo}	0.85		
$K_{standard}$	0.74		
Chance agreement	25		
Quantity agreement	15		
Allocation agreement	44		
Allocation disagreement	7		
Quantity disagreement	9		
Pierce skill score for Boolean case	0.41		
Figure of merit for Boolean case	0.81		

Source: Author

Components

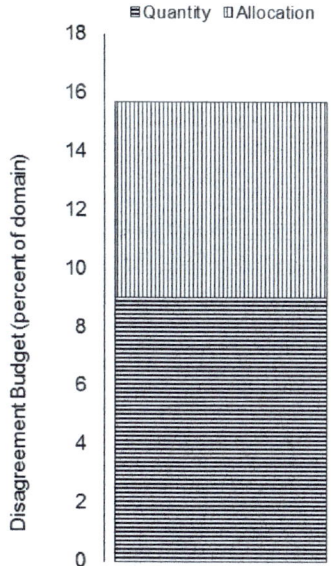

Agreement–Disagreement

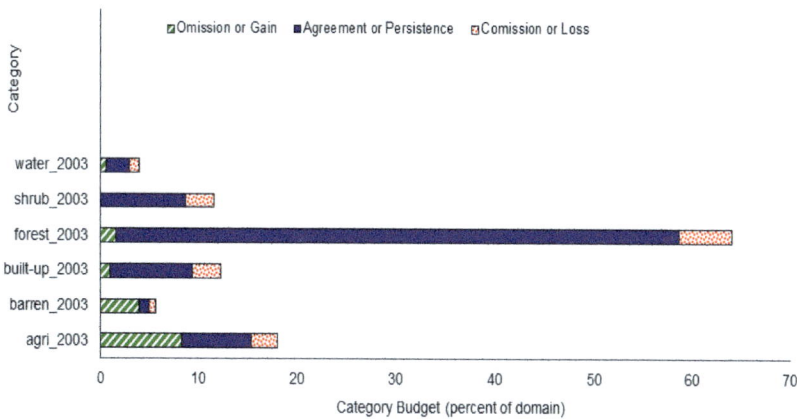

Intensity

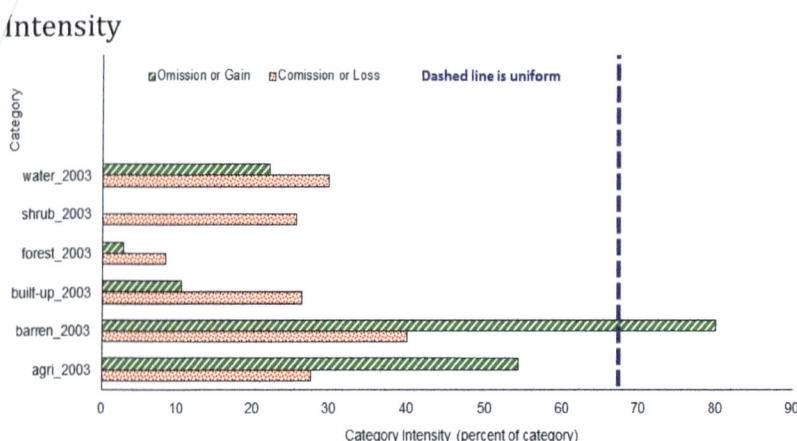

Source: Author

Appendices

LULC 2009

Sample Matrix

Population count	6		Reference or Time2 agri_09	Reference or Time2 barren_09	Reference or Time2 built-up_09	Reference or Time2 forest_09	Reference or Time2 shrub_09	Reference or Time2 water_2009
23	Comparison or Time1	agri_09	14	0	1	8	0	0
5	Comparison or Time1	barren_09	1	4	0	0	0	0
54	Comparison or Time1	built-up_09	4	0	47	2	0	1
179	Comparison or Time1	forest_09	2	0	1	174	0	2
30	Comparison or Time1	shrub_09	6	0	3	0	21	0
9	Comparison or Time1	water_09	0	0	2	0	0	7
300	Reference or Time2	Total	27	4	54	184	21	10
	Reference or Time2	Proportion	0.09	0.01	0.18	0.61	0.07	0.03
		Minimum1 Proportion	0.09	0.01	0.17	0.17	0.07	0.03
		Minimum2 Proportion	0.08	0.01	0.18	0.60	0.07	0.03
		Product Proportion	0.01	0.00	0.03	0.37	0.01	0.00
		Omission or gain intensity	0.48	0.00	0.13	0.05	0.00	0.30
		Allocation Information Perfect	0.54	0.97	1.00			
		Allocation Information Medium	0.49	0.89	0.92			

Appendices

Allocation Information	No Quantity information	0.41 Medium Quantity information	0.42 Perfect Quantity information
No	0.17		
K_{no}	0.87		
$K_{allocation}$	0.86		
$K_{quantity}$	0.93		
K_{histo}	0.94		
$K_{standard}$	0.81		
Chance agreement	17		
Quantity agreement	25		
Allocation agreement	48		
Quantity disagreement	8		
Pierce skill score for Boolean case	3		
Figure of merit for Boolean case	0.93		
	0.93		

Source: Author

Components

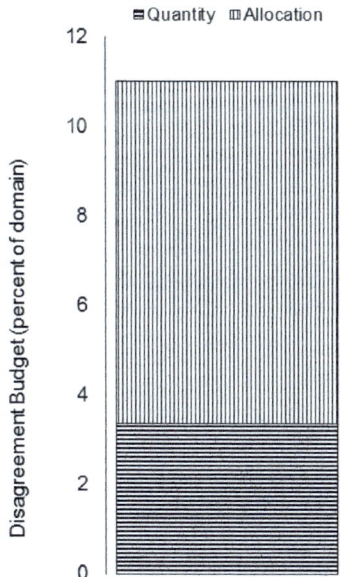

Agreement–Disagreement

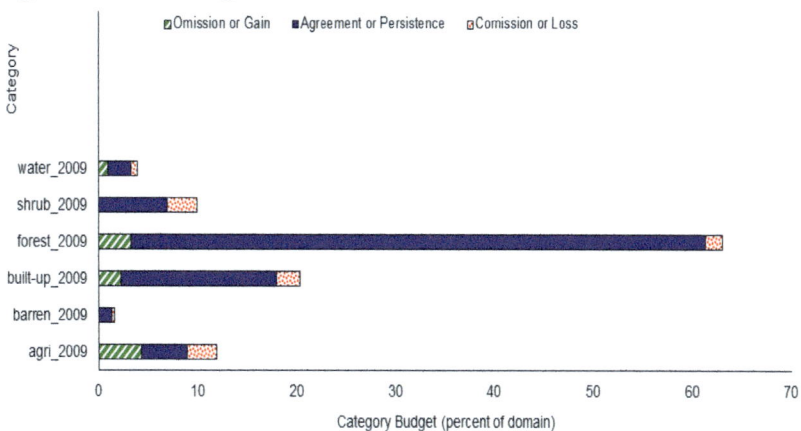

Intensity

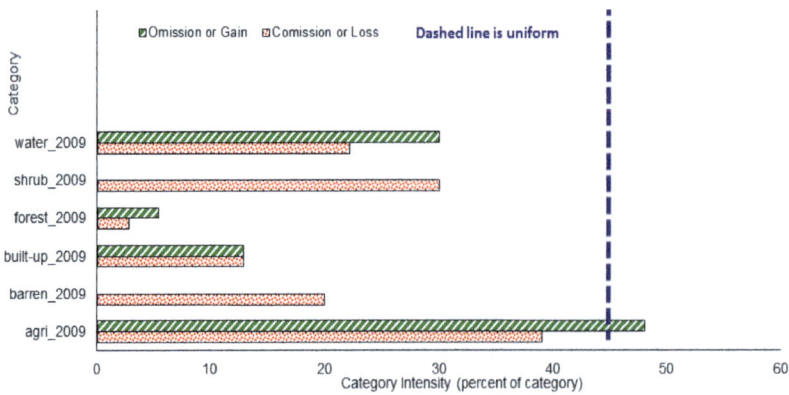

Source: Author

Appendix 2
Scenarios of land-use/cover types from 1996 to 2030

Year	Agriculture	Barren	Urban	Forest	Shrub	Water
1996	10,416.69	3,680.91	7,791.48	58,127.13	14,253.21	2,548.26
1997	10,016.5	3,592.7	8,387.11	58,318.4	13,927.5	2,575.47
1998	9,643.6	3,483.79	8,956.09	58,509.6	13,621.8	2,602.8
1999	9,296.48	3,362.66	9,491.52	58,700.8	13,335.3	26,30.92
2000	8,973.66	3,226.05	9,998.91	58,892.1	13,067.1	2,659.86
2001	8,673.75	2,989.03	10,565.59	59,083.3	12,816.4	2,689.61
2002	8,395.47	2,641.51	11,203.31	59,274.6	12,582.6	2,720.19
2003	8,118.04	24,97.3	11,630	59,467.3	12,322.9	2,782.14
2004	7,932.48	2,377.14	12,843.38	59,205.7	11,644.4	2,814.58
2005	7,767.48	2,275.5	13,911.62	58,945.3	11,069	2,848.78
2006	7,621.99	2,199.49	14,841.04	58,686	10,584.4	2,884.76
2007	7,495.09	2,043.68	15,748.54	58,427.8	10,180	2,922.57
2008	7,385.89	1,823.01	16,629.49	58,170.8	9,846.26	2,962.23
2009	7,293.57	1,733.46	17,296.7	57,914.9	9,575.26	3,003.79
2010	7,054.52	1,959.5	17,934.5	57,647.27	9,218.1	3,003.79
2011	6,903.43	1,582.59	18,921.6	57,426.1	8,980.17	3,003.79
2012	6,740.37	839.22	20,305.8	57,172.6	8,755.9	3,003.79
2013	6,597.62	0	21,722.78	56,920.2	8,573.29	3,003.79
2014	6,474.22	0	22,243.05	56,668.9	8,427.72	3,003.79
2015	6,369.27	0	22,710.9	56,418.6	8,315.12	3,003.79
2016	6,281.93	0	23,130.5	56,169.5	8,231.96	3,003.79
2017	6,211.43	0	23,505.89	55,921.4	8,175.17	3,003.79
2018	6,157.04	0	23,840.36	55,674.4	8,142.09	3,003.79
2019	6,118.1	0	24,129.4	55,428.4	8,137.99	3,003.79
2020	6,094.01	0	24,406.01	55,183.5	8,130.37	3,003.79
2021	5,759.51	0	25,437.79	54,927.8	7,688.79	3,003.79

Year	Agriculture	Barren	Urban	Forest	Shrub	Water
2022	5,458.89	0	26,362.16	54,673.3	7,319.54	3,003.79
2023	5,190.43	0	27,189.34	54,419.8	7,014.32	3,003.79
2024	4,952.51	0	27,928.13	54,167.4	6,765.85	3,003.79
2025	4,743.64	0	28,586.34	53,916.1	6,567.81	3,003.79
2026	4,562.44	0	29,170.97	53,665.8	6,414.68	3,003.79
2027	4,407.59	0	29,687.94	53,416.7	6,301.66	3,003.79
2028	4,277.91	0	30,142.82	53,168.6	6,224.56	3,003.79
2029	4,172.26	0	30,540.3	52,921.6	6,179.73	3,003.79
2030	4,089.62	0	30,884.66	52,675.6	6,164.01	3,003.79

Table A2.1 Demand of land-use/cover types in scenario 1
Source: Author's calculation

Year	Agriculture	Barren	Urban	Forest	Shrub	Water
1996	10,416.69	3,680.91	7,791.48	58,127.13	14,253.21	2,548.26
1997	10,016.5	3,592.7	8,387.11	58,318.4	13,927.5	2,575.47
1998	9,643.6	3,483.79	8,956.09	58,509.6	13,621.8	2,602.8
1999	9,296.48	3,362.66	9,491.52	58,700.8	13,335.3	2,630.92
2000	8,973.66	3,226.05	9,998.91	58,892.1	13,067.1	2,659.86
2001	8,673.75	2,989.03	10,565.59	59,083.3	12,816.4	2,689.61
2002	8,395.47	2,641.51	11,203.31	59,274.6	12,582.6	2,720.19
2003	8,118.04	2,497.3	11,630	59,467.3	12,322.9	2,782.14
2004	7,932.48	2,377.14	12,843.38	59,205.7	11,644.4	2,814.58
2005	7,767.48	2,275.5	13,911.62	58,945.3	11,069	2,848.78
2006	7,621.99	2,199.49	14,841.04	58,686	10,584.4	2,884.76
2007	7,495.09	2,043.68	15,748.54	58,427.8	10,180	2,922.57
2008	7,385.89	1,823.01	16,629.49	58,170.8	9,846.26	2,962.23
2009	7,293.57	1,733.46	17,296.7	57,914.9	9,575.26	3,003.79
2010	6,826.37	1,538.11	18,582.8	57,686.9	9,179.71	3,003.79
2011	6,436.61	1,384.27	19,705.1	57,438.8	8,849.11	3,003.79
2012	6,116.92	1,245.91	20,682.6	57,191.8	8,576.66	3,003.79
2013	5,859.01	1,121.28	21,531.6	56,945.9	8,356.1	3,003.79
2014	5,655.71	1,009.17	22,266	56,701	8,182.01	3,003.79
2015	5,500.82	908.19	22,898	56,457.2	8,049.68	3,003.79
2016	5,388.95	817.34	23,438.1	56,214.5	7,955	3,003.79

2017	5,315.46	735.72	23,895.6	55,972.7	7,894.41	3,003.79
2018	5,276.35	662	24,278.6	55,732.1	7,864.84	3,003.79
2019	5,268.15	595.92	24,593.8	55,492.4	7,863.62	3,003.79
2020	5,287.91	536.3	24,847.4	55,253.8	7,888.48	3,003.79
2021	4,405.16	365.4	26,735.64	55,004.7	7,302.99	3,003.79
2022	3,664.49	211.59	28,367.2	54,756.6	6,814.01	3,003.79
2023	3,048.67	73.16	29,771.28	54,509.6	6,411.18	3,003.79
2024	2,542.73	0	30,922.45	54,263.7	6,085.01	3,003.79
2025	2,133.65	0	31,833.87	54,018.8	5,827.57	3,003.79
2026	1,810.17	0	32,596.85	53,775	5,631.87	3,003.79
2027	1,562.53	0	33,227.21	53,532.3	5,491.85	3,003.79
2028	1,382.27	0	33,738.87	53,290.5	5,402.25	3,003.79
2029	1,262.1	0	34,143.37	53,049.9	5,358.52	3,003.79
2030	1,195.72	0	34,451.24	52,810.2	5,356.73	3,003.79

Table A2.2 Demand of land-use/cover types in scenario 2
Source: Author's calculation

Year	Agriculture	Barren	Urban	Forest	Shrub	Water
1996	10,416.69	3,680.91	7,791.48	58,127.13	14,253.21	2,548.26
1997	10,016.5	3,592.7	8,387.11	58,318.4	13,927.5	2,575.47
1998	9,643.6	3,483.79	8,956.09	58,509.6	13,621.8	2,602.8
1999	9,296.48	3,362.66	9,491.52	58,700.8	13,335.3	2,630.92
2000	8,973.66	3,226.05	9,998.91	58,892.1	13,067.1	2,659.86
2001	8,673.75	2,989.03	10,565.59	59,083.3	12,816.4	2,689.61
2002	8,395.47	2,641.51	11,203.31	59,274.6	12,582.6	2,720.19
2003	8,118.04	2,497.3	11,630	59,467.3	12,322.9	2,782.14
2004	7,932.48	2,377.14	12,843.38	59,205.7	11,644.4	2,814.58
2005	7,767.48	2,275.49	13,911.62	58,945.3	11,069	2,848.78
2006	7,621.99	2,199.48	14,841.04	58,686	10,584.4	2,884.76
2007	7,495.09	2,043.67	15,748.54	58,427.8	10,180	2,922.57
2008	7,385.89	1,823.01	16,629.49	58,170.8	9,846.26	2,962.23
2009	7,293.57	1,733.46	17,296.7	57,914.9	9,575.26	3,003.79
2010	7,161.46	1,538	18,087.4	57,936.2	9,090.83	3,003.79
2011	7,048.16	1,384.19	18,771.91	57,936.2	8,673.43	3,003.79

Year						
2012	6,952.82	1,245.76	19,363.38	57,936.2	8,315.73	3,003.79
2013	6,874.66	1,121.17	19,871.01	57,936.2	8,010.85	3,003.79
2014	6,812.94	1,009.04	20,302.93	57,936.2	7,752.78	3,003.79
2015	6,767	908.12	20,666.28	57,936.2	7,536.28	3,003.79
2016	6,736.22	817.3	20,967.43	57,936.2	7,356.74	3,003.79
2017	6,720.01	735.56	21,211.96	57,936.2	7,210.16	3,003.79
2018	6,703.87	661.99	21,418.81	57,936.2	7,093.02	3,003.79
2019	6,687.59	595.78	21,592.05	57,936.2	7,002.27	3,003.79
2020	6,671.99	536.19	21,734.28	57,936.2	6,935.23	3,003.79
2021	6,411.41	470.93	22,730.71	57,936.2	6,264.63	3,003.79
2022	6,181.66	412.1	23,596.45	57,936.2	5,687.47	3,003.79
2023	5,981.29	359.16	24,344.38	57,936.2	5,192.86	3,003.79
2024	5,808.91	311.5	24,985.98	57,936.2	4,771.29	3,003.79
2025	5,663.26	268.61	25,531.36	57,936.2	4,414.45	3,003.79
2026	5,543.17	230.02	25,989.43	57,936.2	4,115.07	3,003.79
2027	5,447.53	195.28	26,368.07	57,936.2	3,866.81	3,003.79
2028	5,375.35	164.01	26,674.2	57,936.2	3,664.12	3,003.79
2029	5,325.69	135.87	26,913.97	57,936.2	3,502.15	3,003.79
2030	5,297.7	110.55	27,092.77	57,936.2	3,376.67	3,003.79

Table A2.3 Demand of land-use/cover types in scenario 3
Source: Author's calculation

Appendix 3
Logistic regression of land-use/cover types

Value	Land-use/cover type	CLUE name
0	Agriculture	Cov1_0.0
1	Barren	Cov2_0.0
2	Urban	Cov3_0.0
3	Forest	Cov4_0.0
4	Shrub	Cov5_0.0
5	Water	Cov6_0.0

Table A3.1 Available land-use/cover types in logistic regression mode

Value	Driving factor	CLUE name
0	Urban rate	Sc1gr0.fil
1	Mean density of population	Sc1gr1.fil
2	Slope	Sc1gr2.fil
3	Elevation	Sc1gr3.fil
4	Distance to road	Sc1gr4.fil
5	Distance to urban	Sc1gr5.fil
6	Distance to water	Sc1gr6.fil

Table A3.2 Available driving factors in logistic regression mode

	B	S.E.	Wald	df	Sig.	Exp(B)
Step 1[a] sc1gr0.fil	-0.0149190854	0.001	513.110	1	0.000	0.985
sc1gr1.fil	0.0109944723	0.001	218.169	1	0.000	1.011
sc1gr2.fil	-0.0095273290	0.001	144.636	1	0.000	0.991
sc1gr3.fil	-0.0002644512	0.000	99.782	1	0.000	1.000
sc1gr4.fil	-0.0003383414	0.000	1,907.158	1	0.000	1.000
sc1gr5.fil	-0.0001319261	0.000	155.916	1	0.000	1.000
sc1gr6.fil	-0.0000494684	0.000	127.386	1	0.000	1.000
Constant	0.9438244201	0.012	6,038.416	1	0.000	2.570

[a]Variable(s) entered on step 1: sc1gr0.fil, sc1gr1.fil, sc1gr2.fil, sc1gr3.fil, sc1gr4.fil, sc1gr5.fil, sc1gr6.fil.

Table A3.3 Logistic regression for agriculture

	B	S.E.	Wald	df	Sig.	Exp(B)
Step 1a sc1gr0.fil	-0.0046540920	0.001	31.345	1	0.000	0.995
sc1gr1.fil	-0.0086689189	0.001	45.522	1	0.000	0.991
sc1gr2.fil	0.0055618135	0.001	36.023	1	0.000	1.006
sc1gr3.fil	-0.0004720580	0.000	189.136	1	0.000	1.000
sc1gr4.fil	-0.0001496706	0.000	193.121	1	0.000	1.000
sc1gr5.fil	-0.0008809770	0.000	2,507.818	1	0.000	0.999
sc1gr6.fil	-0.0000688887	0.000	124.537	1	0.000	1.000
Constant	1.0548256000	0.015	5,240.184	1	0.000	2.871

[a] Variable(s) entered on step 1: sc1gr0.fil, sc1gr1.fil, sc1gr2.fil, sc1gr3.fil, sc1gr4.fil, sc1gr5.fil, sc1gr6.fil.

Table A3.4 Logistic regression for barren

	B	S.E.	Wald	df	Sig.	Exp(B)
Step 1a sc1gr0.fil	0.0064498058	0.002	16.480	1	0.000	1.006
sc1gr1.fil	-0.0117015352	0.003	18.827	1	0.000	0.988
sc1gr2.fil	-0.0010296843	0.002	0.422	1	0.516	0.999
sc1gr3.fil	0.0003574733	0.000	35.477	1	0.000	1.000
sc1gr4.fil	-0.0002257239	0.000	66.420	1	0.000	1.000
sc1gr5.fil	-0.0292470249	0.000	12,556.409	1	0.000	0.971
sc1gr6.fil	0.0000518170	0.000	8.491	1	0.004	1.000
Constant	2.6309852354	0.029	8,045.194	1	0.000	13.887

[a] Variable(s) entered on step 1: sc1gr0.fil, sc1gr1.fil, sc1gr2.fil, sc1gr3.fil, sc1gr4.fil, sc1gr5.fil, sc1gr6.fil.

Table A3.5 Logistic regression for urban

	B	S.E.	Wald	df	Sig.	Exp(B)
Step 1a sc1gr0.fil	0.0198023206	0.001	553.806	1	0.000	1.020
sc1gr1.fil	-0.0148509094	0.001	225.312	1	0.000	0.985
sc1gr2.fil	0.0168966457	0.001	312.608	1	0.000	1.017
sc1gr3.fil	0.0003982220	0.000	132.819	1	0.000	1.000
sc1gr4.fil	0.0005154539	0.000	2,400.376	1	0.000	1.001
sc1gr5.fil	0.0011781218	0.000	4,849.269	1	0.000	1.001
sc1gr6.fil	0.0001809166	0.000	888.721	1	0.000	1.000
Constant	-2.4199720631	0.018	18,539.638	1	0.000	0.089

[a] Variable(s) entered on step 1: sc1gr0.fil, sc1gr1.fil, sc1gr2.fil, sc1gr3.fil, sc1gr4.fil, sc1gr5.fil, sc1gr6.fil.

Table A3.6 Logistic regression for forest

	B	S.E.	Wald	df	Sig.	Exp(B)
Step 1ª sc1gr0.fil	-0.0184782530	0.001	523.355	1	0.000	0.982
sc1gr1.fil	0.0209688198	0.001	528.641	1+	0.000	1.021
sc1gr2.fil	-0.0173097013	0.001	410.354	1	0.000	0.983
sc1gr3.fil	-0.0005373425	0.000	325.167	1	0.000	0.999
sc1gr4.fil	-0.0003007638	0.000	893.759	1	0.000	1.000
sc1gr5.fil	-0.0009743441	0.000	3,569.740	1	0.000	0.999
sc1gr6.fil	-0.0000489223	0.000	72.376	1	0.000	1.000
Constant	1.4100301112	0.014	10,456.760	1	0.000	4.096

ª *Variable(s) entered on step 1: sc1gr0.fil, sc1gr1.fil, sc1gr2.fil, sc1gr3.fil, sc1gr4.fil, sc1gr5.fil, sc1gr6.fil.*

Table A3.7 Logistic regression for shrub

	B	S.E.	Wald	df	Sig.	Exp(B)
Step 1ª sc1gr0.fil	-0.0063667786	0.004	2.123	1	0.145	0.994
sc1gr1.fil	-0.0094942927	0.006	2.555	1	0.110	0.991
sc1gr2.fil	0.0064991753	0.003	5.074	1	0.024	1.007
sc1gr3.fil	0.0004453436	0.000	20.077	1	0.000	1.000
sc1gr4.fil	-0.0000805535	0.000	6.308	1	0.012	1.000
sc1gr5.fil	0.0001696889	0.000	4.135	1	0.042	1.000
sc1gr6.fil	-0.0189878414	0.000	4,605.810	1	0.000	0.981
Constant	3.1866314025	0.045	4,923.557	1	0.000	24.207

ª *Variable(s) entered on step 1: sc1gr0.fil, sc1gr1.fil, sc1gr2.fil, sc1gr3.fil, sc1gr4.fil, sc1gr5.fil, sc1gr6.fil.*

Table A3.8 Logistic regression for water

Source: Author's calculation

Appendix 4
Area under the curve of land-use/cover types

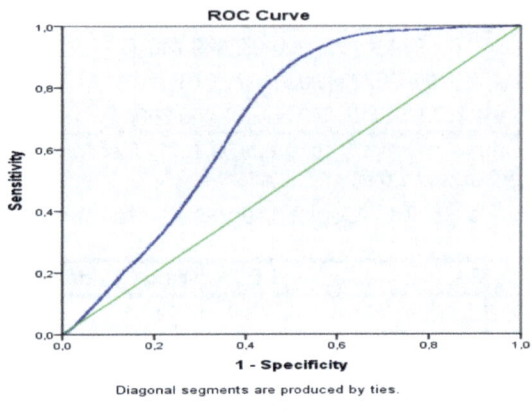

Agriculture

Area
0.697

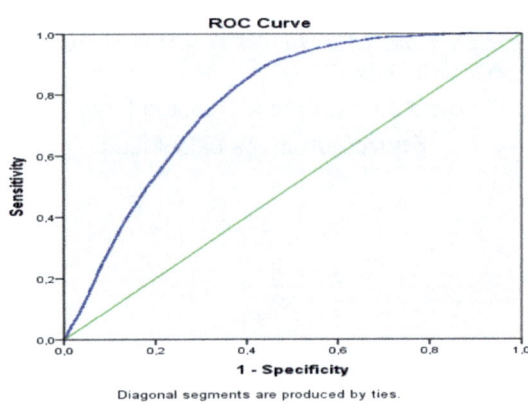

Barren

Area
0.780

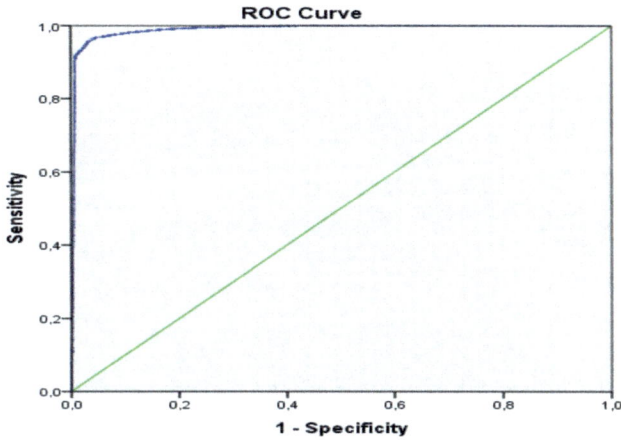

Urban

Area
0.990

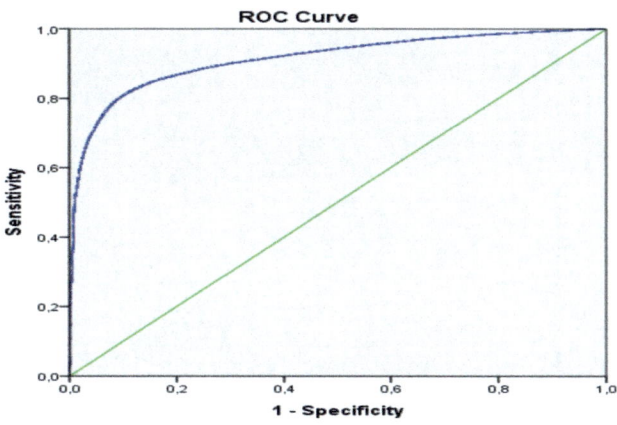

Forest

Area
0.913

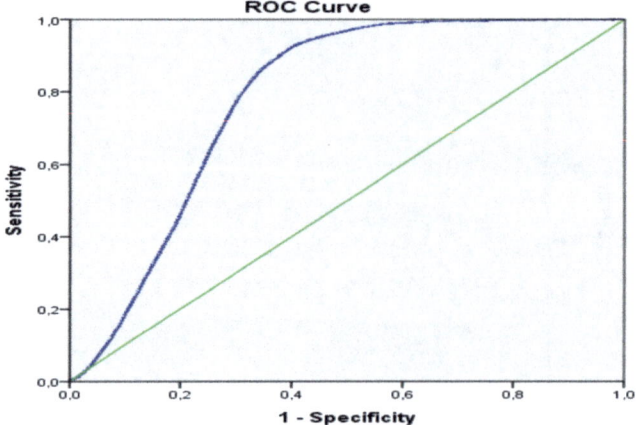

Shrub

Area
0.780

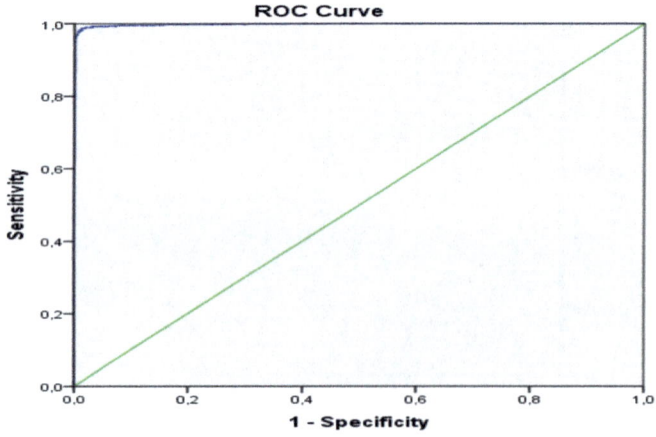

Water

Area
0.998

Source: Author's calculation

Appendix 5
Main parameters of Dyna-CLUE model

Line	Codes	Format	Description
1	6	Integer	Number of land-use/cover type. Maximum 12 different land-use types can be identified
2	1	Integer	Number of regions. Default is 1 and the maximum number of region is 3
3	7	Integer	Maximum number of independent variables in logistic regression equation. The model can handle 20 variables as maximum
4	7	Integer	Total number of driving factors. The model can handle 30 variables as maximum
5	1100	Integer	Number of rows of input grids
6	1800	Integer	Number of columns
7	0.09	Float	Cell area (ha) of the grid cells
8	803145	Float	X-coordinate of the lower left corner
9	1762185	Float	Y-coordinate of the lower left corner
10	0 1 2 3 4 5	Integer	Number coding of the land-use/cover type
11	0.4 0.2 1 0.9 0.6 1	Float	Code for conversion elasticity ranges between 0 and 1 0: all changes of land-use/cover type are allowed >0...<1: changes are allowed, however, the higher the value, the higher the preference given to location 1: grid cell under one land-use type can never be added and removed at the same time
12	0 0.35 3	Float	Iteration variables for output: Iteration mode. Options: 0 (convergence criteria are expressed as a percentage of the demand), 1 (convergence criteria are expressed as absolute values) First convergence criterion: average deviation between demanded changes and actually allocated changes (default for %: 0.35) Second convergence criterion: maximum deviation between demanded changes and actually allocated changes (default for %: 3)
13	1996 2030	Integer	Start and end year of simulation
14	0	Integer	Number and coding of explanatory factors that change every year
15	1	Integer	Output/input file choice 1: ArcView headers will be printed in output files; 0: No headers in output files (suited for, e.g., IDRISI)

Line	Codes	Format	Description
			−2: No headers in output files 2: ArcView—ArcGIS header will be printed in output files 3: ArcGIS/ArcMap extension
16	0	Integer	Choice for a region specific regression 0: No different regression for different regions 1: Different regression for different regions 2: Different regression with different demands
17	1 5	Integer	Initialization of land-use history 0: The initial land-use history will reach from file *age.0* 1: A random number will be assigned to all pixels to represent the number of years that current land-use type is already found at that location according to the standard seed for the random number generator 2: A random number will be assigned to all pixels to represent the number of years that current land-use type is already found at that location with a different random number generator For option 1 or 2 an additional number is added to indicate the maximum number of years that can be generated by the random (default: 5)
18	0	Integer	Choice for using the neighborhood function: 0: Neighborhood function is not used 1: Neighborhood function is used in simulation 2: Only the influences are calculated, the influence files are saved directly, no simulation
19	0	Integer	Variables for location-specific preference addition: 0: not activate the function 1: activate function
20	0.06	Float	Option iteration parameter. The parameter ranges between 0.001 and 0.1. With a somewhat higher value (e.g., 0.06) the iteration is more stable and more likely to find a solution. A lower value (e.g., 0.01) will give a faster convergence although instability is more likely

Source: According to Verburg et al. (2005)

Appendix 6
Main results obtained with ANOVA

A6.1 Landscape level

A6.1.1 Number of patches (NP)

Descriptives								
Value								
	N	Mean	Std. deviation	Std. error	95% Confidence interval for mean		Minimum	Maximum
					Lower bound	Upper bound		
1.00	22	27,035.50	4,059.21	865.42753	25,235.7449	28,835.2551	22,219.00	35,300.00
2.00	22	24,819.00	6,755.59	1,440.29595	21,823.7406	27,814.2594	15,533.00	35,300.00
3.00	22	28,256.36	4,391.18	936.20356	26,309.4218	30,203.3055	21,819.00	35,300.00
Total	66	26,703.62	5,324.77	655.43382	25,394.6295	28,012.6129	15,533.00	35,300.00

ANOVA					
Value					
	Sum of squares	df	Mean square	F	Sig.
Between groups	1.336E8	2	66,802,446.470	2.462	.093
Within groups	1.709E9	63	27,132,558.422		
Total	1.843E9	65			

A6.1.2 Patch density (PD)

Descriptives								
Value								
	N	Mean	Std. deviation	Std. error	95% confidence interval for mean		Minimum	Maximum
					Lower bound	Upper bound		
1.00	22	27.9241	4.19264	.89387	26.0652	29.7831	22.95	36.46
2.00	22	25.6348	6.97763	1.48764	22.5411	28.7285	16.04	36.46
3.00	22	29.1851	4.53552	.96698	27.1742	31.1961	22.54	36.46
Total	66	27.5813	5.49979	.67698	26.2293	28.9334	16.04	36.46

213

Appendices

ANOVA

Value					
	Sum of squares	df	Mean square	F	Sig.
Between groups	142.531	2	71.266	2.462	.093
Within groups	1,823.567	63	28.946		
Total	1,966.098	65			

A6.1.3 Mean proximity (PROX_MN)

Descriptives

Value								
					95% confidence interval for mean			
	N	Mean	Std. deviation	Std. error	Lower bound	Upper bound	Minimum	Maximum
1.00	22	2,996.5684	849.69193	181.15493	2,619.8361	3,373.3007	1,634.17	4,349.57
2.00	22	3,903.4050	2,159.67138	460.44348	2,945.8603	4,860.9496	1,650.94	7,562.04
3.00	22	2,397.6292	621.24526	132.44993	2,122.1845	2,673.0739	1,650.94	3,419.89
Total	66	3,099.2009	1,501.29545	184.79670	2,730.1364	3,468.2653	1,634.17	7,562.04

ANOVA

Value					
	Sum of squares	df	Mean square	F	Sig.
Between groups	25,288,570.038	2	12,644,285.019	6.572	.003
Within groups	1.212E8	63	1,924,034.170		
Total	1.465E8	65			

A6.1.4 Mean area (AREA_MN)

Descriptives

Value								
					95% confidence interval for mean			
	N	Mean	Std. deviation	Std. error	Lower bound	Upper bound	Minimum	Maximum
1.00	22	3.6543	.51643	.11010	3.4254	3.8833	2.74	4.36
2.00	22	4.2291	1.28272	.27348	3.6604	4.7978	2.74	6.23
3.00	22	3.5099	.56686	.12085	3.2586	3.7612	2.74	4.44
Total	66	3.7978	.90529	.11143	3.5752	4.0203	2.74	6.23

Appendices

ANOVA

Value					
	Sum of squares	df	Mean square	F	Sig.
Between groups	6.369	2	3.185	4.278	.018
Within groups	46.901	63	0.744		
Total	53.271	65			

A6.1.5 Interspersion and juxtaposition (IJI)

Descriptives

Value								
					95% confidence interval for mean			
	N	Mean	Std. deviation	Std. error	Lower bound	Upper bound	Minimum	Maximum
1.00	22	77.5856	3.87455	.82606	75.8677	79.3035	69.84	82.18
2.00	22	71.5428	7.64642	1.63022	68.1525	74.9330	57.93	80.95
3.00	22	76.2220	3.47201	.74024	74.6826	77.7614	69.86	80.95
Total	66	75.1168	5.86806	.72231	73.6742	76.5593	57.93	82.18

ANOVA

Value					
	Sum of squares	df	Mean square	F	Sig.
Between groups	441.986	2	220.993	7.751	.001
Within groups	1,796.231	63	28.512		
Total	2,238.217	65			

A6.1.6 Largest patch index (LPI)

Descriptives

Value								
					95% confidence interval for mean			
	N	Mean	Std. deviation	Std. error	Lower bound	Upper bound	Minimum	Maximum
1.00	22	51.3747	0.60625	0.12925	51.1059	51.6435	50.07	52.03
2.00	22	51.4215	0.56660	0.12080	51.1703	51.6727	50.20	52.03
3.00	22	52.0439	0.01637	0.00349	52.0366	52.0511	52.03	52.06
Total	66	51.6134	0.56304	0.06931	51.4750	51.7518	50.07	52.06

ANOVA

Value					
	Sum of squares	df	Mean square	F	Sig.
Between groups	6.141	2	3.070	13.372	0.000
Within groups	14.466	63	.230		
Total	20.606	65			

A6.1.7 Largest shape index (LSI)

Descriptives

Value								
	N	Mean	Std. deviation	Std. error	95% confidence interval for mean		Minimum	Maximum
					Lower bound	Upper bound		
1.00	22	69.5057	4.81447	1.02645	67.3711	71.6403	64.20	80.23
2.00	22	65.0616	8.73264	1.86180	61.1897	68.9334	53.19	80.23
3.00	22	67.2625	7.38207	1.57386	63.9895	70.5355	56.78	80.23
Total	66	67.2766	7.28524	0.89675	65.4857	69.0675	53.19	80.23

ANOVA

Value					
	Sum of squares	df	Mean square	F	Sig.
Between groups	217.263	2	108.631	2.117	0.129
Within groups	3,232.594	63	51.311		
Total	3,449.857	65			

A6.2 Class level

A6.2.1 Agriculture

A6.2.1.1 Number of patches (NP)

ANOVA

Value					
	Sum of squares	df	Mean square	F	Sig.
Between groups	174,265,131.848	2	87,132,565.924	12,847	0.000
Within groups	427,293,152.091	63	6,782,430.986		
Total	601,558,283.939	65			

A6.2.1.2 Patch density (PD)

ANOVA					
Value					
	Sum of squares	df	Mean square	F	Sig.
Between groups	796,869,636,034.576	2	398,434,818,017.288	136,492	0.000
Within groups	183,903,391,208.955	63	2,919,101,447.761		
Total	980,773,027,243.530	65			

A6.2.1.3 Mean proximity (PROX_MN)

ANOVA					
Value					
	Sum of squares	df	Mean square	F	Sig.
Between groups	103,203,134,871.121	2	51,601,567,435.561	9,416	0.000
Within groups	345,256,010,274.409	63	5,480,254,131.340		
Total	448,459,145,145.530	65			

A6.2.1.4 Mean area (AREA_MN)

ANOVA					
Value					
	Sum of squares	df	Mean square	F	Sig.
Between groups	11,865,783.545	2	5,932,891.773	10,751	0.000
Within groups	34,767,550.409	63	551,865.880		
Total	46,633,333.955	65			

A6.2.1.5 Interposition and juxtaposition (IJI)

ANOVA					
Value					
	Sum of squares	df	Mean square	F	Sig.
Between groups	54,455,645,558.273	2	27,227,822,779.136	11,874	0.000
Within groups	144,458,339,717.318	63	2,292,989,519.323		
Total	198,913,985,275.591	65			

A6.2.1.6 Largest patch index (LPI)

ANOVA					
Value					
	Sum of squares	df	Mean square	F	Sig.
Between groups	91,694,116.455	2	45,847,058.227	10,579	0.000
Within groups	273,029,797.136	63	4,333,806.304		
Total	364,723,913.591	65			

A6.2.1.7 Largest shape index (LSI)

Value	ANOVA				
	Sum of squares	df	Mean square	F	Sig.
Between groups	91,694,116.455	2	45,847,058.227	10,579	0.000
Within groups	273,029,797.136	63	4,333,806.304		
Total	364,723,913.591	65			

A6.2.2 Barren

A6.2.2.1 Number of patches (NP)

Value	ANOVA				
	Sum of squares	df	Mean square	F	Sig.
Between groups	18,891,431.545	2	9,445,715.773	4,176	0.020
Within groups	142,492,906.955	63	2,261,792.174		
Total	161,384,338.500	65			

A6.2.2.2 Patch density (PD)

Value	ANOVA				
	Sum of squares	df	Mean square	F	Sig.
Between groups	2,015,361,908.576	2	1,007,680,954.288	4,176	0.020
Within groups	15,201,468,397.364	63	241,293,149.165		
Total	17,216,830,305.939	65			

A6.2.2.3 Mean proximity (PROX_MN)

Value	ANOVA				
	Sum of squares	df	Mean square	F	Sig.
Between groups	2,003,805,662.939	2	1,001,902,831.470	12,186	0.000
Within groups	5,179,593,535.318	63	82,215,770.402		
Total	7,183,399,198.258	65			

A6.2.2.4 Mean area (AREA_MN)

Value	ANOVA				
	Sum of squares	df	Mean square	F	Sig.
Between groups	75,186,612.091	2	37,593,306.045	22,955	0.000
Within groups	103,174,174.273	63	1,637,685.306		
Total	178,360,786.364	65			

A6.2.2.5 Interposition and juxtaposition (IJI)

ANOVA

Value					
	Sum of squares	df	Mean square	F	Sig.
Between groups	4,700,137,146,865.728	2	2,350,068,573,432.864	27,675	0.000
Within groups	5,349,774,565,454.272	63	84,917,056,594.512		
Total	10,049,911,712,320.000	65			

A6.2.6.6 Largest patch index (LPI)

ANOVA

Value					
	Sum of squares	df	Mean square	F	Sig.
Between groups	247,403.273	2	123,701.636	6,152	0.004
Within groups	1,266,727.227	63	20,106.781		
Total	1,514,130.500	65			

A6.2.2.7 Largest shape index (LSI)

ANOVA

Value					
	Sum of squares	df	Mean square	F	Sig.
Between groups	1,289,420,321,581.303	2	644,710,160,790.651	10,269	0.000
Within groups	3,955,111,043,733.182	63	62,779,540,376.717		
Total	5,244,531,365,314.484	65			

A6.2.3 Urban

A6.2.3.1 Number of patches (NP)

ANOVA

Value					
	Sum of squares	df	Mean square	F	Sig.
Between groups	39,903,841.303	2	19,951,920.652	37.100	0.000
Within groups	33,880,550.227	63	537,786.512		
Total	73,784,391.530	65			

A6.2.3.2 Patch density (PD)

ANOVA

Value					
	Sum of squares	df	Mean square	F	Sig.
Between groups	4,257.005	2	2,128.503	37.100	0.000
Within groups	3,614.483	63	57.373		
Total	7,871.488	65			

A6.2.3.3 Mean proximity (PROX_MN)

ANOVA					
Value					
	Sum of squares	df	Mean square	F	Sig.
Between groups	9,848.483	2	4,924.241	8.143	0.001
Within groups	38,098.396	63	604.736		
Total	47,946.878	65			

A6.2.3.4 Mean area (AREA_MN)

ANOVA					
Value					
	Sum of squares	df	Mean square	F	Sig.
Between groups	1,712.009	2	856.005	41.929	0.000
Within groups	1,286.190	63	20.416		
Total	2,998.199	65			

A6.2.3.5 Interposition and Juxtaposition (IJI)

ANOVA					
Value					
	Sum of squares	df	Mean square	F	Sig.
Between groups	50,394.215	2	25,197.108	31.733	0.000
Within groups	50,024.886	63	794.046		
Total	100,419.102	65			

A6.2.3.6 Largest Patch Index (LPI)

ANOVA					
Value					
	Sum of squares	df	Mean square	F	Sig.
Between groups	11,641.065	2	5,820.533	3.293	0.044
Within groups	111,357.387	63	1,767.578		
Total	122,998.452	65			

A6.2.3.7 Largest Shape Index (LSI)

ANOVA					
Value					
	Sum of squares	df	Mean square	F	Sig.
Between groups	330,149.812	2	165,074.906	100.312	0.000
Within groups	103,673.758	63	1,645.615		
Total	433,823.570	65			

A6.2.4 Forest

A6.2.4.1 Number of patches (NP)

Value					
	Sum of squares	df	Mean square	F	Sig.
Between groups	49,541,580.636	2	24,770,790.318	52.297	0.000
Within groups	29,840,375.136	63	473,656.748		
Total	79,381,955.773	65			

ANOVA

A6.2.4.2 Patch density (PD)

Value					
	Sum of squares	df	Mean square	F	Sig.
Between groups	4,099.111	2	2,049.555	23.245	0.000
Within groups	5,554.893	63	88.173		
Total	9,654.004	65			

ANOVA

A6.2.4.3 Mean proximity (PROX_MN)

Value					
	Sum of squares	df	Mean square	F	Sig.
Between groups	43,088.591	2	21,544.296	33.465	0.000
Within groups	40,558.896	63	643.792		
Total	83,647.487	65			

ANOVA

A6.2.4.4 Mean area (AREA_MN)

Value					
	Sum of squares	df	Mean square	F	Sig.
Between groups	85,704.203	2	42,852.102	34.269	0.000
Within groups	78,779.983	63	1,250.476		
Total	164,484.186	65			

ANOVA

A6.2.4.5 Interposition and juxtaposition (IJI)

Value					
	Sum of squares	df	Mean square	F	Sig.
Between groups	333,278.779	2	166,639.389	5.959	0.004
Within groups	1,761,889.863	63	27,966.506		
Total	2,095,168.641	65			

ANOVA

A6.2.4.6 Largest patch index (LPI)

ANOVA					
Value					
	Sum of squares	df	Mean square	F	Sig.
Between groups	613.801	2	306.900	13.366	0.000
Within groups	1,446.576	63	22.962		
Total	2,060.377	65			

A6.2.4.7 Largest shape index (LSI)

ANOVA					
Value					
	Sum of squares	df	Mean square	F	Sig.
Between groups	76,627.413	2	38,313.706	55.378	0.000
Within groups	43,587.039	63	691.858		
Total	120,214.452	65			

A6.2.5 Shrub

A6.2.5.1 Number of patches (NP)

ANOVA					
Value					
	Sum of squares	df	Mean square	F	Sig.
Between groups	27,406,294.576	2	13,703,147.288	5.825	0.005
Within groups	1.482E8	63	2,352,467.721		
Total	1.756E8	65			

A6.2.5.2 Patch density (PD)

ANOVA					
Value					
	Sum of squares	df	Mean square	F	Sig.
Between groups	2,923.824	2	1,461.912	5.825	0.005
Within groups	15,810.893	63	250.967		
Total	18,734.717	65			

A6.2.5.3 Mean proximity (PROX_MN)

ANOVA					
Value					
	Sum of squares	df	Mean square	F	Sig.
Between groups	98,737.931	2	49,368.965	2.228	0.116
Within groups	1,396,115.475	63	22,160.563		
Total	1,494,853.406	65			

A6.2.5.4 Mean area (AREA_MN)

ANOVA					
Value					
	Sum of squares	df	Mean square	F	Sig.
Between groups	2.731	2	1.366	5.676	0.005
Within groups	15.158	63	0.241		
Total	17.890	65			

A6.2.5.5 Interposition and juxtaposition (IJI)

ANOVA					
Value					
	Sum of squares	df	Mean square	F	Sig.
Between groups	255,842.186	2	127,921.093	12.220	0.000
Within groups	659,474.231	63	10,467.845		
Total	915,316.418	65			

A6.2.5.6 Largest patch index (LPI)

ANOVA					
Value					
	Sum of squares	df	Mean square	F	Sig.
Between groups	7.296	2	3.648	4.693	0.013
Within groups	48.973	63	0.777		
Total	56.269	65			

A6.2.5.7 Largest shape index (LSI)

ANOVA					
Value					
	Sum of squares	df	Mean square	F	Sig.
Between groups	187,964.401	2	93,982.201	5.829	0.005
Within groups	1,015,710.376	63	16,122.387		
Total	1,203,674.777	65			

A6.2.6 Water

A6.2.6.1 Number of patches (NP)

ANOVA					
Value					
	Sum of squares	df	Mean square	F	Sig.
Between groups	0.000	2	0.000	.	.
Within groups	0.000	63	0.000		
Total	0.000	65			

A6.2.6.2 Patch density (PD)

Value	ANOVA				
	Sum of squares	df	Mean square	F	Sig.
Between groups	0.000	2	0.000	0.000	1.000
Within groups	0.000	63	0.000		
Total	0.000	65			

A6.2.6.3 Mean proximity (PROX_MN)

Value	ANOVA				
	Sum of squares	df	Mean square	F	Sig.
Between groups	0.000	2	0.000	0.000	1.000
Within groups	0.000	63	0.000		
Total	0.000	65			

A6.2.6.4 Mean area (AREA_MN)

Value	ANOVA				
	Sum of squares	df	Mean square	F	Sig.
Between groups	0.000	2	0.000	0.000	1.000
Within groups	0.000	63	0.000		
Total	0.000	65			

A6.2.6.5 Interposition and juxtaposition (IJI)

Value	ANOVA				
	Sum of squares	df	Mean square	F	Sig.
Between groups	0.000	2	0.000	0.000	1.000
Within groups	0.000	63	0.000		
Total	0.000	65			

A6.2.6.6 Largest patch index (LPI)

Value	ANOVA				
	Sum of squares	df	Mean square	F	Sig.
Between groups	0.000	2	0.000	0.000	1.000
Within groups	0.000	63	0.000		
Total	0.000	65			

A6.2.6.7 Largest shape index (LSI)

ANOVA						
Value						
	Sum of squares	df	Mean square	F	Sig.	
Between groups	0.000	2	0.000	0.000	1.000	
Within groups	0.000	63	0.000			
Total	0.000	65				

Source: Author's calculation

ERDSICHT - EINBLICKE IN GEOGRAPHISCHE UND GEOINFORMATIONSTECHNISCHE ARBEITSWEISEN

Schriftenreihe des Geographischen Instituts der Universität Göttingen, Abteilung Kartographie, GIS und Fernerkundung

Herausgegeben von Prof. Dr. Martin Kappas

ISSN 1614-4716

1 *Claudia Sültmann*
   GIS- und Satellitenbildgestützte Landnutzungsklassifikation mit Change detection im Westen der Côte d'Ivoire
   ISBN 3-89821-356-0

2 *Katharina Feiden*
   GIS - gestützte Analyse der zeitlichen und räumlichen Verteilung der Niederschlagsjahressummen (1961 - 1990) in der Dominikanischen Republik
   Charakteristika und Trends
   ISBN 3-89821-368-4

3 *Nicole Erler*
   GIS- und fernerkundungsgestützte Bewertung von „Natural Hazards" im oberen Einzugsgebiet des Rio Yaque del Norte (Dominikanische Republik)
   ISBN 3-89821-409-5

4 *Martin Kappas, Frank Schöggl*
   Bodenerosion in der Dominikanischen Republik
   Eine vergleichende Studie zum Bodenabtrag auf Argrarflächen mit und ohne Erosionsschutzmassnahmen
   ISBN 3-89821-423-0

5 *Randy Thomsen*
   Change Detection – fernerkundungsgestützte Methoden zur Ableitung des Landnutzungswandels in den Tropen (Fallbeispiel Dominikanische Republik)
   ISBN 3-89821-433-8

6 *Sören Steinbach*
   Visualisierung und Quantifizierung von Überschwemmungsbereichen am Mittellauf der Elbe
   GIS-gestützte Modellierung von Überschwemmungen
   ISBN 3-89821-530-X

7 *Jobst Augustin*
   Das Seegangsklima der Ostsee zwischen 1958 und 2002 auf Grundlage numerischer Daten
   ISBN 3-89821-572-5

8   *Martin Kappas*
    Naturraumpotential und Landnutzung im Oudalan – eine Fallstudie aus dem Sahel
    Burkina Fasos zur Anwendbarkeit von Fernerkundungsmethoden im regionalen
    Maßstab
    ISBN 3-89821-664-0

9   *Ortwin Kessels*
    Qualitätsanalyse verschiedener digitaler Geländemodelle und deren Eignung für die
    Prozessierung von Satellitenbilddaten in den Tropen
    ISBN 3-89821-603-9

10 *Christian Knieper*
    Remote Sensing Based Analysis of Land Cover and Land Cover Change in Central
    Sulawesi, Indonesia
    ISBN 3-89821-646-2

11 *Mareike Lehrling*
    Klimaentwicklung in Alaska - eine GIS-gestützte Erfassung und Analyse der raum-
    zeitlichen Entwicklung von Temperatur und Niederschlag
    ISBN 3-89821-670-5

12 *Daniel Karthe*
    Trinkwasser in Calcutta
    Versorgungsproblematik einer indischen Megastadt
    ISBN 3-89821-661-6

13 *Enrico Kalb*
    Landnutzungsinterpretation und Erosionsmodellierung der Küstenregion von Nordost
    Bali, Indonesien
    ISBN 3-89821-666-7

14 *Anke Gleitsmann*
    Exploiting the Spatial Information in High Resolution Satellite Data and Utilising
    Multi-Source Data for Tropical Mountain Forest and Land Cover Mapping
    ISBN 3-89821-727-2

15 *Arno Krause*
    Einführung eines GIS für die Landwirtschaftsverwaltungen der BRD auf Grundlage
    EU-rechtlicher und nationaler Verordnungen
    unter besonderer Berücksichtigung des Bundeslandes Mecklenburg-Vorpommern
    ISBN 3-89821-738-8

16 *Pavel Propastin*
    Remote sensing based study on vegetation dynamics in dry lands of Kazakhstan
    ISBN 978-3-89821-823-8

17 *Matthias Stähle*
    Trinkwasser in Delhi
    Versorgungsproblematik einer indischen Megastadt
    ISBN 978-3-89821-827-6

18 *Roland Bauböck*
    Bioenergie im Landkreis Göttingen
    GIS-gestützte Biomassepotentialabschätzung anhand ausgewählter Kulturen, Triticale und Mais
    ISBN 978-3-89821-959-4

19 *Wahib Sahwan*
    Geomorphologische Untersuchungen mittels GIS- und Fernerkundungsverfahren unter Berücksichtigung hydrogeologischer Fragestellungen
    Fallbeispiele aus Nordwest Syrien
    ISBN 978-3-8382-0094-1

20 *Julia Krimkowski*
    Das Vordringen der Malaria nach Mitteleuropa im Zuge der Klimaerwärmung
    Fallbeispiel Deutschland
    ISBN 978-3-8382-0312-6

21 *Julia Kubanek*
    Comparison of GIS-based and High Resolution Satellite Imagery Population Modeling
    A Case Study for Istanbul
    ISBN 978-3-8382-0306-5

22 *Christine von Buttlar, Marianne Karpenstein-Machan, Roland Bauböck*
    Anbaukonzepte für Energiepflanzen in Zeiten des Klimawandels
    Beitrag zum Klimafolgenmanagement in der Metropolregion Hannover-Braunschweig-Göttingen-Wolfsburg
    ISBN 978-3-8382-0525-0

23 *Daniel Karthe, Sergey Chalov, Nikolay Kasimov, Martin Kappas (eds.)*
    Water and Environment in the Selenga-Baikal Basin:
    International Research Cooperation for an Ecoregion of Global Relevance
    ISBN 978-3-8382-0853-4

24 *Hoang Khanh Linh Nguyen*
    Detecting and Modeling the Changes of Land Use
    and Land Cover for Land Use Planning in Da Nang City, Vietnam
    ISBN 978-3-8382-1136-7

***ibidem**.eu*